First World War
and Army of Occupation
War Diary
France, Belgium and Germany

17 DIVISION
Divisional Troops
93 Field Company Royal Engineers
15 July 1915 - 31 March 1919

WO95/1993/3

The Naval & Military Press Ltd
www.nmarchive.com
Published in association with The National Archives

Published by

The Naval & Military Press Ltd

Unit 10 Ridgewood Industrial Park,

Uckfield, East Sussex,

TN22 5QE England

Tel: +44 (0) 1825 749494

www.naval-military-press.com

www.nmarchive.com

This diary has been reprinted in facsimile from the original. Any imperfections are inevitably reproduced and the quality may fall short of modern type and cartographic standards.

© Crown Copyright
Images reproduced by permission of The National Archives, London, England, 2015.

Contents

Document type	Place/Title	Date From	Date To
Heading	WO95/1993/3 Jul 1915-Mar 1919 93 Field Coy RE		
Heading	17th Division 93rd Field Coy R.E. 1915 July-1919 Mar To 6 Div Troops Rhine Army		
Heading	17th Division 93rd F.C.R.E. Vol I July-15 Oct		
War Diary	Horsley	15/07/1915	15/07/1915
War Diary	Le Havre	16/07/1915	16/07/1915
War Diary	Lumbres	17/07/1915	18/07/1915
War Diary	L'Hoffland	19/07/1915	22/07/1915
War Diary	Camp F	27/07/1915	27/07/1915
War Diary	H34a.9 0	30/07/1915	31/07/1915
War Diary	H 23g.58	01/08/1915	01/08/1915
War Diary	H 34a 9.0	26/08/1915	26/08/1915
War Diary	H 34a 9.0		
War Diary	H 34a 9.0	01/09/1915	14/09/1915
War Diary	Godewaer	06/10/1915	06/10/1915
War Diary	Godewaer Svelde	17/10/1915	23/10/1915
War Diary	H27b 62	24/10/1915	31/10/1915
Heading	17th Div Division Nov 15 93th F.C.R.E. Vol.2		
War Diary	H 27b 6.2	03/11/1915	07/11/1915
War Diary	H.23 G	09/11/1915	09/11/1915
War Diary	I.N To I27d 27	12/11/1915	28/11/1915
Heading	93rd F.C.R.E. Vol 3		
War Diary	H27b.6.2	01/12/1915	31/12/1915
Heading	93rd F.C.R.E. Vol 4 Jan 16		
War Diary	Dicke-Busch	01/01/1916	05/01/1916
War Diary	Zermezeele	06/01/1916	07/01/1916
War Diary	Monnecove	12/01/1916	27/01/1916
Heading	War Diary 93rd Field Co R.E. February 1916 93rd F.C.R.E. Vol 5		
War Diary	Monecove	04/02/1916	07/02/1916
War Diary	Ouderdom	08/02/1916	08/02/1916
War Diary	Monecove	08/02/1916	08/02/1916
War Diary	Ouderdom	08/02/1916	10/02/1916
War Diary	Scottish Wood	10/02/1916	14/02/1916
War Diary	Scottish Wood & Ouderdom.	14/02/1916	16/02/1916
War Diary	Scottish Wood	16/02/1916	16/02/1916
War Diary	Ouderdom	16/02/1916	18/02/1916
War Diary	Scottish Wood	16/02/1916	28/02/1916
War Diary	Ouderdom	29/02/1916	29/02/1916
Heading	War Diary Of 93rd Field Company R. E. From 1-3-16 To 31-3-16 Vol 6		
War Diary	Ouderdom	01/03/1916	11/03/1916
War Diary	Outtersteene	12/03/1916	22/03/1916
War Diary	Armentieres	18/03/1916	24/03/1916
Heading	War Diary Of 93rd Field Company R.E. From 1-4-16 To 30-4-16 Vol 7		
War Diary	Armentieres	01/04/1916	30/04/1916
Heading	War Diary Of 93rd Field Company R.E. From 1-5-16 To 31-5-16 Vol 8		
War Diary	Armentieres	01/05/1916	16/05/1916

War Diary	Estaires	17/05/1916	17/05/1916
War Diary	Steenbecque	18/05/1916	18/05/1916
War Diary	Wardrecques	19/05/1916	19/05/1916
War Diary	Leulinghem	19/05/1916	08/06/1916
War Diary	Allonville	09/06/1916	27/07/1916
War Diary	Ribemont	28/07/1916	30/07/1916
War Diary	Bois Des Tailles	01/07/1916	02/07/1916
War Diary	Morlancourt	02/07/1916	03/07/1916
War Diary	Fid 10.9	04/07/1916	04/07/1916
War Diary	Becourt Valley	05/07/1916	08/07/1916
War Diary	Meaulte	09/07/1916	10/07/1916
War Diary	Oissy	11/07/1916	15/07/1916
War Diary	L'Eloile.	16/07/1916	23/07/1916
War Diary	Dernancourt	24/07/1916	31/07/1916
Heading	93rd Field Company R. E. August 1916		
Heading	War Diary Of 93rd Field Company R.E From 1-8-16 To 31-8-16 Vol 11		
War Diary	Dernancourt	01/08/1916	11/08/1916
War Diary	S.16.a.b. S.17.a	12/08/1916	20/08/1916
War Diary	Fonquevillers Sheet 57 D NE E.21., E.27., E.28 a & c (Patt) K3 (except Patts b & d) and K9	20/08/1916	31/08/1916
War Diary	Fonquevillers.	01/09/1916	13/09/1916
War Diary	Bayencourt	14/09/1916	23/09/1916
War Diary	Gapennes	24/09/1916	03/10/1916
War Diary	Mezerolles	04/10/1916	04/10/1916
War Diary	Halloy	05/10/1916	19/10/1916
War Diary	Le Souich	20/10/1916	22/10/1916
War Diary	Allonville	23/10/1916	23/10/1916
War Diary	Daours	24/10/1916	27/10/1916
War Diary	Sandpits Camp.	28/10/1916	30/10/1916
War Diary	S.24.I.	31/10/1916	31/10/1916
War Diary	Waterlot Farm.	01/11/1916	13/11/1916
War Diary	A.8.a. (Albert)	14/11/1916	19/11/1916
War Diary	A.8.b.	20/11/1916	30/11/1916
War Diary	Carnoy Camp.	01/12/1916	08/12/1916
War Diary	Morlancourt.	09/12/1916	13/12/1916
War Diary	Treux.	14/12/1916	14/12/1916
War Diary	Corbie	15/12/1916	23/12/1916
War Diary	S.30.a.8.5	24/12/1916	31/12/1916
War Diary	Trones Wood	01/01/1917	15/01/1917
War Diary	La Houssoye	16/01/1917	19/01/1917
War Diary	Daours	20/01/1917	27/01/1917
War Diary	Combles	28/01/1917	31/01/1917
War Diary	Combles	01/02/1917	20/02/1917
War Diary	Mansell. Camp.	21/02/1917	21/02/1917
War Diary	Daours.	22/02/1917	02/03/1917
War Diary	Herissart.	03/03/1917	13/03/1917
War Diary	Beauval	14/03/1917	14/03/1917
War Diary	Beauvoir.	15/03/1917	15/03/1917
War Diary	Haravesnes.	16/03/1917	22/03/1917
War Diary	Remaisnil	23/03/1917	23/03/1917
War Diary	Beaudricourt	24/03/1917	25/03/1917
War Diary	Oppy	26/03/1917	04/04/1917
War Diary	Houvin.	05/04/1917	06/04/1917
War Diary	Beaufort	07/04/1917	07/04/1917
War Diary	Simencourt.	08/04/1917	09/04/1917

War Diary	Arras	10/04/1917	13/04/1917
War Diary	Feuchy	14/04/1917	25/04/1917
War Diary	Arras.	26/04/1917	26/04/1917
War Diary	Ivergny.	27/04/1917	01/05/1917
War Diary	Laresset	02/05/1917	02/05/1917
War Diary	Arras. G.17.b. Sheet No 51.b.	03/05/1917	08/05/1917
War Diary	S. of. Gavrelles.	09/05/1917	22/05/1917
War Diary	Railway Cutting	23/05/1917	30/05/1917
War Diary	Humbercourt	31/05/1917	02/06/1917
War Diary	Wanquetin.	03/06/1917	12/06/1917
War Diary	Arras.	13/06/1917	30/06/1917
War Diary	Sheet No.51.b G.16.b.2.3.	01/07/1917	31/08/1917
War Diary	G.16.b.2.3 Sheet 51. B Near Arras	01/09/1917	22/09/1917
War Diary	Hauteville	23/09/1917	24/09/1917
War Diary	Hermaville	25/09/1917	26/09/1917
War Diary	Bouquemaison	27/09/1917	29/09/1917
War Diary	Humbercourt	30/09/1917	03/10/1917
War Diary	Proven.	04/10/1917	09/10/1917
War Diary	Elverdinghe.	10/10/1917	13/10/1917
War Diary	Boesinghe.	14/10/1917	25/10/1917
War Diary	Elverdinghe	26/10/1917	31/10/1917
Miscellaneous	C.R.E. 17th Division Appendix I	12/10/1917	12/10/1917
Miscellaneous	C.R.E. 17th Division Appendix III	14/10/1917	14/10/1917
Miscellaneous	C.R.E. 17th Divn Appendix IV	15/10/1917	15/10/1917
War Diary	Sheet. 28 A.11.b.4.4.	01/11/1917	07/11/1917
War Diary	Canal. Bank.	08/11/1917	30/11/1917
War Diary	Canal. Bank. C19.a. Sheet 28	01/12/1917	05/12/1917
War Diary	Portland Camp.	06/12/1917	08/12/1917
War Diary	Louches	09/12/1917	11/12/1917
War Diary	Moulle	12/12/1917	14/12/1917
War Diary	Sappers Camp	15/12/1917	16/12/1917
War Diary	Lechelle	17/12/1917	22/12/1917
War Diary	Grand Ravine K.29.d.1.1.	23/12/1917	23/12/1917
War Diary	Grand Ravine	24/12/1917	31/12/1917
War Diary	Horse Lines At P.17.a. K 29 d 1.1.	01/01/1918	10/01/1918
War Diary	K.22.C.6.8	11/01/1918	20/01/1918
War Diary	K.27.a.1.8.	21/01/1918	31/01/1918
Heading	War Diary. The Officer i/c A.G's Office At The Base		
Heading	93 Id Coy RE Vol 29		
War Diary	In The Field Forward Billets K.27.a.1.7 Horse Lines P.17d.	01/02/1918	28/02/1918
War Diary	93rd Field Company R.E. March 1918		
War Diary	K.27.a.1.7.	01/03/1918	31/03/1918
Miscellaneous	Appendices 1 To 28.		
Miscellaneous	17th Divisional Engineers & Pioneers Progress Report Ending 6 a.m. 1-3-18		
Miscellaneous	Progress Report		
Miscellaneous	17th Divisional Engineers & Pioneers Progress Report Ending 6 a.m. 3-3-18 Appendix 3		
Miscellaneous	17 Programme Engineers & Pioneers Progress Report Ending 6 a.m. 6-3-18 Appendix 4	06/03/1918	06/03/1918
Miscellaneous	17 Divisional Engineers & Pioneers Progress Report Ending 6 a.m. 7-3-18	07/03/1918	07/03/1918
Miscellaneous	17 Divisional Engineers & Pioneers Progress Report Ending 6 a.m. 8-3-18	08/03/1918	08/03/1918

Miscellaneous	17 Divisional Engineers & Pioneers Progress Report Ending 6 a.m. 9-3-18	09/03/1918	09/03/1918
Miscellaneous	17 Divisional Engineers & Pioneers Progress Report Ending 6 a.m. 10-3-18	10/03/1918	10/03/1918
Miscellaneous	17 Divisional Engineers & Pioneers Progress Report Ending 6 a.m. 11-3-18	11/03/1918	11/03/1918
Miscellaneous	17th Divisional Engineers & Pioneers Progress Report Ending 6 a.m. 12-3-18	12/03/1918	12/03/1918
Miscellaneous	17th Divisional Engineers & Pioneers Progress Report Ending 6 a.m. 13-3-18	13/03/1918	13/03/1918
Miscellaneous	17th Divisional Engineers & Pioneers Progress Report Ending 6 a.m. 14-3-18	14/03/1918	14/03/1918
Miscellaneous	17th Divisional Engineers & Pioneers Progress Report Ending 6 a.m. 15-3-18	15/03/1918	15/03/1918
Miscellaneous	17th Divisional Engineers & Pioneers Progress Report Ending 6.a.m. 16-3-18 Appendix 12	16/03/1918	16/03/1918
Miscellaneous	17th Divisional Engineers & Pioneers Progress Report Ending 6.a.m. 17-3-18	17/03/1918	17/03/1918
Miscellaneous	17th Divisional Engineers & Pioneers Progress Report Ending 6 a.m. 18-3-18	18/03/1918	18/03/1918
War Diary	17th Divisional Engineers & Pioneers Progress Report Ending 6 a.m. 19-3-18	19/03/1918	19/03/1918
Miscellaneous	17th Divisional Engineers & Pioneers Progress Report Ending 6 a.m. 19-3-18	19/03/1918	19/03/1918
Miscellaneous	17th Divisional Engineers & Pioneers Progress Report Ending 6 a.m. 20-3-18	20/03/1918	20/03/1918
Miscellaneous	C.R.E. 17th Division Appendix 23		
Miscellaneous	C.R.E. 17th Division Appendix 24	28/03/1918	28/03/1918
Miscellaneous	C.R.E. 17th Division Appendix 25	29/03/1918	29/03/1918
Miscellaneous	C.R.E. 17th Division Appendix 26	30/03/1918	30/03/1918
Miscellaneous	C.R.E. 17th Division Appendix 27	31/03/1916	31/03/1916
Miscellaneous	C.R.E. 17th Division Appendix 28	01/04/1918	01/04/1918
Heading	93rd Field Company R. E. April 1918		
Heading	War Diary Of 93rd Field. Company R.E. From 1-4-18 To 30-4-18 Vol 31		
War Diary	Senlis.	01/04/1918	01/04/1918
War Diary	Contay	02/04/1918	03/04/1918
War Diary	Villers-Bocarge	04/04/1918	05/04/1918
War Diary	Fieffes.	06/04/1918	10/04/1918
War Diary	Toutencourt	11/04/1918	14/04/1918
War Diary	Forceville	15/04/1918	30/04/1918
Miscellaneous	Progress Report Ending 6am 19-4-18		
Miscellaneous			
Miscellaneous	Progress Report Ending 6.a.m. 21-4-18		
Miscellaneous	C.R.E. 17th Divn		
Miscellaneous	Progress Report Ending 6.a.m. 24-1-18		
Miscellaneous	C.R.E. 17th Div	30/04/1918	30/04/1918
Miscellaneous	Progress Report Ending 1-5-18		
Heading	War Diary Of 93rd Field Coy. R.E. From 1-5-18 To 31-5-18		
War Diary	Forcville	01/05/1918	07/05/1918
War Diary	Acheux.	08/05/1918	25/05/1918
War Diary	P.17.a.4.2.	26/05/1918	30/05/1918
War Diary	Acheux	31/05/1918	31/05/1918
Miscellaneous	17th Divisional Engineers & Pioneers Progress Report Ending 6 a.m. 2-5-18	02/05/1918	02/05/1918

Miscellaneous	17th Divisional Engineers & Pioneers Progress Report Ending 6a.m. 3-5-18 Appendix 2		
Miscellaneous	17th Divisional Engineers & Pioneers Progress Report Ending 6a.m. 4-5-18 Appendix 3		
Miscellaneous	17th Divisional Engineers & Pioneers Progress Report Ending 6a.m. 5-4-18 Appendix 4		
Miscellaneous	17th Divisional Engineers & Pioneers Progress Report Ending 6a.m. 6-4-18 Appendix 5.		
Miscellaneous	17th Divisional Engineers and Pioneers Progress Report Ending 6a.m. 7-5-18 Appendix 6.		
Miscellaneous	17th Divisional Engineers & Pioneers Progress Report Ending 6a.m. 8-5-18 Appendix 7.		
Miscellaneous	17th Divisional R.E. and Pioneers Progress Report Appendix 8	27/05/1918	27/05/1918
Miscellaneous	17th Divisional R.E. And Pioneers Appendix 9	28/05/1918	28/05/1918
Miscellaneous	17th Divisional R.E. And Pioneers Appendix 10	29/05/1918	29/05/1918
Miscellaneous	17th Divisional R.E. And Pioneers Appendix 11	30/05/1918	30/05/1918
Miscellaneous	17th Divisional R.E. And Pioneers Appendix 12	31/05/1918	31/05/1918
Miscellaneous	17th Divisional R.E. And Pioneers Appendix 13	01/06/1918	01/06/1918
Heading	War Diary Of 93rd (Field) Coy R.E. From 1-6-18 To 30-6-18 Vol 33		
War Diary	P17a47	01/06/1918	23/06/1918
War Diary	T.6.d.2.5.	24/06/1918	30/06/1918
Miscellaneous	17th Division R.E. And Pioneers Progress Report for 24 hours ending 6 a.m. 2-6-18	02/06/1918	02/06/1918
Miscellaneous	17th Division R.E. And Pioneers Progress Report for 24 hours ending 6 a.m. 3-6-18	03/06/1918	03/06/1918
Map	17th Division R.E. And Pioneers Progress Report for 24 hours ending 6 a.m. 4-6-18	04/06/1918	04/06/1918
Miscellaneous	17th Division R.E. And Pioneers Progress Report for 24 hours ending 6 a.m. 5-6-18	05/06/1918	05/06/1918
Miscellaneous	17th Division R.E. And Pioneers Progress Report for 24 hours ending 6 a.m. 6-6-18	06/06/1918	06/06/1918
Miscellaneous	17th Division R.E. And Pioneers Progress Report for 24 hours ending 6 a.m. 7-6-18	07/06/1918	07/06/1918
Miscellaneous	17th Division R.E. And Pioneers Progress Report for 24 hours ending 6 a.m. 8-6-18	08/06/1918	08/06/1918
Miscellaneous	17th Division R.E. And Pioneers Progress Report for 24 hours ending 6 a.m. 9-6-18	09/06/1918	09/06/1918
Miscellaneous	17th Division R.E. And Pioneers Progress Report for 24 hours ending 6 a.m. 10-6-18	10/06/1918	10/06/1918
Miscellaneous	17th Divisional Engineers & Pioneers Diary Progress Report for 24 hrs ending 6 a.m. 11-6-18	11/06/1918	11/06/1918
Miscellaneous	17th Division R.E. And Pioneers Progress Report for 24 hours ending 6 a.m. 12-6-18	12/06/1918	12/06/1918
Miscellaneous	17th Divisional R.E. And Pioneers	13/06/1918	13/06/1918
Miscellaneous	17th Divisional R.E. And Pioneers	14/06/1918	14/06/1918
Miscellaneous	17th Division R.E. And Pioneers Progress Report for 24 hours ending 6 a.m. 15-6-18	15/06/1918	15/06/1918
Miscellaneous	17th Division R.E. And Pioneers Progress Report for 24 hours ending 6 a.m. 16-6-18	16/06/1918	16/06/1918
Miscellaneous	17th Division R.E. And Pioneers Progress Report for 24 hours ending 6 a.m. 17-6-18	17/06/1918	17/06/1918
Miscellaneous	17th Division R.E. And Pioneers Progress Report for 24 hours ending 6 a.m. 18-6-18	18/06/1918	18/06/1918

Type	Description	Start	End
Miscellaneous	17th Division R.E. And Pioneers Progress Report for 24 hours ending 6 a.m. 19-6-18	19/06/1918	19/06/1918
Miscellaneous	17th Division R.E. And Pioneers Progress Report for 24 hours ending 6 a.m. 20-6-18	20/06/1918	20/06/1918
Miscellaneous	17th Division R.E. And Pioneers Progress Report for 24 hours ending 6 a.m. 21-6-18	21/06/1918	21/06/1918
Miscellaneous	17th Divisional Engineers + Pioneers	22/06/1918	22/06/1918
Miscellaneous	17th Divisional R.E. Daily Progress	23/06/1918	23/06/1918
Heading	War Diary Of 93rd Field Coy R.E. From 1-7-18 To 31-7-18 Vol 34		
War Diary	Sheet.57.D.T.G.d.2.5.	01/07/1918	10/07/1918
War Diary	V.7.b.6.2.	11/07/1918	15/07/1918
War Diary	Sheet.57.D.V.7.b.6.2.	16/07/1918	18/07/1918
War Diary	V.10.d.	19/07/1918	19/07/1918
War Diary	V.17 Cent.	20/07/1918	31/07/1918
Heading	93rd Field Co. Royal Engineers, August 1918		
Heading	War Diary 93rd Fd. Coy R.E. From 1-8-18 To 31-8-18 Vol 35		
Miscellaneous			
War Diary	V.17.cent. Sheet 57.D.	01/08/1918	08/08/1918
War Diary	Herissart.	07/08/1918	08/08/1918
War Diary	Bois L'Abbaye	09/08/1918	09/08/1918
War Diary	Corbie	10/08/1918	12/08/1918
War Diary	Q.21.I. Sheet.62.D.2.8.	13/08/1918	13/08/1918
War Diary	Sheet 62.D. Q.21.b.2.8.	14/08/1918	16/08/1918
War Diary	Daours.	17/08/1918	17/08/1918
War Diary	Herissart.	18/08/1918	18/08/1918
War Diary	Beauquesne.	19/08/1918	20/08/1918
War Diary	Acheux.	21/08/1918	24/08/1918
War Diary	Sheet.57.D. Q.17.c.0.5.	25/08/1918	25/08/1918
War Diary	R.32.b.2.3.	26/08/1918	27/08/1918
War Diary	Sheet 57 C. M.25.b.0.6	28/08/1918	28/08/1918
War Diary	M.25.b.0.6.	29/08/1918	30/08/1918
War Diary	Flers	31/08/1918	31/08/1918
Miscellaneous	Appendix I		
Miscellaneous	17th Divisional R.E And Pioneers Appendix II	03/08/1918	03/08/1918
Miscellaneous	17th Division R.E. And Pioneers Progress Report for 24 hours ending 6 a.m. 4-8-18 Appendix III	04/08/1918	04/08/1918
Miscellaneous	Appendix IV		
Miscellaneous	Appendix V		
Miscellaneous	17th Divisional R.E. And Pioneers Appendix VI	05/08/1918	05/08/1918
Miscellaneous	17th Divisional R.E. And Pioneers Appendix VII	16/06/1918	16/06/1918
Miscellaneous	17th Division R.E. and Pioneers Appendix VIII		
Map	C R E 17th Divisional Appendix IX	25/08/1915	25/08/1915
Miscellaneous	C.R.E. 17th Divn Appendix X	26/08/1918	26/08/1918
Miscellaneous	C.R.E. 7th Division Appendix XI		
Miscellaneous	C.R.E. 17th Divisional Appendix XII		
Miscellaneous	C.R.E. 17th Division Appendix XII	28/08/1918	28/08/1918
Miscellaneous	C.R.E. 17th Division Appendix XIII	29/08/1918	29/08/1918
Miscellaneous	C.R.E. 17th Division Appendix XIV	30/08/1918	30/08/1918
Miscellaneous	C.R.E. 17th Division Appendix XV	31/08/1918	31/08/1918
Miscellaneous	C.R.E. 17th Division Appendix XV		
Heading	War Diary Of 93rd Field Co. R.E. From 1-9-18-to 30-9-18 Vol 36		
War Diary	Flers	01/09/1918	03/09/1918
War Diary	Le Transloy	04/09/1918	07/09/1918

War Diary	U.6.b.	08/09/1918	08/09/1918
War Diary	U.6.b. (57.c.)	09/09/1918	11/09/1918
War Diary	Le Transloy.	12/09/1918	17/09/1918
War Diary	57.c. V.7.b.7.6	18/09/1918	19/09/1918
War Diary	W.3.c.7.6.	20/09/1918	25/09/1918
War Diary	V.7.b.7.6.	26/09/1918	26/09/1918
War Diary	57.c. V.7.b.7.6.	27/09/1918	30/09/1918
War Diary	Etricourt	01/10/1918	01/10/1918
War Diary	Railton Dump	02/10/1918	05/10/1918
War Diary	Escault. R.	06/10/1918	06/10/1918
War Diary	Honnecourt	07/10/1918	07/10/1918
War Diary	W.16.C.7.8.	08/10/1918	08/10/1918
War Diary	Concentration Camp.	08/10/1918	08/10/1918
War Diary	X.3.a.6.2	09/10/1918	09/10/1918
War Diary	Haut. Fm.	10/10/1918	10/10/1918
War Diary	J17c 3.5	11/10/1918	13/10/1918
War Diary	J.37.c.3.5.	14/10/1918	15/10/1918
War Diary	Audencourt	16/10/1918	22/10/1918
War Diary	Inchy	23/10/1918	27/10/1918
War Diary	Vendegies-au-Bois	28/10/1918	29/10/1918
War Diary	Neuvilly	30/10/1918	02/11/1918
War Diary	Near Poix-Du-Nord	03/11/1918	05/11/1918
War Diary	Locquignol	06/11/1918	07/11/1918
War Diary	Aymeries	08/11/1918	08/11/1918
War Diary	Bachant	09/11/1918	14/11/1918
War Diary	Engle Fontaine	15/11/1918	15/11/1918
War Diary	Beaumont	16/11/1918	16/11/1918
War Diary	Inchy	17/11/1918	08/12/1918
War Diary	Laleu	09/12/1918	12/12/1918
War Diary	Croquoison	13/12/1918	28/02/1919
Miscellaneous	C.R.E. 17th Division Appendix 1	01/09/1918	01/09/1918
Miscellaneous	C.R.E. 17th Division Water Supply Report To 10pm 1-9-18 Appendix2		
Miscellaneous	C.R.E 17th Division Appendix II	02/09/1918	02/09/1918
Miscellaneous	C R E 17th Division Appendix III	03/09/1918	03/09/1918
Miscellaneous	C R E 17th Division Appendix III		
Miscellaneous	C R E 17th Division Appendix IV		
Miscellaneous	C R E 17th Division Appendix V	06/09/1918	06/09/1918
Miscellaneous	C R E 17th Division Appendix VI	06/09/1918	06/09/1918
Miscellaneous			
Miscellaneous	C R E 17th Division App VII	08/09/1918	08/09/1918
Miscellaneous	C R E 17th Division App VIII	09/09/1918	09/09/1918
Miscellaneous	C R E 17th Division App IX	10/09/1918	10/09/1918
Miscellaneous	C R E 17th Division App X	11/09/1918	11/09/1918
Miscellaneous	C R E 17th Division App XI	14/09/1918	14/09/1918
Miscellaneous	17th Division R.E. And Pioneers Progress Report for 24 hours ending 6 a.m. 20-9-18 App XII	20/09/1918	20/09/1918
Miscellaneous	17th Division R.E. And Pioneers Progress Report for 24 hours ending 6 a.m. 21-9-18 App XIII	21/09/1918	21/09/1918
Miscellaneous	17th Division R.E. And Pioneers Progress Report for 24 hours ending 6 a.m. 22-9-18 Appendix XIV	22/09/1918	22/09/1918
Miscellaneous	17th Division R.E. And Pioneers Progress Report for 24 hours ending 6 a.m. 23-9-18 App XV	23/09/1918	23/09/1918
Miscellaneous	17th Division R.E. And Pioneers Progress Report for 24 hours ending 6 a.m. 24-9-18 App XVI	24/09/1918	24/09/1918

Miscellaneous	17th Division R.E. And Pioneers Progress Report for 24 hours ending 6 a.m. 25-9-18 App XVII	25/09/1918	25/09/1918
War Diary	Croquoison.	01/03/1919	12/03/1919
War Diary	Croquoison Hangest.	13/03/1919	16/03/1919
War Diary	Hangest.	17/03/1919	28/03/1919
War Diary	Hangest Bourdon.	29/03/1919	31/03/1919

WO95 1993/3

Jul 1915 - MAR 1919.

93 Field coy RE.

17TH DIVISION

93RD FIELD COY R.E.
~~JLY 1915 AUG 1919~~

1915 July — 1919 Mar

To 6 Div Troops

Rhine Army

17th Division

121/7432

93rd F.C.R.E.
Vol I

July 15 to Aug 19
Oct.

CONFIDENTIAL

WAR DIARY

of

93rd Field Company RE

from 15-7-1915 to 31-7-1915

Hour, Place, Date	Summary of Events	Remarks
15-7-15 7.30 AM HURSLEY	1. The Coy. started for Southampton, strength:- 6 officers, 223 OR (including 1 ASC attached): horses and mules 81 (including 2 ASC).	
12.30 pm	2. The Company embarked on S.S. African Prince, with the exception of 70 men under Lieut A.S. Culham RE, who embarked on S.S. Queen Empress. Both ships sailed during the afternoon	P.H
16.7.15 10 am - 1.30 pm LE HAVRE	3. The Company disembarked at LE HAVRE and were unloading transport	
	4. ~~Five~~ men were detained in hospital because of bad vaccination arms.	

Hour, Date	Summary of Events	Remarks
LE HAVRE 16-7-15 4.30 PM	5. The Company entrained at Point 4 and the train left at 8.20 PM	PH
17.7.15 LUMBRES 4.0 PM	6. The Company detrained, marched to HALLINES and went into billets	PH
18.7.15 LUMBRES 8.5 am	7. The Company marched via ARQUES and HAZEBROUCK and billeted in a farm at L'HOFFLAND	PH
19.7.15 L'HOFFLAND 10.0 AM	8. The Company marched via CAESTRE to GODEWAERSVELDE and bivouaced in a field by the farm of VERHAERUE.	PH
21.7.15 9 PM	9. The Company marched via WESTOUTRE and LA CLYTTE	PH
22.7.15 3.40 AM	10. The Company arrived at hutments at Camp F H 19 b 4 4	Sheet 28 1/40.000 PH
27.7.15 Camp F 7 PM	11. The Company marched to a billet at H 34 a 9 0	PH

page 3

Hour Date Place	Summary of Events	Remarks
H 34 a 9.0 30.7.15 10 PM	12. Orders were received for the Company to march at once & join the 52nd Bde at the Chateau at H 23 b 5 8	P.H.
H.34.a 9.0 31.7.15 2.30 am	13 The Company marched off, reached the above Chateau at 3.15 am & went into bivouac.	P.H.
	P Hogg Major RE O.C. 93rd Field Co RE	

CONFIDENTIAL

WAR DIARY OF
93rd Field Coy. RE
from 1-8-1915 to 31-8-1915

Hours, date, place	Summary of Events	Remarks
1-8-15 H 23b 58 10.30 PM	1. The Company marched back to its former billet at H 34 a 90 arriving at 11.30 PM	See Sheet 2P 1/40,000 PH
H 34 a 90	2. During this month the Coy. was employed on various works which may well be described in one paragraph (a) Owing to cramped space in the billet, dug outs were constructed at night on various dates. (b) The work of improving or revetting the communication trench running through the BOIS CARRÉ went on all the month (c) The work of improving the road across the DICKEBUSCH ETANG went on all the month; the edges of the road were	

Date/hour place	Summary of Events	Remarks
H34a90	2(c)(cont⁻ᵈ) strengthened by beams obtained from ruined houses in DICKEBUSCH and the surface was improved with brick rubble from the same source. At the same time all the culverts were re-built & maintained.	
	(d) From the 20th a wooden tramway was commenced, starting at the dump at GORDONS FARM, N5a34 & continuing through RIDGE WOOD it was about 100 yards beyond the wood at the end of the month. The wooden track was supplemented in many places with steel track salved from a light railway near the ETANG; several pairs of truck wheels were also salved & truck bodies made. It was noticed that the wooden track deteriorated rapidly, especially round curves.	PH.
H34a90	3. Three men were evacuated sick on 6th, 14th & 25th respectively	PH

← page 3

Hour date place	Summary of Events	Remarks
H 34 a 90 10. am 26.8.15	4. A high explosive shell burst over the billet and one man inside a barn was wounded & evacuated	PN
21.8.15	5 A reinforcement of 4 men joined the Company	PN.
26.8.15	6 Orders were received to tape out a line in front of our trenches so that a V shaped ditch might be dug. It was to be laid out in re-entrants in such a way that it could be enfiladed from our parapets. The work resolved itself into 2 sectors, a right and a left sector Lieut D.S. CULHAM and 2nd Lieut C.C. KIDD laid out the right sector tape on nights of 26/27 & 27/28 without any difficulty. Lieut C.G. MITCHELL and 2nd Lt. D.C. BLYTH laid out the left hand sector on nights of 27/28 & 28/29 ; on the	

page 4

Date Hour Place	Summary of Events	Remarks
	6 (cont') first night they were discovered by an enemy listening post & heavily fired at & compelled to desist, on the second night they completed half their line & on starting the remainder noticed that a covering patrol of 12.Bn Manchester Regt were not out as far as they should have been, they however determined to complete the work, were seen by an enemy listening post and 2nd Lieut D.C BLYTH was shot.	P.H
	P.H Ogg. Major R.E. O.C 93rd F.Co R.E	

CONFIDENTIAL

WAR DIARY OF
93rd Field Co RE
from 1-9-1915 to 30.9.1915

Hour Date Place	Summary of Events	Remarks
H34a90	1. As in the previous month, the Company had some definite works which went on all the month & can be described in one paragraph. (a) No I Section was employed all the month in revetting & improving the Bois Carré communication trench. (b) No II Section had its (a) subsection at work improving the main communication trench between the WYTSCHAETE BEEK and N8 and its (b) sub section at work improving the road across the DICKEBUSCH ETANG, towards the latter end of the month some good poles being obtained, the work of corduroying this road was started. (c). No III Section worked on the tramway	

page 2

Hour date place	Summary of Events	Remarks
	1.0.(cntd) and by the end of the month it was 100 yards inside the BOIS CARRE	
	(d) No V Section had half its section at work revetting & improving the POPPY LANE communication trench, leading from VIERSTRAAT to the M trenches; the other half were laying a pipe line from N.E corner of DICKEBUSCH ETANG to the BOIS CARRE. The pipe was a 2" steel pipe, the engine was a Merewether radiant combined engine & pump; the pipe line had reached the BOIS CARRE by the end of the month.	P.H
H34a90 3-9-15	2. II Lieut A.E. WOOD joined the Company.	P.H
10.9.15	3. One man owing to an accident had to be evacuated	P.H
12.9.15	4. One man was wounded & evacuated & afterwards died on 21.9.15	P.H

page 3

Date Hour Place	Summary of Events	Remarks
1.9.15	5. One man was transferred to the 182nd Tunnelling Co	PH.
	6. Early in the month Lieut. A.S. CULHAM was put in charge of the BRASSERIE defences, the work was done under direct orders from the division	PH
3.9.15	7. A Reinforcement of 3 men joined	PH
14.9.15	8. A reinforcement of 3 men joined	PH.

P Hogg.
Major RE
OC 93. Field Co RE

CONFIDENTIAL

WAR DIARY of
93rd Field Co. RE
from 1-10-15 to 31-10-15

Hour date place	Summary of Events	Remarks
H34a9, 1-2/10/15	1. The Co carried on the works enumerated in para 1 of Diary for September - after the 2nd the Co. did no more work on the lines	PH
1.10.15	2. One man evacuated with a bad knee	PH
2.10.15	3. One man evacuated sick	PH
4.10.15	4. One man evacuated sick	PH
5.10.15 6 PM	5. The Co'y marched off to join the 52nd Bde in rest billets via RENINGHELST	PH
12.30 PM 6.10.15 GODEWAER	6. The Company arrived & went into close billets; both officers & men were very much crowded & very uncomfortable	PH

page 2

Hour date place	Summary of Events	Remarks
RODEWAER SVELDE 17.10.15	7. A reinforcement of 5 men joined	PH
20.10.15	8. 2nd Lieut W.G. JOHNSON joined the Company – he replaced Capt. F.P. HEATH who became Adjutant 17. Div. R.E on 5-10-15	PH
22.10.15	9. 2 men were evacuated sick	PH
22.10.15 1.15pm	10. The Company marched into bivouac at G5c83	PH
23.10.15 1.0PM	11. The Company marched into a hut camp vacated by 56th Field Co RE at H27 6 6 2	PH
H27 6 62 24.10.15	12. The OC was taken round new works to be done by CRE	PH
H27 6 62 25.10.15	13. The OC & 2nd in command took the subaltern officers round to point them out their work	PH

page 3

Hour date Place	Summary of Events	Remarks
H.27 c 62 26.10.15	14. The Company started work as follows :— No I Section with ½ Co. of Pioneers building dug outs at W. edge of ZILLEBEKE ETANG. No III & ½ No II Section building dug outs near BELGIAN CHATEAU H.23 c 44 ½ No II building horse lines in Camp. No IV Section with 1 Co Pioneers building a tramway from KRUISTRAAT to ZILLEBEKE A man in No I Section was wounded & evacuated	P/L
27-31	15 Work as above was carried on. One man evacuated sick.	P/L
31.10.15	16 One man went home for munition work	P/L

P Hogg
Major R.E.
O.C. 937 Co R.E.

93-L.F.C.R.E.
Vol. 2.

B/
7693

17/h/15 Marin

K

2 Nov 15

CONFIDENTIAL

WAR DIARY of
93rd Field Co. RE
from 1-11-15 — 30-11-15

Hour date place	Summary of Events.	Remarks
I. 27 b 6.2.	The Company carried on the work enumerated in Diary of October until 6-11-15 inclusive	GJR
3-11-15	One driver joined.	GJR
4-11-15	Received one L D Horse.	GJR
	Promotions 49732 Sgt Staniforth to be ?CQMS. 49330 Cpl Hinton to be a/Sergt 46797 LceCpl Cole " a/2nd Cpl 49855 Spr Beaton " Lce Cpl all to date from 1-11-15 Auth. RE Records letter R2P/074	GJR
	SSM Young to be CSM dated 23-10-15.	GJR
7-11-15 H.23.b	No I Section taken from ZILLEBEKE dugouts and put to work on Belgian Chateau dugouts.	GJR
9-11-15	No II Section moved to work at French Steel dugouts at HALFWAY Ho. at I 17 c 5.7. under 78th Co RE	GJR

Page 2.

Hour Place	Summary of Events	Remarks
7=20	The RMRE 2nd Company (Siege) supplied a party for clearing Brickstock, Rank & Routelbeek, under supervision of this Company	CRE
20.11.15	No I & No II moved into YPRES Quarters at H.12.d.35	CRE
21.11.15	Above 15 sections commenced work on Oxford Street C.T. as far as junction with Regent Street. This trench having fallen in badly needs draining & revetting. Some portions being too bad to repair a sandbag parapet is under construction. 2 sappers evacuated sick	CRE
22.11.15	One L/C Hoye & one L/C Park evacuated	CRE
23.11.15	2 drivers evacuated sick	CRE
25.11.15	One private evacuated sick	CRE
26.11.15	One sapper & one driver evacuated sick. One driver evacuated result of accident	CRE
28.11.15	No II Section moved into billets in YPRES in Rue de HAGUE	CRE
13/1 - 29/11	Major HAGG RE officiated as CRE. Lt MITCHELL officiated as O.C. Co.	PA signed OC 2/ OS 2E CRE

93rd ½ Co R.E.
fol: 3

121/7935

17 R/5/13

WAR DIARY or INTELLIGENCE SUMMARY

Army Form C. 2118.

Place	Date	Hour	Summary of Events and Information	Remarks and references to Appendices
H27 k.6.2	1/12/15	—	Company carried on following work. No 1 Section } Oxford Street Communication Trench No 3 Section } west of REGENT ST. Revetting and building breastwork where breastwork impossible. No 2 Section. Trench Shel Dugouts at HALFWAY HO (I.7.c.37) No 4 Section Trench Tramway from KRUISTRAAT to GORDON HO. (I.1.b & 1.h.)	JM JM JM
	4/12/15	—	No 4 Section moved into cellars in KRUISTRAAT (H.18.d.8.5)	JM
	11/12/15	—	One Sapper evacuated sick.	JM
	12/12/15	—	One sapper evacuated sick. One sapper, one pioneer, and four drivers joined the Company. Received 1 L.D. Horse & 1 L.D. Mule.	JM
	16/12/15	—	No 2 Section & No 4 Section taken from dugouts and trench tramway respectively and worked with No 1 & No 3 on a diversion from OXFORD ST to UNION ST. consisting partly of sandbag breastwork, partly of trench revetted with thumb frames and having a three foot sandbag parapet. The western part of OXFORD ST. had been shelled in several places and abandoned. This new diversion could not be easily seen.	JM
	19/12/15	—	One sapper killed in action. One sapper evacuated.	JM
	13/12/15	—	One driver rejoined Company	JM

WAR DIARY or INTELLIGENCE SUMMARY

Army Form C. 2118.

(Erase heading not required).

Place	Date	Hour	Summary of Events and Information	Remarks and references to Appendices
H 27.6.6.2	22/12/15	—	One sapper killed in action, one sapper wounded in action, & two sappers evacuated (wounded).	JMcR
	23/12/15	—	One sapper evacuated sick.	JMcR
	24/12/15	—	One driver evacuated sick.	JMcR
	26/12/15	—	One riding cob lost in YPRES.	JMcR
	27/12/15	—	One L.D. Horse received.	JMcR
	28/12/15	—	One L.D. Horse died.	JMcR
	3/1/15	—	The Company still working on that OXFORD ST Comm. Trench & breastwork.	JMcR

J McRitchie
Lieut RE
O.C. 93rd Field Coy RE

93rd F.C. R.E.
fol: 4
Tank

Page 1.

WAR DIARY
or
INTELLIGENCE SUMMARY

93rd Field Coy RE from 1.1.16 to 31.1.16

(Erase heading not required.)

Army Form C. 2118

Place	Date	Hour	Summary of Events and Information	Remarks and references to Appendices
DICKE-BUSCH	1.1.16		Last day of work on the line	ppt
"	3.1.16	11.0 AM	Dismounted portion of Company proceeded by motor lorries to MONNECOVE. MAJOR P.G.H. HOGG R.E. took on duties of C. RE.	ppt
"	5.1.16	10.0 AM	Mounted men & transport proceeded to ZERMEZEELE	ppt
ZERMEZ-EELE	6.1.16		Mounted men & transport rested	ppt
"	7.1.16	9.0 PM	Mounted men & transport proceeded to MONNECOVE. Two Sappers joined	ppt
MONNE-COVE	12.1.16		One Sapper transferred to Railway operating department.	ppt
"	15.1.16		Received 2 horses + 1 mule on remounts.	ppt
"	18.1.16		One Sapper and one L.D. horse evacuated	ppt
"	25.1.16		Evacuated one driver.	ppt

Page 2

Army Form C. 2118

WAR DIARY
~~INTELLIGENCE SUMMARY~~
(Erase heading not required.)

Instructions regarding War Diaries and Intelligence Summaries are contained in F.S. Regs., Part II. and the Staff Manual respectively. Title Pages will be prepared in manuscript.

Place	Date	Hour	Summary of Events and Information	Remarks and references to Appendices
MONINE COVE	27·1·16		MAJOR P.G.H. HOGG RE resumed command and (temp) Lieut C.G. MITCHELL RE one NCO left the company to proceed to ENGLAND for a temporary commission in the RE.	PH

(P Hogg)
Major RE
i/c 70 Co RE
or 93

31/1/16

93ʳᵈ F.C. R.E.
1) Vol: 5

War Diary.

93ʳᵈ Field Co. R.E.

February 1916.

WAR DIARY or INTELLIGENCE SUMMARY

Army Form C. 2118

Place	Date	Hour	Summary of Events and Information	Remarks and references to Appendices
MONECOVE	4-2-16		Major P.G.H. Hogg RE had to go to hospital at ST OMER as a result of accident whilst riding	O.S.C.
"	4-2-16		1 L.D. Rose evacuated	O.S.C.
"	5-2-16	8.0 PM	Advance Party, Lt Wood R.E. and 6 O.R., left rail area by 10 P.M. train from WATTEN	O.S.C.
"	6-2-16	8-30 PM	Mounted portion of Company including cyclists and lorries on forage cart left rail area. Lt Kidd RE in charge	O.S.C.
"	6-2-16		2 mules left at NOORDPEENE, evacuated,	O.S.C.
"	"		1 O.R. N° 44904 evacuated sick	O.S.C
"	7-2-16	12 NOON	Sections 2 & 3. 11 Lt Johnson in charge. Left rail area by motor buses and proceeded to forward billets in SCOTTISH WOOD Company took over section of line, work billets of the Cheshire Field C.R.E. T.F.	O.S.C.
OUDERDOM	8-2-16			O.S.C
MONECOVE	"	4.0 A.M	Remainder dismounted men & on forage cart left rail area by 7-39 train from AUDRUICQ. Arrived at camp OUDERDOM 12-30 PM	O.S.C.

WAR DIARY
INTELLIGENCE SUMMARY

(Erase heading not required.)

Army Form C. 2118

Place	Date	Hour	Summary of Events and Information	Remarks and references to Appendices
OUDERDOM	8-2-16	1 PM	Mounted portion of Company arrived at Camp.	O.S.C.
"	"	"	4 men y L Y&L's attached to Company as Telephone Operators	G.S.C.
"	10-2-16		1 O.R. No. 46209 returned to Coas for munition work	O.S.C.
SCOTTISH WOOD	10.2.16 to 14.2.16		Sections 2 & 3 from SCOTTISH WOOD carried on the following works: 1/ Communication trenches, Supports and assistance given in front line work to P.Q. & R trenches. 2/ Building steel dugouts for Corps Signals at DICKEBUSCH LAKE & BRASSERIE Station at BRASSERIE. 3/ Building steel dugout for dressing station at SCOTTISH WOOD. 4/ Building dugouts in SCOTTISH WOOD.	GR
" & OUDERDOM	14.2.16		Orders received to stand to as enemy were said to have broken thro' near the BLUFF. The normal programme of work was suspended.	GR
"	15.2.16	11.0 pm	The two back Sections received orders to proceed at once to Brigade Workshops on the DICKEBUSCH ROAD to detonate Mill's Grenades.	GR
"	16.2.16	1.0 pm	These two Sections returned to camp having detonated whole supply.	GR
SCOTTISH WOOD	16.2.16	noon	Two forward Sections received orders for work to be resumed. Assistance to be given to 98th Fd. Co. R.E. in CONVENT LANE & running from CONVENT LANE to SPOILS BANK.	GR

Army Form C. 2118.

WAR DIARY
or
INTELLIGENCE SUMMARY
(Erase heading not required).

Instructions regarding War Diaries and Intelligence Summaries are contained in F. S. Regs., Part II, and the Staff Manual respectively. Title Pages will be prepared in manuscript.

Place	Date	Hour	Summary of Events and Information	Remarks and references to Appendices
OUDERDOM	16.2.16	—	Received 1 L.D. Horse.	GMK
"	18.2.16	—	1 O.R. transferred to Base Depot.	GMK
"	18.2.16	—	Two wagons with teams & drivers attached to company from 19th D.A.C.	GMK
SCOTTISH WOOD	16.2.16 to 29.2.16	—	Work forward continued as usual. Work began on R.S. Trench 19.2.16.	GMK
"	22.2.16	—	No 1 Section relieved No 3 in forward trieto.	GMK GMK
"	23.2.16	—	No 4 Section relieved No 2 in forward trieto.	GMK
"	27.2.16	—	1 O.R. evacuated wounded.	GMK
OUDERDOM	29.2.16	—	1 O.R. struck off strength of company as permanently away on extra regimental employment.	GMK
"	29.2.16	—	Four sappers joined as reinforcements.	GMK

Signature — Capt. RE
OC 93rd Field Co RE
29.2.16.

93 FCRE
Vol 6/

CONFIDENTIAL

WAR DIARY

of

93rd FIELD COMPANY R.E.

From 1-3-16 to 31-3-16

Army Form C. 2118.

WAR DIARY
INTELLIGENCE SUMMARY
(Erase heading not required).

93rd Field Co. R.E.   March 1916

Place	Date	Hour	Summary of Events and Information	Remarks and references to Appendices
OUDERDOM	1st	2.30am	Major P.G.H. HOGG R.E. rejoined & resumed command	PH.
		4.30am	Lieut C.C. KIDD R.E. & No IV Section returned to Headquarters from forward billets in SCOTTISH WOOD	
	2nd	2.0PM	Lieut C.C. KIDD R.E. & No IV Section went into huts near DICKEBUSCH & commenced work of revetting Rs.	PH.
	4th	2.0PM	Lieut A.E. WOOD & II Section w/ Lieut W.G. JOHNSON with No I & III Sections went into forward billets in Canal bank near Bridge 18: Their work was (a) clearing ammunition trenches leading to the BLUFF (+) consolidating & digging communication trenches to the BEAN.	PH.
	6th	6.3PM	1 Sergeant & 4 men of No III Section were wounded by shell fire.	PH.

Army Form C. 2118.

WAR DIARY
or
INTELLIGENCE SUMMARY
(Erase heading not required).

Part 2. 93rd Field C. RE

Place	Date	Hour	Summary of Events and Information	Remarks and references to Appendices
OUDERDOM	7th	10.30 am	Lieut - A.S. CULHAM & No II section relieved Lieut C.C. KIDD & No IV section - the latter returned to Headquarters. 4 Reinforcements joined.	P.H.
	8th		One of the men wounded on the 6th died of his wounds in hospital.	P.H.
	10th	4.0am	No I & IV sections returned to headquarters & are relieved by 56th Field C. RE. 1 man to hospital & evacuated.	P.H.
		11.0am	No II section returned to Headquarters.	
	11th	7.30 am	The Company marched via GODEWAERSVELDE and CAESTRE to billets at F9c50 near OUTTERSTEENE	P.H. Map 36A 1/40,000
OUTTERSTEENE	12th to 22nd		The Company remained in rest billets. 1 man evacuated.	P.H.

Army Form C. 2118.

WAR DIARY
—or—
INTELLIGENCE SUMMARY
(Erase heading not required).

93rd Field Coy RE

March 1916

Place	Date	Hour	Summary of Events and Information	Remarks and references to Appendices
ARMENT-IERES	18	8 am	The OC with Lieut AEWOOD & Mr I Doden marched to ARMENTIÈRES as a forward party to take over billets &c.	PA
	22	10 am	Remainder of Company marched to ARMENTIÈRES.	PA
	24		The Company started work on the line — They are on the left their northern boundary being the RIVER LYS their southern boundary the PONT BALLOT Road. The work chiefly consists of revetting communication trenches & support lines, relaying wooden logs, cementing 2 machine gun emplacements.	PA

Ph 099
Ingale
OC 93rd Fd Coy RE

31.3.16

CONFIDENTIAL

War Diary

of

93rd Field Company, R.E.

from 1-4-16 to 30-4-16

WAR DIARY
or
INTELLIGENCE SUMMARY

(Erase heading not required).

Army Form C. 2118.

93rd Field Co. RE
April 1916

Place	Date	Hour	Summary of Events and Information	Remarks and references to Appendices
ARMENTIERES	1		Owing to a change in Battalion fronts, the Southern Boundary of "C" area is now to Junction of 81·82 T west wall of ORCHARD, GLOUCESTER Avenue as far as PONT BALLOT Road exclusive. The following are the more important works being carried out: (a) Machine gun emplacements in house 1841 T84 (b) Retaining post C. CAMBRIDGE Avenue, SS 87 — S 86 (c) Improving SS 88 · S 82 (d) pulling traverses in EDMEADES Avenue (e) The FRY PAN defence scheme.	
	2nd		MAJOR P.G.H.HOGG R.E. officiating as CRE during leave of absence of Lt Colonel C.M. CARPENTER RE	PH PH

WAR DIARY
or
INTELLIGENCE SUMMARY

(Erase heading not required)

Army Form C. 2118.

93rd Field Co. RE

Place	Date	Hour	Summary of Events and Information	Remarks and references to Appendices
ARMENTIÈRES	2nd		Captain C.G. MITCHELL officiates as O.C.	Apt
	6th	9.0pm	Lieut C.C. KIDD RE was wounded and is left for a Casualty Clearing Hospital	Apt
	10th	4.30pm	Lieut L.E. TRAVERS joined the Company	Apt
	11th	AM	MAJOR P.G.H. HOGG RE resumed command	Apt
	13th		The 7th York & Lancashire Regt (Pioneers) took over the work of widening S 82. The O.C. went round with the Brigadier Commanding 52nd Yards Role the ados for 4 Aug 16 & machine gun teams were fixed.	Apt
	24th	AM	One II Cpl was wounded and one sapper was killed.	Apt
	25th		Considerable enemy artillery activity. T88 was machined HMLs	Apt
	26th	PM	at IRISH AVENUE on badly damaged. One section was sent to work on T88 at 11.50pm	Apt

WAR DIARY
or
INTELLIGENCE SUMMARY 93rd Field C.R.E.
(Erase heading not required).

Army Form C. 2118.

Pp 2

Place	Date	Hour	Summary of Events and Information	Remarks and references to Appendices
ARMENTIERES	27.	PM	A section out all night clearing IRISH AVENUE. It's not clear enough to be used in daylight.	PP
	29/30		The Co. ? was chiefly employed on clearing drainage done by hostile bombardment in different parts of the line	PP

J. Mogg ?
Major R.E.
O.C. 93 Field C.R.E.
30.4.1916

XVII
XVIII 93 F C R E
Vol 8

CONFIDENTIAL

WAR DIARY

of

93rd Field Company. R.E.

from 1-5-16 to 31-5-16.

WAR DIARY or INTELLIGENCE SUMMARY

Army Form C. 2118.

93rd Field C. v. RE

May 1916

Place	Date	Hour	Summary of Events and Information	Remarks and references to Appendices
ARMENTIERES	1st–15th		The Company carried on the same work as last month and handed over to 3rd New Zealand Field Company.	App.K
"	16th	9.30 pm		[S]
ESTAIRES	17th	1.30 am	The Company marched to ESTAIRES	[S]
"	17th	1.0 pm	The Company arrived at ESTAIRES	[S]
STEENBECQUE	18th	6.30 pm	The Company marched to STEENBECQUE STATION arriving at 6.30 pm	[S]
WARDRECQUES	19th	6.0 am	The Company marched to WARDRECQUES arriving at 10.30 AM.	[S]
LEULINGHEM	19th–31st	6.31	The Company marched to LEULINGHEM arriving at 10.45 am	[S]
			The Company underwent training details in rest area.	App.T

31-5-1916

(signature)
Major RE
OC 93 Field C RE

Army Form C. 2118.

June
Vol 9

WAR DIARY
or
93rd Field Co. ? RE
XVII
INTELLIGENCE SUMMARY

(Erase heading not required).

June 1916

Instructions regarding War Diaries and Intelligence Summaries are contained in F. S. Regs., Part II, and the Staff Manual respectively. Title Pages will be prepared in manuscript.

Place	Date	Hour	Summary of Events and Information	Remarks and references to Appendices
LEULINGHEN	1st to 7th	7.E	Training in rest area. 1 L.D Horse & 1 mule evacuated on 5th	P.H
" "	8th		2 L.D. Hides received on 7th. Marched to ST OMER and entrained. One sapper transferred to base	P.H
" "	9th		Detrained at LONGUEAU and marched to billets in ALLONVILLE	P.H
ALLONVILLE			One sapper evacuated	
"	10th to 13th		Employed on water supply in Corps rest area, also in cutting timber in a neighbouring wood	P.H
"	14		No. 2 Section under Lieut A.S. CULHAM went forward to billets at MEAULTE	P.H
"	16th		No. 3 Section under 2nd Lieut W.G. JOHNSON went forward to camp near HAPPY VALLEY for employment in preparation of dumps of S.I & 52 nd Infantry Brigade	P.H
"	16th		One driver evacuated.	P.H
"	19th		No. 3 Section returned to ALLONVILLE	P.H
"	20th		1 sapper evacuated.	P.H

Army Form C. 2118.

WAR DIARY or INTELLIGENCE SUMMARY

93rd Field Co. R.E.

June 1916   Page 2

(Erase heading not required).

Place	Date	Hour	Summary of Events and Information	Remarks and references to Appendices
ALLONVILLE	21st		Our Sapper Transferred home for work on munitions. 1 L.D horse evacuated	O.P.H.
"	22nd		Sh. 2 Section returned to ALLONVILLE. Our sapper transferred home for work on munitions	O.P.H.
"	25th		No 4 Section under Lieut L. E. TRAVERS went forward to camp near HAPPY VALLEY for work on building support trenches. 1 L.D horse received	O.P.H
"	26th		1 mule evacuated	O.P.H
"	14th to 27th		Sections at head quarters were employed on making preparations for the following offensive viz:- packed into ice containers entanglements, S.A.A carriers, food & water carriers, L Gun charge carriers & Petroleum. Received orders at 5.15 PM to march that night (27/2), left at 9.0 PM	O.P.A
RIBEMONT	28th		Arrived 12.30 AM, went into billets at the SUCRERIE; received orders at 1.50 PM to march that night, received counter-orders at 4.0 PM to stand fast till further orders. No 4 Section reported at 10.0 PM	O.P.H

WAR DIARY or INTELLIGENCE SUMMARY

93rd Field Co. R.E.

June 1916 Page 3

Army Form C. 2118.

Place	Date	Hour	Summary of Events and Information	Remarks and references to Appendices
RIBEMONT	29th		Halted	Opt
"	30	10.0pm	March to BOIS DE TAILLES, reaches MORLANCOURT at midnight	Opt

P. Hogg
Major R.E.
O.C 93rd Field Co R.E.
1-7-16

WAR DIARY of INTELLIGENCE SUMMARY

Army Form C. 2118.

93rd Field Co. R.E.

July 1916

Vol 10

Place	Date	Hour	Summary of Events and Information	Remarks and references to Appendices
BOIS DES TAILLES	1st	12.30 am	Arrived from RIBEMONT & went into camp. Received orders to be ready to march at 10.0am or at any subsequent time at half an hour's notice. Halted all day	PH
"	2nd	12.30 am	Received orders to march to MORLANCOURT	PH
MORLANCOURT	2nd	6.45 am	Arrived at MORLANCOURT & went into billets. Under orders to march at ½ an hour's notice. Halted all day.	PH
"	3rd		Received orders from 52nd Bde at 4.30pm to march at 5.10 pm to CARNOY via FARM (E.18.a.4.6) – did so, but received orders at MEAULTE from CRE to return to MORLANCOURT – got back at 7.15 pm	Sheet 62 NE D 1/20,000 PH
F.12.10.9	4th		Marched at 9.30 am under orders (CRE & took men dug outs at F.12.10.9 east of BECORT WOOD. Major HOGG & Lieut WOOD with 2 NCO's went forward at 10.30 am to reconnoitre strong points by ROUND WOOD & BIRCH TREE WOOD X.21.d	MONTAUBAN X.5.c.10.10
"		9pm	Capt C.G. Mitchell with Sections 3 & 4 paraded marched to SUNKEN ROAD by LOZENGE WOOD. Stood by awaiting orders to make strong points in QUADRANGLE TRENCH at head of SHELTER ALLEY & BOTTOM ALLEY. No orders received as QUADRANGLE TRENCH not taken till morning of 5th.	PH

Army Form C. 2118.

WAR DIARY
or
INTELLIGENCE SUMMARY
(Erase heading not required.)

93rd Fd Co. R.E.   July 1916

Place	Date	Hour	Summary of Events and Information	Remarks and references to Appendices
BÉCOURT VALLEY	5.	10 am	Major P.G.H. Hogg with Nos 1 & 2 Sections worked on CRUCIFIX TRENCH & strong points, returning 4 pm. Major Hogg discussed to have a knee ahutter to Adv. Dressing Station FRICOURT. Capt. C.G. Mitchell took over command.	JR
		10 pm	Capt MITCHELL & No 3 Section started by for work in SUNKEN ROAD. No 3 worked on SHELTER ALLEY & No 4 on finishing strps in QUADRANGLE ALLEY. Nos 1 & 2 returned to Camp 2 am 6th. Lieut HOLBROW temporarily attached.	JR
	6.			JR
	7.	1 am	No 1 Section under LIEUT. WOOD paraded for consolidation of ACID DROP COPSE. Nos 2, 3 & 4 stood by in FRICOURT for strong pts in QUADRANGLE	JR
		12 noon	TRENCH shunts QUADRANGLE Sy SUPPORT be taken.	JR
		12.30 pm	Nos. 1, 3 & 4 ordered forward as QUADRANGLE SUPPORT thought to be taken. Enemy still in position so no work done. 2 men wounded.	
	8.	2 pm	Marched company to MÉAULTE & then over fields of 77/15 Fd G RE. One mule killed by to shell fire.	JR
MÉAULTE	9.	6 pm	Orders received to report at FRICOURT at 7 pm for work. On arriving sent back as company not required.	JR
	10.	10 am	Company moved up for work on strong pts BOTTOM WOOD.	JR

BSD - B. M351/22/11. 12/15. 2000

WAR DIARY
or
INTELLIGENCE SUMMARY

July 1916   93rd 2d Co R.E.

Army Form C. 2118.

Place	Date	Hour	Summary of Events and Information	Remarks and references to Appendices
MÉAULTE	10th	6.30pm	Capt MITCHELL handed over to Capt W.J.N GLASGOW RE who has arrived to command company	JM
OISSY	11th	6.00A	Coy move into Res Billets. No train available in 3.30pm. Coy (less Mounted Sec) overcome at SALEUX and marches 13 mls to OISSY, arriving midnight. The Mounted Section proceeds by rail via QUERRIEU and ABBEVILLE arriving at billets at 9pm. Check parade only held, men allowed to rest.	WJG
"	12th			WJG
"	13th		Company put into training. Reveille 6 AM: followed by Physical exercises, bayonet fighting and arm drill till midday. Afternoon future either short rest march or fatigue.	WJG
"	14th		As above	
"	15th			WJG
"	16th	7.31AM	Change Billets to l'Étoile marching into Sims Ay Pde, arriving 11 AM. Sunday, Check parade only.	WJG
L'Étoile	17th			
"	18th		Company training continues as indicated above.	WJG
"	19th			WJG
"	20th			WJG
"	21st		Spent into field, including Summary Chemistry Competition, Company training.	WJG
"	22nd	7.AM	Mounted Section marches into Bois de Warnimont to Billets via DERNANCOURT (by night) arriving afternoon of 23rd at E.19.b.	WJG
"	23rd	9.30	Dismounted Section marches to HANGEST MERRICOURT SUR ANCRE at 6.30pm + proceed into billets (E.19 b) by arriving at 9.30pm. Lieut Johnsons M.G.'s left to join 30th searching Coy RE.	WJG
DERNANCOURT	24th		Former Billets are Cuffies on Company training.	WJG

Army Form C. 2118.

WAR DIARY
—or—
INTELLIGENCE SUMMARY
(Erase heading not required).

JULY 1916   83rd Bn. H. Q. R.E.

Instructions regarding War Diaries and Intelligence Summaries are contained in F. S. Regs., Part II, and the Staff Manual respectively. Title Pages will be prepared in manuscript.

Place	Date	Hour	Summary of Events and Information	Remarks and references to Appendices
DERNANCOURT	25th	–	Company training proceeded with. First Reinforcement received from No. 4 G. Base Depôt.	M.S.
"	26th	–	Shooting a Course of Musketry at 100yds Quarry range. 1st reinforcement men.	M.S.
"	27th	–	2/Lieut. G.D. Bevington joined from 7th Field Coy. R.E. Company training.	M.S.
"	28th	–	} Company training.	M.S.
"	29th	–	}	
"	30th	–	}	
"	31st	–	Lieut L.E. Towers R.E. taken to 53rd. Casualty Clearing Station (suspected measles). Preparations made for move into line. To relieve the 1/2 Durham Fd. Eng. 7th Div. O.C. carried on reconnaissance of work in hand, to seem between BAZENTIN-LE-GRAND and LONGUEVAL. Strength of Company — 5 Officers; 205 other ranks; 76 horses.	M.S.

BSD - B. M351/22/11. 12/15. 2000

17th Divisional Engineers

93rd FIELD COMPANY R. E.

AUGUST 1 9 1 6

Vol 11

CONFIDENTIAL

War Diary

of

93rd Field Company. RE

from 1-8-16. to. 31-8-16.

Army Form C. 2118

WAR DIARY
INTELLIGENCE SUMMARY
(Erase heading not required.)

93rd Field Company R.E.
AUGUST 1916

Place	Date	Hour	Summary of Events and Information	Remarks and references to Appendices
DERNANCOURT	1/8	8.10 pm	Orders from CRE to move into hills five miles of MAMETZ. F.10 a 9.9. Sappers (Hq Sect, Nos 1, 2, & 4) billeted in Se German dft dugouts but transport sent here to BECORDEL on account of shelling fire (heavy). Men Conducted by 11.30 pm. No4 Section sent to BELLEVUE FARM (17th Div Hqrs) for work on dugouts etc. Strength 5 Officers; 203 O.R; 7 Sick in France + 1 Sick in trans.	MB
	2/8	7.00 am	No1 Section to work in tramp mtp at S 20 d 5.9 fr 52nd & 80th RFA Bdys	MB
			No2 — to 52nd Inf Bde	
			No3 — to accompany No1 Section. Two men wounded by H.E. shrapnel.	
	3/8		Work as above. 5th Div Inf Bde 0.7. No 86 killed 6.15 pm. RE not involved. No4 Sect. Less Sjt & 14 O.R rejoined at 10 pm. Weather very hot. Much sickness from diarrhoea in Coy.	MB
	4/8		Work as above but No2 at Manchester Rus Hq. (S 26 d 04) + No4 Secy at S2 m Inf Bde Hq. at S 26. d 3.6. — Very hot. Two men slightly wounded by shrapnel on duty	MB
	5/8		Work as for 4.8.16	MB
	6/8		do — "	MB
	7/8		do — " — Except No2 at work in LONGUEVAL VILLAGE consolidation. 1 Sec Sappers in hut & one killed	MB
	8/8		do — :2 Officers + 6 O.R supervising digging of C.T.'s (YORK ALLEY etc) by Inf working parties	MB
	9/8		do — 2.50 etc.	MB
	10/8		do — Sect. No 1.3.+4 in Se German 2nd line. No2 in material in Camp. 1 killed Went out at 6.30 pm for work at Battle Hq etc at Junction of PONT ST + BLACK WATCH 2 Officers + 6 Sappers supervising Inf working parties (480 for return of 7th etc.) ALLEN on Se 2nd & 3rd German 2nd line Consolidation. One killed 1 wounded. Strength 5 Officers (1 R.C.M) + 200 O.R.	MB

II.

WAR DIARY or INTELLIGENCE SUMMARY

Army Form C. 2118

3rd Fd Coy RE

AUGUST 1916

Place	Date	Hour	Summary of Events and Information	Remarks and references to Appendices
S.16 a. b / S.17 a	12		Sections 1, 2, 3 & 4 on Bc German 2nd line Christendom. 1/2 No 1 Section broken up & 1/2/16 in PEAR ST.	
	13	8.15pm	Coy not any more held to British at DERNANCOURT. 2/Lt E.C. HARRIS joins Company. Strength 6 Officers (1 sick in hosp) 200 OR. Sgt S/Nos + 7 men rejoined. Church parade Raining.	
	14		Raining. Re Stns by No. S.0, No 76 & 93.	
	15		Transport marched to CANDAS at 6 am. Remainder Entrained at 5 pm as MERRICOURT aux alieux CANDAS at 1 am 16/8/16	
	16		Marched to MEZEROLLES at 3 pm. arrived 5.30 pm Billeted at TRAVERS Lejourn. Res Sec Fd Bn OC No 94 Fd.	
	17		Marched to LUCHEUX at 8.00 AM arrived at 11.30 AM.	
	18		Lt TRAVERS & CULHAM & 28 ORs sent to BAVENCOURT to find with 1/4 EDINBURGH Fd Cy RE	
	19		Lt OLIHAM admitted to hospital (dysentery) long serving Major Cyril J Lyle (?) Saffron in PAS - alarm (3hr away)	
	20		Coy marched to BAVENCOURT at 8.00 AM - Sappers in marched sections via HALLOY - AUTHIE - COIGNEUX there have been no casualties.	

WAR DIARY or INTELLIGENCE SUMMARY

Army Form C. 2118

93 Rd Fd. Coy RE
AUGUST 1916

Place	Date	Hour	Summary of Events and Information	Remarks and references to Appendices
FONQUEVILLERS SHEET 57DNE — E.21.; E.27.; E.28 a + c (last) K3 (04ch last F+4) over K.9.	20.		Hq. Sect. & Nos 1, 2, 3 marches to FONQUEVILLERS at 7pm arrivi 8pm	
	21.		Started work on trench reclamation Huts, dugouts. Strength 6 Officers 205 OR + 178 horses	
	22 23 24 25 26		As for 21.8.16	
	27		No 1 Sect. Sent back to BAYENCOURT + No 2 Sect. brought up to FONQUEVILLERS 8pm	
	28 29 30 31		Work as for 21.8.16 — Rain much colder every day. Rendering work in trenches very slow. Strength 6 Officers 204 OR + 44 horses	

M. McGlashan
Capt RE
O.C. 93rd Fd Coy

Army Form C.2118

WAR DIARY or **INTELLIGENCE SUMMARY**

93rd Field Company R.E.

September 1916

(Erase heading not required.)

Instructions regarding War Diaries and Intelligence Summaries are contained in F.S. Regs., Part II. and the Staff Manual respectively. Title Pages will be prepared in manuscript.

Place	Date	Hour	Summary of Events and Information	Remarks and references to Appendices
FONQUEVILLERS	1.9	—	Three Sections of Coy. at work on deep dugout & trench reclamation in FONQUEVILLERS - HEBUTERNE front. Fourth Section Mining Section at BAYENCOURT. Coy strength: 5 off. + 205 O.R. + 80 horses. Company assisted by 3 Mining Platoons of 30 O.R. each (10 Bn Lanc. Fus.; 11th Bn Northumberland Fus.; 17th Bn Manchester Regt.)	
"	2.9	do dtto		
"	3.9	do dtto		
"	4.9	do dtto		
"	5.9	do dtto		
"	6.9	do dtto		
"	7.9	do dtto		
"	8.9	do dtto		
"	9.9	do dtto		
"	10	do dtto		
"	11	do dtto		
"	12	do dtto		
"	13	do dtto	The Company (less one Section) marched at 8.0 pm to field billets at BAYENCOURT, being relieved by the 222nd Field Coy. R.E. of the 33rd Div. Mining Section Sent back to their proposition lines at SAUSSIGNY.	
BAYENCOURT	14		Company labour now while at 9.0 AM. Reconnaissance of way ahead via Russian trenches in	
"	15	do to 14th		
"	16	do to 14th		
"	17		Work on Russian Sap at HEBUTERNE (YIDDISH ST.; WURZEL ST.; NEW WOMAN ST. and WHISKEY ST.; NEW WOMAN ST. and WHISKEY ST.) — one section mining a tunnel at BAYENCOURT and the other at shops at BAYENCOURT and HEBUTERNE made a cycle & tool party to clear journey. When BAYENCOURT and HEBUTERNE make a cycle & tool party (5 Officers, 207 O.R. and 79 horses) joined by above mentioned Mining Platoons less one from the 9th West Riding Regt. — one billeted at BAYENCOURT (the 10 Lanc. Fus.) has the remainder at HEBUTERNE (30 men each) the other Mathis who having was gently	
	18			P.T.O

WAR DIARY or INTELLIGENCE SUMMARY

Army Form C. 2118

September 1916

93rd Field Company R.E.

Place	Date	Hour	Summary of Events and Information	Remarks and references to Appendices
BAYENCOURT	19	—	Company bivouac as on Monday 18th inst. Very hot weather.	M/-
"	20	—	As for the 19th. Re. Lt Mining Platoon sent back when Inspector Bros. on duty was relieved by Vicars M. Eng. Rs. of 33rd Divn.	M/-
"	21	—	Company marched at 5.00 am for CAUMESNIL via HENU aux PAS. arriving at 2 pm. (Billets & bivouac). Strength. 5 Officers. 206 OR and 79 horses.	Lens 11½ Sheet 1/10000
"				M/- M/-
"	22	—	Company marched at 7.45 am for MEZEROLLES via DOULLENS. arriving at 10 am. Company marched at 7.45 am for FERME DE L'ABBAYE D'HIMONT near CONTEVILLE arriving at 2 pm.	M/- M/-
"	23	—	Company marched at 9.30 am for GAPENNES (MILLEVILLE SHEET)	M/-
GAPENNES	24	—	Company training. Strength 6 Officers. (Lt M.G. MacQuarrie (Army) 208 OR 79 horses. Rifle and Bayonet wg. took on in rifle range & his horses fighting course & dismounted	M/-
"	25	—	Company training in Engineers wk. 10 West Riding Rn.	M/-
"	26	—	Do - with 12th Bn Manchester Regt.	M/-
"	27	—	Do - with 10th Lanc. Fusiliers.	M/-
"	28	—		M/-
"	29	—	Company Calcium chloride trench lining Scheme.	M/-
"	30	—	Company Strength. 7 Officers, Lt. M.S.Cultram rejoins his day. 203 O Ranks 79 horses.	M/-

W.H. Blackmore

A.D.C.R.E. 2nd Div R.E.

ORIGINAL

WAR DIARY OCTOBER 1916
INTELLIGENCE SUMMARY — 93rd Field Coy R E
Army Form C. 2118. (Sheet 1)

VH 113

Place	Date	Hour	Summary of Events and Information	Remarks and references to Appendices
GAPENNES	1-10-16		Strength, 6 Officers 203 O.R. 79 Horses	ASC
"	3-10-16	1.0 PM	Company left GAPENNES at 1.0 PM and marched to MEZEROLLES arrived MEZEROLLES at 8.15 PM	ASC
"	"		Sappers BUTCHER H. and SOUTHAM admitted to hospital	ASC
MEZEROLLES	4-10-16	10 AM	Company left MEZEROLLES at 10 0 AM and reached HALLOY at 2.0 PM	ASC
"	"		Strength 6 Officers 201 OR 79 Horses	ASC
HALLOY	5-10-16		Company started work on hutments and drainage of Camps	ASC
"	6-10-16	2.30 PM	Capt W.J.N. GLASGOW M.C. R.E. Officer Commanding Company was wounded at HEBUTERNE	ASC
"	"		Lt A.S. CULHAM R.E. temporarily ith command of company	ASC
"	"		1 OR transferred to Base for munitions	ASC
"	7-10-16		Capt W.J.N. GLASGOW M.C. R.E. died of wounds in hospital	ASC
"	"		Lt A.E. WOOD. R.E. transferred to England sick	ASC
"	"		2. O.R. joined Company as reinforcements	ASC
"	"		Strength 6 officers 202 O.R. 79 Horses	ASC
"	8-10-16	8.30 AM	No 2 Section marched to HEBUTERNE and commenced work the same day on Russian Saps.	ASC
"	"		Work on hutments continued by remainder of Company	ASC
"	"		1 Horse attached to No 2 Section died on road between SAILLY and HEBUTERNE	ASC
"	"		Experiments in forming communication trenches by high explosives carried out	ASC

BSD - B. M351/23/11.12/15. 2000

ORIGINAL

WAR DIARY
INTELLIGENCE SUMMARY

Army Form C. 2118.

93rd Field Co R.E.
OCTOBER 1916 (Sheet 2)

Place	Date	Hour	Summary of Events and Information	Remarks and references to Appendices
HALLOY	9-10-16	3.0 PM	Capt W.J.N.GLASGOW M.C. R.E. buried at cemetery D.26. central MAP 57d NE	O/C
"	"	"	G.O.C. 19th Division visited Camp to see experiments in making a communication trench by high explosive carried out.	O/C
"	"	—	Strength 6 Officers 202 O.R. 78 Horses	O/C O/C
HALLOY	11-10-16		3 O.R. joined Company as reinforcements	O/C
			Strength 6 Officers 205 O.R. 78 Horses	O/C
HALLOY	12.10.16		Capt. C.G. Mitchell R.E. struck off Coy. Strength	R.C.L.
	12.10.16		Lt. R.C. LUNDIE R.E. S.R. took over Command of the Company	R.C.L. R.C.L.
"	13.10.16		No 3 Section relieved No 2 Section on Russian Sap at HEBUTERNE	R.C.L.
	14.10.16		Work in trenches at HALLOY.	
	15.10.16		1 O.R. joined Coy from H.Q. R.E. 19th Divn. Strength 206 O.R. 6 Officers. 78 horses	R.C.L.
	16.10.16		Capt. C.G. Mitchell R.E. on return from leave to U.K. reported immediately to C.E.	R.C.L.
	18.10.16		Lt. R. St C. REID R.E. (T.C.) joined Coy from 3rd Pontoon Park bringing VIIth Corps kit, through his changes in addition 4 O.R. joined Coy as reinforcements.	R.C.L.
			No 3 Section under Lt. Beauford returned from HEBUTERNE.	R.C.L.
			Strength 6 Officers 210 O.R. 79 horses.	
HALLOY.	19.10.16		Coy marched out of HALLOY at 3.10 p.m. arriving at LE SOUICH about 6 pm.	
			Transferred to Bosque MAISON at 6.30 p.m. accidentally injured on line of march & No G.9979 Sapper Ritchie D. returning about 10 p.m. removed to hospital.	R.C.L.

Army Form C. 2118.

Sheet (3)

WAR DIARY 93rd (Fd.) Coy. RE.
INTELLIGENCE SUMMARY OCTOBER 1916.

(Erase heading not required).

Instructions regarding War Diaries and Intelligence Summaries are contained in F.S. Regs., Part II, and the Staff Manual respectively. Title Pages will be prepared in manuscript.

Place	Date	Hour	Summary of Events and Information	Remarks and references to Appendices
LE SOUICH	20.10.16		Coy in billets at Le Souich. Sapper Ritchie reported died in hospital. (43rd C.C.S.)	R.C.L.
"	21.10.16		Court of Enquiry held on accidental injury to No. 69977 Sapper Ritchie D.	R.C.L.
"	22.10.16		Coy moved to Allonville. Transport by road. Remainder by bus. 1 O.R. admitted to Hosp. 1 Mule left at Le Souich lame. Strength 6 officers, 209 O.R.	R.C.L.
ALLONVILLE	23.10.16		Coy proceeded by march route to Daours. 79 horses.	R.C.L.
DAOURS	24.10.16		Coy resting in billets	R.C.L.
"	25.10.16		1 O.R. admitted to Hosp. on 25.10.16	R.C.L.
"	26.10.16			R.C.L.
"	27.10.16		Coy proceeded by march route to Sandpits Camp, Meaulte. Bridging equipment dumped at Sucerie Ribemont with 1 O.R. in charge.	R.C.L.
SANDPITS CAMP	28.10.16		Coy encamped at Sandpits Camp. Survey commenced for hutting under direction of C.E. XIV Corps.	R.C.L.
"	29.10.16		Coy moved to billets at S.24.d. (Sheet 57c 1/40,000) O.C. taken over from 15th Coy R.E.	R.C.L.
"	30.10.16		Coy improving billets & R.E. Dump in Guillemont. O.C. made H.Q. 32nd Inf. Bde.	R.C.L.
S.24.d.	31.10.16			R.C.L.

R.C. Lundie (Lt. R.E.(S.R.))
O.C. 93rd (Fd.) Coy. R.E.

WAR DIARY
INTELLIGENCE SUMMARY

93rd (Hull) Coy. R.E.

NOVEMBER

Vol/4

Place	Date	Hour	Summary of Events and Information	Remarks and references to Appendices
WATERLOT FARM.	1/11/16		O.C. visits Left Bn. H.Q. with G.O.C. 52nd Bde. Strength, 6 officers, 209 O.R., 78 horses & mules	Rct.
	2/11/16		No. 4 Section goes into bivouac billets at AID POST DUMP. O.C. visits CRE at Div. H.Q.	R.C.
	3/11/16		O.C. visits advanced section and visits CRE at Div.H.Q. (BERNEFAY WOOD) & FAREHAM Rct. 12th Bn. Manchester Regt. relieves detachments of 52nd Inf. Bde. for work under Rct. Sapping platoons commence work.	
	4/11/16		CRE goes round work in Left Bde. Sector with O.C. Sapping Platoons. 1 O.R. Killed in action & 1 wounded at duty (both shell-fire). Work & progress report to Strength. 6 officers. 208 O.R. 78 horses & mules. rendered to C.R.E.	App. I
	5/11/16		No. 2 Section relieves No. 4 Section. O.C. visits H.Q. 52nd Bde & CRE. Works Report. Lt. Reid comes forward from home lines I.O.R. accidentally injured, takes charge of all work on duckwalk track. Lt. MacSwain replaces him at horse lines. Works Report. Strength. 6 officers. 209 O.R. 78 horses & mules	App. II Rct. R.Ct. App. III
	6/11/16		Works Report.	Rct. App. IV
	7/11/16		No. 3 Section relieved No. 2 Section at AID POST DUMP. O.C. visits Advanced Section. Works Report.	Rct. App. V
	8/11/16		One L.D. horse shot. 1 L.D. horse evacuated. Strength 6 officers 209. O.R. 76 horses & mules	Rct. App. VI
	9/11/16		Works Report.	Rct. App. VII
	10/11/16		Works Report.	

Army Form C. 2118

WAR DIARY or INTELLIGENCE SUMMARY

(Erase heading not required.)

93rd (J.U.L) Coy R.E.

NOVEMBER 1916

Place	Date	Hour	Summary of Events and Information	Remarks and references to Appendices
WATERLOT FARM.	10/11/16		Advanced Section returned to WATERLOT FARM after work. Lt REID returned to move. Landing over to S.S. Coy R.E. to take charge of transport arrangements. Works Refets. Reconnaissance commenced.	R.C.t. App'x VIII & IX
"	12/11/16		Coy on the march to CITADEL en route for PICQUIGNY when intercepted by orders from C.R.E. and sent to hutments at A.8.a. C.R.E. instructed by D.A.A. & Q.M.G. 33rd Div. Report of work	R.C.t. App'x X
A.8.a. (ALBERT)	13/11/16		Coy resting & making improvements. A.D.V.S. & C.R.E. visits Coy. 1 L.D. horse & 1 Mule (horse suspected mange). Strength 6 Officers ? 209 O.R. 74 horses & mules. Three Sections hutting under C.E. XIV Corps. 1 Section working in camp.	R.C.t.
"	14/11/16		Work as on 14th. O.C. visits C.R.E. 8th Div. & C.R.E. 8th Div. and visited camp. Is working under instruction. 2 O.R. admitted to hospital.	R.C.t.
"	15/11/16		2 Sections hutting under C.R.E. 8th Div. & 2 Sections hutting under C.R.E. & in work in 8th Div. 1 O.R. admitted to hospt.	R.C.t.
"	16/11/16		Orders received to carry on work on 4" Water Main. all four sections being used to carry on water main work. O.C. & Lt Graham reconnoitred line.	R.C.t.
"	17/11/16		Coy working on pipe line. 1 O.R. admitted to hosp. Sick	R.C.t.
"	18/11/16		Coy continues work on pipe line. Camp vacated & attention turned over to MONTAUBAN–CARNOY Rd. at A.8.2.8.	R.C.t.
"	19/11/16		Work on pipe line. 2 O.R. admitted to hospital.	R.C.t.
A.8.6.	29/11/16		1 O.R. returned to duty from hospital	R.C.t.

WAR DIARY — 93rd (Field) Coy RE

NOVEMBER 1916

INTELLIGENCE SUMMARY

Page III

Place	Date	Hour	Summary of Events and Information	Remarks and references to Appendices
21.11.16 A.3.b.	21.11.16		Work on Rifle laying. 1 O.R. reinforcement joined unit. Strength 6 Officers, 210 O.R., 74 horses. O.C. visited Junction & Jute Equipment at RIBEMONT. Lt CULHAM left for 4th Army Inf. School.	R.C.L.
"	22.11.16		Three Sections on Rifle laying. One to MEAULTE for batts. Lt MacQueen commences experiments on blowing camouflets under Stumps under orders of C.E. XIVth Corps. 1 O.R. admitted to Hospital.	R.C.L.
"	23.11.16		Whole company on Rifle laying.	R.C.L.
"	24.11.16		Two Sections to MEAULTE for batts. Two sections on laying Rifles. Experiments on Stumps continued. 2 O.R. admitted to Hospital. 1 O.R. rejoined from Hospital.	R.C.L.
"	25.11.16		One Section to Batts. Remainder on Rifle laying. 2 O.R. shewn in D.R.O. as evacuated. Strength 6 Officers, 208 O.R., 74 horses. 1 O.R. admitted to Hospital. Experiments on Stumps concluded. Orders received to hand over Rifle line work to ANZAC Corps after work on 28.11.16. Work interrupted by bad weather.	R.C.L.
"	26.11.16		One Section to Batts. Remainder on Rifle laying. O.C. visits Stumps.	R.C.L.
"	27.11.16		Rifle laying. O.C. visits new work in A.5. with Lt DURHAM R.E.	R.C.L.
"	28.11.16		Rifle laying. 1 Officer & 20 men hutting with 1 Officer & 20 men under C.R.E. 29th Divn. O.C. visits C.R.E. 29th Divn. 1 Section to Batts. One section on YMCA Hut in MONTAUBAN. Remainder on Rifle laying. O.C. hands over Rifle line to CAPT. VESEY R.E. & visits Stumps. Reconnaissance new work. 1 L.D. horse evacuated. Strength 6 Officers, 208 O.R. 73 horses.	R.C.L. App. XI
"	29.11.16		One Section to Batts. One section hutting. Two sections on digging Mat.trench in A.5. 2 O.R. reinforcements joined.	R.C.L.
"	30.11.16		One section to Batts. One hutting under 29th Div. Two digging Mat.trench & laying Rifles.	R.C.L. R.C.L.

R.E. Lieuten. Capt. R.E.
O.C. 93rd (Field) Coy R.E.

WAR DIARY
or
INTELLIGENCE SUMMARY

(Erase heading not required).

93rd (Field) Coy. R.E.

DECEMBER 1916

Vol 15

Army Form C. 2118.

Place	Date	Hour	Summary of Events and Information	Remarks and references to Appendices
CARNOY. CAMP.	1/12/16		One Section to Batts. One Section under C.R.E. 29th Divn. Remainder hut laying. 1 O.R. evacuated. 1 O.R. admitted to Hosp. Strength, 6 Officers, 269 O.R., 73 horses. Works Report.	R.C.L. APP. I. R.C.L.
	2/12/16		One Section hutting. Remainder hut laying. 10 O.R. admitted to hospital.	R.C.L.
	3/12/16		One Section hutting. Remainder hut laying	R.C.L.
	4/12/16		" " "	R.C.L.
	5/12/16		" " "	
	6/12/16		1 O.R. admitted to Hospital	R.C.L.
	7/12/16		Work as above. O.C. proceeds to AMIENS to confer with C.R.E. 1 O.R. evacuated. Strength 6 Officers. 208 O.R.'s 73 horses. Works Report. (Hut week completed.) Whole Company hutting.	APP II & III & IV
	8/12/16		1 L.D. horse destroyed. 3 L.D. horses evacuated. Strength 6 Officers. 208 O.R. 69 horses	R.C.L. R.C.L.
MORLANCOURT.	9/12/16		Coy. moved into Billets at MORLANCOURT. O.C. visits XIVth Corps H.Q.	R.C.L.
	10/12/16		Kit- & Ball Helmet Inspections carried out. 10 L.D. horses obtained from IVth Army H.Q. at QUERRIEU. Strength 6 Officers 208 O.R. 79 horses.	
	12/12/16		Camp Sanitation & Camp Improvements.	R.C.L.
	13/12/16		Coy. moved to VIEUX d-TREUX	R.C.L.
TREUX.	14/12/16		Coy. moved to CORBIE. Three (O.R.) men have presently joined. Strength 6 Officers, 211 O.R. 79 horses	R.C.L. R.C.L.
CORBIE.	15/12/16		Camp Improvements.	
	16/12/16		No.1 Section proceeded to DAOURS under Lt Plowin for work on 14th Corps R.A. School. Remainder on Camp Improvements & work in ANZAC CORPS Supply Depot. Sixteen troops from RISEMONT & dumped near DAOURS. 3 O.R. & 3 L.D. horses evacuated. Strength 6 Officers. 208 O.R. 76 horses.	R.C.L.

WAR DIARY or INTELLIGENCE SUMMARY

93rd (Field) Coy. R.E.
DECEMBER 1916.

Army Form C. 2118

Place	Date	Hour	Summary of Events and Information	Remarks and references to Appendices
CORBIE	17/12/16		No 1 Section at DAOURS. No 2 Section working under ADJT. R.E. 17th Div. No 3 & 4 Sections on Stables & Sully Dump. 1 N.C.O.'s Rider & two mules evacuated. Strength. 6 Officers 208 O.R's. 73 horses.	Rct.
"	18/12/16		Work as for 17.12.16	Rct.
"	19/12/16		Work as for 18.12.16	Rct.
"	20.12.16		Work as for 17.12.16. Letter from B.G. R.A. XIV Corps re Section at DAOURS.	Rct. APP. V
"	21.12.16		Work as for 17.12.16. Report of work in CORBIE to H.Q. 51st Bde.	Rct. APP. VI
"	22.12.16		No 1 Section returns from DAOURS. Batt. for remainder. 1 Rider & 2 L.D. mules drawn from 29th M.V.S. Strength. 6 Officers, 208 O.R. 76 horses.	Rct.
"	23.12.16		Advanced party sent to 5.30.a.8.5. Coy moved to Camp at 5.30.a.8.5. Dismounted portion by bus to FRICOURT Cemetery. O.C. reconnoitred new line with C.R.E. & O.C. 84th Coy R.E. from whom L took over.	Rct.
5.30.a.8.5.	24.12.16		Whole Coy on Camp improvements. 5 O.R's admitted to Hospital.	Rct.
"	25.12.16		XMAS DAY. Camp improvements. Left day only worked. 2 Units of Beer (Free) for men. C.R.E. & M.O. ½ R.E. lunched in Coy mess. 2 O.R's admitted to Hospital. 2 O.R. reinforcements joined. Strength. 6 Officers. 210 O.R's. 76 horses.	Rct.
"	26.12.16		1 O.R. admitted to Hospital. Works Report.	Rct. APP. VII
"	27.12.16		No 2 & 4 Sections on ground work. Remainder Camp Improvements & 52nd Bde H.Q. Works Report.	Rct. APP. VIII
"	28.12.16		1 O.R. admitted to Hospital. 1 L.D. mule died. Strength. 6 Officers. 210 O.R. 75 horses. Works Report.	APP. IX Rct.
"	29.12.16		1 O.R. proceeded to U.K. to take commission. Works Report.	APP. X Rct.
"	30.12.16		2 O.R. returned to duty from Hosp. Works Report.	APP. XI Rct. APP. XII Rct.
"	31.12.16		Works Report.	

R.C. Lambli. Capt R.E.
O.C. 93rd (Field) Coy. R.E.

WAR DIARY
or
INTELLIGENCE SUMMARY

(Erase heading not required.)

Army Form C. 2118

93rd Field Company R.E.

Sheet No 1

Place	Date	Hour	Summary of Events and Information	Remarks and references to Appendices
Trones Wood	1/1/17		Work as for 31/12/16	① R.H. R.H. R.H.
"	"		1 O.R. Evacuated, and 2 O.Rs returned to duty from Hospital.	
"	"		Strength:– 6 Officers 208 O.Rs 75 Animals.	
"	2/1/17	9.00 a.m.	No 3 Section proceeds to adjoining trenches in Sunken Road near Morval and continues erection of corrugated steel shelters for troops and works on Cable Bell's HQ.	② R.H.
"	"		No 1, 2 and 4 Sections work as for 1/1/17.	
"	"		1 Mule sick	
"	"		Strength:– 6 Officers 208 O.R. 74 Animals.	R.H.
"	3/1/17		Work as for 2/1/17	③ R.H.
"	"		1 O.R. returned to duty from Hospital	R.H.
"	"		Strength:– 6 Officers 208 O.Rs 74 Animals	R.H.
"	4/1/17		Work as for 3/1/17	④ R.H.
"	5/1/17		Work as for 4/1/17	R.H.
"	"		1 O.R. wounded by shellfire	R.H.
"	"		4 Animals wounded	R.H.
"	"		Strength:– 6 Officers 207 O.Rs 70 Animals.	⑤ R.H.
"	"	9 a.m.	1 N.C.O. and men of No 1 Section proceed to advanced trills	R.H.

Sheet 2
Army Form C. 2118

WAR DIARY
or
INTELLIGENCE SUMMARY
(Erase heading not required.)

Place	Date	Hour	Summary of Events and Information	Remarks and references to Appendices
TRONES WOOD	6/1/17	9am	Remainder of No 1 Section proceeds to advanced billets — Work as for 5/1/17	⑥ EH
"	7/1/17		Work as for 6/1/17 1 Driver reinforcement joined unit Strength — 6 Officers 208 O.R. 70 Animals	⑦ EH EH
"	8/1/17		7 N.C.O's & men of No 4 section proceed to advanced billets — Work as for 7/1/17 and section in advanced billets commences work in Reserve line trenches 2 O.R's evacuated Strength — 6 Officers 206 O.R. 70 Animals	⑧ EH Feb EH
"	9/1/17		Remainder of No 4 section proceeds to advanced billets and No 3 section returns to D.H.Q. Work as for 8/1/17 No 2 & 3 sections went for baths No 2 section commences wiring new Reserve Line.	⑨ EH EH EH
"	10/1/17	6pm	Work as for 9/1/17 1 O.R. evacuated Strength. — 6 Officer 205 O.R. 70 Animals	EH EH EH
"	11/1/17	6pm	Whole company proceeds to Reserve line and works on apron fence wiring. 2 O.R's joined unit Strength. — 6 Officers 207 O.R. 70 Animals	⑩ EH EH

Sheet 3

Army Form C. 2118

WAR DIARY
or
INTELLIGENCE SUMMARY 93rd Field Company, R.E.
(Erase heading not required.)

Instructions regarding War Diaries and Intelligence Summaries are contained in F.S. Regs, Part II. and the Staff Manual respectively. Title Pages will be prepared in manuscript.

Place	Date	Hour	Summary of Events and Information	Remarks and references to Appendices
TRONES WOOD	12/1/17	6 p.m.	Company continued night wiring on/for 11/7. 2 O.R. Wounded 2 Light draught horses evacuated. Strength :- 6 Officers 205 - OR 62 animals	S.M. ⑩ S.M.
"	13/1/17		No 4 Section returns from advanced billets - O.R.HQ. 2 O.R. admitted to hospital.	S.M. ⑪
"	14/1/17		No 4 Section returns from advanced billets - O.R.HQ. 5 Mules and 3 light draught horses drawn from Remounts. Strength :- 6 Officers 205 OR. 75 animals.	S.M. ⑫
"	15/1/17		Company proceeded to Divisional Reserve. No 1 section left TRONES WOOD and arrives LA HOUSSOYE at 4.30 p.m.	S.M.
		9.30 a.m.	mains column left TRONES WOOD and arrives LA HOUSSOYE 9.20 p.m.	S.M. ⑬
		12.N p.m.	Remainder of Company left PLATEAU returning at BUIRE Mense en fort. returning at PLATEAU returning at billets - chief officers incapacitated	S.M.
LA HOUSSOYE	16/1/17		Company works on improvement of billets - chief officers incapacitated accommodation for all ranks.	
"	17/1/17		Work as for 16/7. 1 O.R. pioneer unit 1 O.R. admitted to hospital. 1 O.R. Pioneer 1 O.R. joined unit	S.M.
"	18/1/17		Work as for 17/7.	S.M.
"	19/1/17	0.30	Company moves from LA HOUSSOYE to DAOURS arriving at 4 p.m.	S.M. ⑬
DAOURS	20/1/17		Company commenced work at XIV Corps R.A. School constructing Stabling and camp buildings. 1 O.R. rejoined unit.	S.M.

Sheet 4
Army Form C. 2118

WAR DIARY
or
INTELLIGENCE SUMMARY 93rd FIELD Coy. R.E.

(Erase heading not required.)

Instructions regarding War Diaries and Intelligence Summaries are contained in F.S. Regs., Part II. and the Staff Manual respectively. Title Pages will be prepared in manuscript.

Place	Date	Hour	Summary of Events and Information	Remarks and references to Appendices
DAOURS	21/7/17		Work as for 20/7/17. Corpl Smith and 2 O.R. proceeds to C.C.S. Neilly. In moves in N° 1,2,6 & 3 Secs. Corpl Lancaster appointed acting Sergeant N° 4 Section.	B.H. (13)
"	22/7/17		Sgt Lacey & 8 O.R. proceeds to Reilly for work as 21/7. Remainder of Company notes on R.E. School Camp. 3 O.R. evacuated 1 Light Draught horse evacuated.	B.H. (13)
"	23/7/17		Strength:- 8 Officers 202 O.R. 74 animals. 1 Corpl & 6 O.R. proceeds to Reilly for work on CCS. Work as for 23/7/17.	B.H.
"	24/7/17		Lt. Morris and 6 O.R. proceeds to COMBLES to take over from 96 K Fd Coy R.E. - Remainder of Company work as for 24/7/17.	S.H. (13)
"	25/7/17		1 O.R. admitted to Hospital. Party from REILLY returns to DAOURS.	S.H. (13)
"	26/7/17		2 O.R. admitted to Hospital. Dismounted section left DAOURS and proceeds to COMBLES entraining at 8.30 am, arrives 2.0 p.m. went into billets - 3 Section in COMBLES and one section (N°4) at WEDGEWOOD.	B.H.
"	27/7/17		Mounted section left DAOURS 9.00 am arrives WEDGEWOOD at 6 p.m. 9 Light Draught Horses drawn from Remounts. Strength:- 6 Officers 202 O.R. 83 animals.	B.H.

Stubs
Army Form C. 2118

WAR DIARY
or
INTELLIGENCE SUMMARY

93rd Field Company R.E.

(Erase heading not required.)

Instructions regarding War Diaries and Intelligence Summaries are contained in F. S. Regs., Part II. and the Staff Manual respectively. Title Pages will be prepared in manuscript.

Place	Date	Hour	Summary of Events and Information	Remarks and references to Appendices
COMBLES	28/7/17		No.1 Section on Daywork — FREGICOURT. No.2 & 3 Sections on Nightwork — Support line area. No.4 Section on Daywork improving WEDGEWOOD reconnaissance. 1 O.R. admitted to Hospital. 1 Light Draught stores received. Strength — 6 officers 202 O.R. 82 animals.	(14)
"	29/7/17		Work as for 28th inst 1/17	Sen (14)
"	30/7/17		Work as for 29th inst 1/17. 3 O.R. admitted to Hospital.	824 (14)
"	31/7/17		Work as for 30/7/17. 1 O.R. killed in action. 1 O.R. wounded. 1 O.R. returned to England to take up Commission. Strength — 6 officers 199 O.R. 82 animals.	Pgl. (14)

G.S. Culham P/R.E
O.C. 93rd Field Co R.E.

WAR DIARY
or
INTELLIGENCE SUMMARY.
(Erase heading not required.)

Army Form C. 2118.

Shex. M.1.
93rd Field Coy. R.E.
Vol 17

Place	Date	Hour	Summary of Events and Information	Remarks and references to Appendices
Gueudecourt COMBLES.	1.2.17.		No. 1. Section on day work. Nos. 2 & 3. on night work. No. 4 section attached 78th Fd. Coy. for work in back area. Strength:— 6 Officers — 199. O.R's. 82 animals.	G. D. 13.—
"	2.2.17.		Work as for 1st. 1 horse died. 1. O.R. evacuated. Strength. 6 Officers. 198. O.R's. 81 animals.	G. D. 13.
"	3.2.17.		Work as for 2nd. Works report from 1st — 3rd inclusive.	Appendix 1. G.D.13.
"	4.2.17.		Work as above. Works report.	Appendix 2. G.D.13.
"	5.2.17.		Work as above. 6. O.R's evacuated. Strength. 6 Officers. 192. O.R's. 81 animals. Works report.	Appendix 3. G.D.13.
"	6.2.17.		Work as above. 1 horse died. Strength. 6 Officers. 192. O.R's. 80 animals. Daily Works report.	Appendix 4. G.D.13.
"	7.2.17.		Work as above. Daily Works report.	Appendix 5. G.D.13.
"	8.2.17.		Work as above. Also working captured position of Sudenum Trench. 1. O.R. killed, 1. O.R wounded (multiple) Strength. Work report	Appendix 6. G.D.13.
"	9.2.17.		Work as for 8th inst. 1. S.D. horse evacuated. Strength. 6 Officers. 190. O.R's. 80 animals. Work report.	Appendix 7. G.D.13.—
"	10.2.17.		Work as for 9th inst. No. 2. section reduced. No. 4. section on work in back areas by agreement with O.C. 78th Fd. Cy. Work report.	Appendix 8. G.D.13.
"	11.2.17.		Work as above. 1. O.R. killed (Rifle fire) Strength. 6 Officers. 189. O.R's. 79 animals. Daily Work report.	Appendix 9. G.D.13.
"	12.2.17.		Work as above. Daily works report.	Weekly Report. G.D.13
"	13.2.17.		Work as above. 2nd Lt. Culham admitted to hospital. 1. S.D. horse died. Strength. 5 Officers. 189. O.R's. 78 animals. Daily work Report.	Appendix 10. G.D.13.—
"	14.2.17.		Work as above. 3. O.R's. reinforcements (drivers) joined Coy. ?/Lt. Long awarded M.M. Strength. 5 Officers. 192. O.R's. Daily Works report.	Appendix 11. G.D.13.
"	15.2.17.		Work as above. Daily Works report.	Appendix 12. G.D.13.—
"	16.2.17.		Work as above. 2nd Lt. A.S. Culham R.E. evacuated sick. Strength. 5 Officers. 192. O.R's. 78 animals. Daily Works Report.	Appendix 13. G.D.13.

Army Form C. 2118.

WAR DIARY
or
INTELLIGENCE SUMMARY.
(Erase heading not required.)

Sheet No. 2.
93rd Field Coy. R.E.

Place	Date	Hour	Summary of Events and Information	Remarks and references to Appendices
COMBLES	17.2.17		Work on as for 16.2.17. 6 O.R.'s evacuated. 1 S.D. horse evacuated. Strength: 5 Officers 187 O.R.'s & 77 animals	Appendix No.
"	18.2.17		Work as above. 1 civilian destroyed. Strength 5 Officers 187 O.R.'s 78 animals. Daily with report	A.T.B. Appendix 4.
"	19.2.17		Work as above. 3 S.D. horses & mules evacuated. Strength 5 Officers 187 O.R.'s 72 animals.	A.D.B.R.
"	20.2.17		Advanced Sections arrived with 9 Coy. at 4 P.M. Pulled up & marched to Mansell Camp. 4 O.R.'s reinforcements. Strength 6 Officers 191 O.R.'s 72 animals.	C.D.B.
MANSELL CAMP	21.2.17		Nos 1 and 2 sections returned to Combles under T.D. Beaupré. Remainder of Coy. proceeded by road & billets at Daours. 4 O.R.'s 72 animals	C.D.B.
DAOURS	22.2.17		1 O.R. proceeded to Base depot. Strength 5 Officers 190 O.R.'s 72 animals. Improvements to billets. Workshops XIV Corps R.O. staff.	C.D.B.
"	23.2.17		Nos. 1 and 2 Sections worked on dugouts, Maricourt - Chateau - ILR, Y.A. Jacquez R.F. joined Coy. Strength 6 Officers 190 O.R.'s 72 animals.	C.D.B.
"	24.2.17		Work as above. 2 mules evacuated. Strength 6 Officers 190 O.R.'s 70 animals.	C.D.B.
"	25.2.17		Work as above. Nos 1 & 2 sections rejoined Coy. 2/Lt G.D. Beaupré R.E. arrived. Shelby Cpl. 57056 2/Cpl J. Beaumont arrived. 3 B.E.M. 2nd Lt from 17th D.R.O. N.P.16.01. & 23 others.	Appendix 18. C.D.B.
"	26.2.17		Work as above. 2 S.D. horses evacuated. Strength 6 Officers 190 O.R.'s 68 animals.	C.D.B.
"	27.2.17		Work as above. 2 N.C.O's & 10 men went to Corveney to work a field rly.	C.D.B.
"	28.2.17		Work as above. Coy. had men live respirator fitted in gas chamber under supervision of Divl. Gas N.C.O. Men in detachment agreed with.	C.D.B.

C.D. Beaupré 2 Lt. R.E.
IV Corps 93rd Field Coy R.E.

Army Form C. 2118.

WAR DIARY
or
INTELLIGENCE SUMMARY.
(Erase heading not required.)

93rd Field Coy. R.E.
SHEET No. 1 Vol. 18

Instructions regarding War Diaries and Intelligence Summaries are contained in F.S. Regs., Part II. and the Staff Manual respectively. Title pages will be prepared in manuscript.

Place	Date	Hour	Summary of Events and Information	Remarks and references to Appendices
DADOURS	1.3.17		Work on XIV Corps Artillery School. 2 O.R's evacuated. Strength 6 Officers 188 O.R's. 68 Animals.	S.D.B.
"	2.3.17	8.45 A.M.	Left DADOURS and marched to HERISSART arriving 2.30 p.m.	G.D.B.
HERISSART	3.3.17		Company training started.	G.D.B.
"	4.3.17		As for 3.3.17. 1 O.R. evacuated. 1 Mdr. I.L.D. evacuated. Strength 6 Officers 187 O.R's. 61 animals	G.D.B.
"	5.3.17		As for 4.3.17. 1 O.R. evacuated. Strength 6 Officers 186 O.R's 66 animals.	G.D.B.
"	6.3.17		As for 5.3.17. 6 reinforcements joined unit. Strength 6 Officers 192 O.R's. 66 horses animals. G.D.B.	
"	7.3.17		As for 6.3.17. 1 O.R. evacuated. Strength 6 Officers 191 O.R's. 66 animals	G.D.B.
"	8.3.17		As for 7.3.17	G.D.B.
"	9.3.17		As for 8.3.17	G.D.B.
"	10.3.17		As for 9.3.17. Preliminary parade held by C.R.E. No 1 Section paraded to Rubempré for work from.	G.D.B.
"	11.3.17		C.R.E. inspected Coy. at 10 A.M. 2 L.D. & 3 Cable drawn from 295 Bristol Yd. Section. Strength 6 Officers 196 O.R's. 66 animals. 1 O.R (diary) evacuated.	G.D.B.
"	12.3.17		Company training in morning. Paraded & Baths Strength 6 Officers 195 O.R's. 71 animals at Contay in afternoon.	G.D.B.
"	13.3.17	10.15 A.M.	Company marched out of HERISSART at 10.15 A.M. arrived BEAUVAL 2.15 p.m.	G.D.B.
BEAUVAL	14.3.17	8.30 A.M.	Company marched out of BEAUVAL at 8.30 A.M. arrived BEAUVOIR 2.30 p.m.	G.D.B.
BEAUVOIR	15.3.17	9 A.M.	Company marched out of BEAUVOIR at 9 A.M. arrived HARAVESNES at 12.30 p.m. 1 O.R. evacuated	G.D.B.
HARAVESNES	16.3.17		Company started training. Strength 6 Officers 194 O.R's. 71 animals.	G.D.B.
"	17.3.17		As for 16.3.17.	S.G.B.
"	18.3.17		As for 17.3.17. 1 Rider and 13 L.D. cast by A.D.V.S. Strength 6 Officers 194 O.R's. 57 animals	G.D.B.
"	19.3.17		As for 18.3.17. 2nd Lt. Hornby & Lt. Harris from Abermad R.E. joined unit. 1 O.R. joined unit. Strength 7 Officers 195 O.R's. 57 animals. 4 N.C.O's went for Gas course. 4 N.C.O's & sappers sent to Battn: as instructors.	G.D.B.
"	20.3.17		As for 19.3.17	G.D.B.

Army Form C. 2118

WAR DIARY
or
INTELLIGENCE SUMMARY
(Erase heading not required.)

Instructions regarding War Diaries and Intelligence Summaries are contained in F.S. Regs, Part II. and the Staff Manual respectively. Title Pages will be prepared in manuscript.

Place	Date	Hour	Summary of Events and Information	Remarks and references to Appendices
HARAVESNES	21.3.17		Company training	R.C.L.
"	22.3.17	10.15 AM	Marched out of HARAVESNES. Arrived at REMAISNIL at 3 p.m.	R.C.L.
REMAISNIL	23.3.17	9.30 AM	Dismounted portion marched out. Stopped at BOUQUEMAISON for 4 hours to repair roads under orders from G.S. 17th Div. Arrived at BEAUDRICOURT at 6.15 p.m.	
		9.45 AM	Mounted portion marched out of REMAISNIL at 9.45 a.m. Arrived BEAUDRICOURT 4.15 p.m.	R.C.L.
BEAUDRICOURT	24.3.17		L.D. horse destroyed. 4 O.R. reinforcements joined. Strength 7 officers. 199 O.R.'s. 70 animals.	R.C.L.
"	25.3.17	9.30 AM	Coy. marched to OPPY. Summer time instituted. (Time advanced 60 min.)	R.C.L.
OPPY	26.3.17		Coy. training & overhauling vehicles & equipment.	R.C.L.
	27.3.17		"	R.C.L.
	28.3.17		" 1 L.D. mule died.	R.C.L.
	29.3.17		" Strength 7 officers. 199 O.R.'s. 69 animals.	R.C.L.
			10 O.R. sent to work at XVIIIth Corps workshop under C.R.E's. orders.	R.C.L.
	30.3.17		As for 29.3.17. 2 O.R's evacuated. 3 O.R's joined unit. Strength 7 officers. 200 O.R.'s. 69 animals.	Q.D.B.
	31.3.17		As for 30.3.17. 1 O.R. returned from hospital after being evacuated. 1 O.R. joined unit. 1 O.R. admitted to hospital. Strength 7 officers. 202 O.R.'s. 69 animals.	Q.D.B.

R.E.P. Lunde
Maj. R.E.
O.C. 93rd Coy R.E.

Army Form C. 2118

93rd (Jd) Coy RE

APRIL 1917.

WAR DIARY
or
INTELLIGENCE SUMMARY

(Erase heading not required.)

Instructions regarding War Diaries and Intelligence Summaries are contained in F.S. Regs., Part II. and the Staff Manual respectively. Title Pages will be prepared in manuscript.

Place	Date	Hour	Summary of Events and Information	Remarks and references to Appendices
OPPY.	1.4.17.		Coy. Training and refitting Coy. Equipment. Strength. 7 officers. 202 O.R's. 69 animals.	G.D.B.
"	2.4.17.		As above. No. 4. Section out on fall day. 3 O.R's joined unit. Strength. 7 officers. 205 O.R's. 69 animals.	G.D.B.
"	3.4.17.		As above. No 1. Section out on fall day. 2 O.R's joined unit. I.L.D. mule joined unit.	G.D.B.
"	4.4.17		As above. Transport out on full day. 1 O.R evacuated. Strength. 7 officers. 207 O.R's. 70 animals.	G.D.B.
HOUVIN.	5.4.17.	2.15 p.m.	Company marched out of OPPY. at 12.30. p.m. arrived HOUVIN. at 2.15. p.m. 2 L.D. Mules joined unit. Strength. 7 officers. 206 O.R's. 70 animals.	G.D.B.
"	6.4.17.		Kit inspection held. I.L.D Horse shot under V.O's orders. 2 O.R's joined unit. 1 O.R injured aft. kit inspection. 1 O.R evacuated. Strength. 7 officers. 208 O.R's. 71 animals.	G.D.B.
BEAUFORT.	7.4.17.	1.15 p.m.	Company marched out of HOUVIN at 10 A.M. arrived at BEAUFORT. at 1.15. p.m.	G.D.B.
SIMENCOURT.	8.4.17	2.30 p.m.	Company marched at BEAUFORT at 10.35 A.M. arrived at SIMENCOURT. at 2.30. p.m. 1 L.D Horse shot. Strength. 7 officers. 208 O.R's 70 animals.	G.D.B.
"	9.4.17.		Battle kit inspection. Coy. divided into echelons. A.P.B. echelon marched out at 4.45. p.m. 1 O.R to ARRAS admitted to hospital.	G.D.B.
ARRAS	10.4.17.		C. Echelon marched to BERNEVILLE. 2 O.R's admitted to hospital. I.L.D. mule died. Strength. 7 officers. 208 O.R's. 69 animals. A & B Echelons at ARRAS	G.D.B.
"	11.4.17.		A. & B. Echelons at ARRAS. C. echelon at BERNEVILLE awaiting return 1 O.R admitted to Aug. Strength. 7 officers. 209 O.R's. 69 animals.	G.D.B.
"	12.4.17	5 P.M.	A. Echelon marched out of ARRAS.	R.C.L.
"	13.4.17	4 A.M.	A. Echelon arrived at FEUCHY & went into Billets Work commenced in and around FEUCHY. Works Report. 2 O.R evacuated. Strength. 7 officers. 206 O.R. 69 animals.	App. I R.C.L.

WAR DIARY
or
INTELLIGENCE SUMMARY

(Erase heading not required.)

Army Form C. 2118

53rd (Sd) Coy RE
APRIL 1917

Place	Date	Hour	Summary of Events and Information	Remarks and references to Appendices
FEUCHY	14.4.17	9 A.M.	C Echelon marched from BERNEVILLE to ARRAS, & joined B Echelon. Work continued behind MONCHY & on ORANGE HILL LINE.	App. II R.E.
	15.4.17		1 O.R. killed. 1 O.R. wounded, 1 O.R. wounded at duty, 1 O.R. admissions. Strength 7 Off. 204 O.R. 68 horses	App. III R.E. App. IV R.E. Works Report.
	16.4.17		Work on ORANGE HILL LINE. No work in MONCHY CHATEAU WOOD. Wire no letter 2nd/Lieut. M. E. THOMAS wounded (at duty). 1 O.R. wounded. Strength 7 Off. 203 O.R. 71 animals. Three L.D. Mules received.	R.E.I.
	17.4.17		1 Mule & 1 L.D. Horse destroyed. 1 Mule & 3 horses evacuated. Strength 203 O.R. 7 Officers. 65 animals	App. V R.E.I.
	18.4.17 19.4.17		Strength as above. No night work. 3 O.R. wounded. Strength 7 Off. 200 O.R. 65 admissions. Works Report.	R.E.I.
	20.4.17		Strength as above. Works Report.	App. VI R.E.
	21.4.17		1 Rider evac. 4 horses & G.L.D. Mules joined. Strength 7 Off. 203 O.R. 70 animals.	App. VII R.E. Works Report
	22.4.17		2 O.R. wounded. 5 Sappers joined. Strength 7 Off. 206 O.R. 70 animals.	App. VIII R.E. App. VIIIA Report on ORANGE HILL LINE
	23.4.17	6.30 A.M. 10 P.M.	Coy and C. Coy 7th Bn Seaforth Regt. moved into "BROWN LINE" Orders for night work received by O.C. 2nd Bde H.Q. (50th). 2 O.R. evacuated. 1 O.R. wounded. 10 animals joined.	R.E. App. IX R.E.I
	24.4.17		Strength 7 Officers. 204 O.R. 70 animals. 3 O.R. joined. Strength 7 Off. 207 O.R. 70 animals.	Works Report. App. X R.E.I Works Report.

Army Form C. 2118

WAR DIARY
or
INTELLIGENCE SUMMARY

(Erase heading not required.)

93rd (Id) Coy R.E.

APRIL 1917

Place	Date	Hour	Summary of Events and Information	Remarks and references to Appendices
FEUCHY	25.4.17		Work & Billets taken over by 69th (Id) Coy R.E. 1 O.R. Wounded. Echelon A returned to billets in ARRAS. 2 L.D. horses received. Strength 7 Officers, 206 O.R. 72 animals.	RCL
ARRAS.	26.4.17	10. A.M. 9. A.M.	Dismounted Portion entrained for SAULTY & ARRAS STATION. Arrived IVERGNY 4 P.M. Mounted Portion marched to IVERGNY arriving 4.30 P.M. 1 O.R. evacuated. Strength 7 Off. 205 O.R. 72 animals.	RCL.
IVERGNY.	27.4.17		Coy. resting. Kit etc. infested. Men paid. 2 O.R. (prev. evac.) rejoined. Strength 7 Off. 207 O.R. 72 animals. Baths.	RCL.
	28.4.17		3 Riders 4 L.D. Mules received. Strength 7 Off. 207 O.R. 79 animals. Baths.	RCL.
	29.4.17		Coy. resting. Warning order re movement to XVIIth Corps Area received.	RCL.
	30.4.17		Instructions for movement completed.	

R.C. Dundas
Maj. R.E.
O.C. 93rd (Id) Coy R.E.

Army Form C. 2118.

Sheet No. 1.

WAR DIARY
~~INTELLIGENCE SUMMARY~~

(Erase heading not required.)

93rd (Field) Coy. R.E.

Place	Date July	Hour	Summary of Events and Information	Remarks and references to Appendices
IVERGNY	1		Dismounted portion of company embussed at 6·00 a.m. at cross roads EAST of IVERGNY arrived at LARESSET HUTS at 9·00 a.m. Mounted portion of company marched out of IVERGNY at 9·00 a.m. arrived at LARESSET HUTS at 3·15 p.m. Strength 7 Officers. 207 O.R. 79 animals (B) sheet No 51.b.	3/4 W. Scarpe. 3/4 W. Scarpe.
LARESSET	2		Company marched out at 3·00 p.m. arrived G17·B·6·A at 5·30 p.m. 2 O.R. joined company. Strength 7 Officers. 209 O.R. 79 animals.	3/4 W. Scarpe.
ARRAS. G.17.b. sheet No 51.b.	3		Company awaiting orders. Improvements to camp &c. 1. O.R. evacuated. Strength 7 Officers. 208 O.R. 79 animals.	3/4 W. Scarpe.
-do-	4		As for 3rd.	3/4 W. Scarpe.
-do-	5		As for 3rd.	3/4 W. Scarpe.
-do-	6		As for 3rd. 2. O.R. evacuated. Strength 7 Officers. 206 O.R. 79 animals.	3/4 W. Scarpe.
-do-	7		As for 6th.	3/4 W. Scarpe. B.
-do-	8		As for 6th. O.C. visited H.Q. and through Sector J 90's Field. Coy. R.E. with view to taking over. C.R.E. B. 2. O.R. evacuated. Strength 7 Officers. 204 O.R. 79 animals.	3/4 W. Scarpe.

Army Form C. 2118.

WAR DIARY
INTELLIGENCE SUMMARY.
(Erase heading not required.)

93rd (Field) Coy. R.E. Sheet. No 2.—

Place	Date	Hour	Summary of Events and Information	Remarks and references to Appendices
S. OF AVRELLES	9.5.17	2 A.M.	Coy: relieved 90th Field Coy: Dismounted portion left at 9 p.m. for forward billets. 7 men went to work under D.O.R.E. 1. Section worked all night on O.P.—	G.D.B.
"	10.5.17		As for 9.5.17. Dismounted worked for O.C. R.E. Strength. 7 Offrs. 202 O.R's. 79 animals. Wehrspel alf? 3 A.M. O.C. reinforcement section with B.M. 52nd Bde. F.O.C. 10th Armd. Divn. O.P. finished.— (C.L. 91, 32, 93.)	Appendix I G.D.B.
"	11.5.17		As for 10.5.17. Wehr spel alf? (C.L. 96)	Appendix II G.D.B.
"	12.5.17		As for 11.5.17. Wehr spel alf? (C.L. 98)	Appendix III G.D.B.
"	13.5.17		As for 12.5.17. 1.O.R. joined unit. 1.L.D. Horse evacuated. I.L.D. Horse evacuated. Strength 7 Offrs. 202 O.R's. 79 animals. O.C. ord. new Batt? H.Q. with O.C. 9 S.N.F. 2nd Lt. Off D? Murchlett? Wehrspel alf?	Appendix IV G.D.B.
"	14.5.17		As for 13.5.17. 2.O.R's (joined unit) Strength 7 Offrs. 204 O.R's. 79 animals. Wehr spel alf?— (C.L.2,3,?4)	Appendix V G.D.B.—
"	15.5.17		As for 14.5.17. II Lieut. Beresford returned to Horse Lines. 1.L.D. Mule evacuated. 2.O.R's. evacuated. Strength 7 Offrs. 202 O.R's. 77 animals.	G.D.B Appendix VI
"	16.5.17		As for 15.5.17. No 3. Section came back to adv. H.Q. (Horse Lines) No 3. Section. H.Q. Section. Pioneers Section paid. II Lt. Jacques came back to adv. H.Q. (5 Pioneers Amps)	G.D.B Appendix VII
"	17.5.17		As for 16.5.17. No 3. Section worked on Camp improvements. II Lieut. Macquaine went forward. II Lt. Harris returned to adv. H.Q.	G.D.B.
"	18.5.17		As for 17.5.17. Capt. Reid wounded near H.Q. during afternoon, returned to forward H.Q. with II Lt. Beresford and No 3. Section. II Lt Jacques admitted to hospital. No 1. Jackson returned to adv H.Q. arrived at 11.30 a.m.	G.D.B.
"	19.5.17		As for 18.5.17. No 1. section paid. 1.O.R wounded (bullets). Inspection of horses by A.D.V.S. 1 mule shot. 4.L.D horses evacuated Strength 7 Offrs. 201 O.R's. 72 animals.	Appendix VIII G.D.B.
"	20.5.17		As for 19.5.17. No 1. section went forward at 8 p.m. No 2. section returned to adv H.Q at 11.30 p.m. Capt. Reid returned to adv. H.Q. at 2. p.m. 3.O.R's joined unit. 1.O.R evacuated Strength 7 Offrs. 203. O.R's. 72 animals.	Appendix IX G.D.B
"	21.5.17		As for 20.5.17. II Lt. Yeoman came back to Read? H.Q. No 2. Section paid. 2. O.R's evacuated. Strength 7 Offrs. 201. O.R's. 72 animals.	G.D.B Appendix XI

A3834 Wt.W4973/M687 750,000 8/16 D.D.& L. Ltd. Forms/C.2118/13.

WAR DIARY or INTELLIGENCE SUMMARY

Army Form C. 2118.

93rd Field Company R.E. May 1917

Place	Date	Hour	Summary of Events and Information	Remarks and references to Appendices
Cap Groville	22/5/17	—	Relief of 93rd R.E. by 77th Fld Coy R.E. Company took over work and billets of 77th Coy R.E. Nos 1,2&3 sections in billets in Ry Cutting and No.4 Section in billets at Rear H.Q. C.O. at Rear H.Q. 3 O.R's wounded. Strength 7 officers 198 O.Rs 72 animals. — Works Report	S.M. Appendix XII / XIII
Railway Cutting	23/5/17	—	No.1,2&3 Sections on time duty – one Sec to do S.I. Butalf. No.4 Section at H.Q. (R.H.). —	Appendix XIV / XV B.M.
"	24/5/17	—	As for above. Strength 7 Officers 197 O.Rs 72 animals – Works Report. 1 O.R. wounded	Appendix XVI B.M.
"	25/5/17	—	As for above. 1 O.R. sent base wounded. Command proceeds on leave. Sec in Command proceeds to Rear H.Q.	Appendix XVI B.M.
"	26/5/17	—	As for above. O.C. + Lt McQuarie + 2 O.R. proceed on leave. Works Report.	B.M.
"	27/5/17	—	No.1,2&3 sections on duty. (No.4 section on limed dug-out to billeting and commencement of new Strength 7 Officers 197 O.R's 71 animals. Works Report. in Ry Cutting to accommodate 1 Inf Coy. 1 B.O. ft'ce received	Appendix XVIII B.M.
"	28/5/17	—	As for above — Officer from relieving unit inspects billets + work in hand – Works Report.	Appendix XIX B.M.
"	29/5/17	—	Nos 1,2&3 sections on time work as above. No.9 Section at H.Q. preparing moving to move. "H." Mess and all equip and baggage proceeds from Ry Cutting to Rear H.Q. — Works Report. Strength 7 Officers 196 O.R's 72 animals	Appendix XX B.M.
"	30/5/17	—	Morning parties march-in at 7.30 am. HUMBERCOURT at 3 p.m. Damaged prior. Old Rly CUTTING at 5 am – arrived near H.Q. at 10.15 am (tram) at ARRAS goods Station at 4 p.m. – tram started detrainment at SAULTY at 5.15 p.m. – arrived HUMBERCOURT at 7.15 p.m. and into Billets. Company employed improving billets – Company was back 4 O.R's joined unit.	B.M.
HUMBERCOURT	31/5/17	—	Company employed improving billets translation. Strength 7 Officers 200 O.R's 72 animals.	B.M.

R.S. McLeod
Major
O.C 93rd Field Coy R.E

Army Form C. 2118.

WAR DIARY or INTELLIGENCE SUMMARY.

(Erase heading not required.)

93rd Field Coy R.E.   SHEET No. 1

Place	Date	Hour	Summary of Events and Information	Remarks and references to Appendices
HUMBERCOURT	1.6.17.	3 p.m.	Company worked on improving billets. 2nd Lieut. Thomas & Sergt. Coe. proceeded to WANQUETIN. to take over work from Chestnut Hill Coy. 2nd Lieut Thomas returned to HUMBERCOURT. Sergt Coe. stayed at WANQUETIN. 1 officer evacuated. (2nd LIEUT. A. JACQUES). 1 O.R. evacuated. Strength 6 officers 199. O.R's. 72 animals.	G.D.B.
"	2.6.17.		Coy. went to baths at HUMBERCOURT. Advanced party of 4 men proceeded to WANQUETIN. 1 O.R. joined unit.	G.D.B.
WANQUETIN.	3.6.17.	3 p.m.	Coy marched out of Humbercourt at 10.30 A.M. arrived WANQUETIN. 2.30 p.m. and went into billets. 2nd Lt. HARRIS. joined. 1 + 4. A.T. Coy. R.E.	G.D.B.
"	4.6.17.		Sappers started work on repair of horses at WANQUETIN. Officer preparing for Divisional Horse Show. Works report C.E. XVIII Corps.	G.D.B. Appendix 1
"	5.6.19.		As for 4th inst. 3. O.R's. evacuated. Strength. 6 officers. 196. O.R's. 72 animals. (Works Report.)	Appendix 2. G.D.B.
"	6.6.17.		As for 5th inst. Waggons & horses went to Divisional Horse Show. at MONDICOURT. (Works Report)	Appendix 3 G.D.B.
"	7.6.17.		As for 6th inst. Horse Show. Pontoon Waggon and mule team obtained 1st Prize. C.O. returned from leave. (Works Report)	Appendix 4. G.D.B.
"	8.6.17.		As for 7th inst. (Works Report)	Appendix 5. G.D.B.
"	9.6.17.		As for 8th inst. 7. O.R's. joined unit. Strength. 6 officers. 203. O.R's. 72 animals. (Works Report)	Appendix 6. G.D.B.
"	10.6.17.		As for 9th inst. Maunsell section had a company concert and dinner in the evening. (Works Report)	Appendix 7. G.D.B.
"	11.6.17.		As for 10th inst. 4. O.R's. joined unit. Strength. 6 officers. 207. O.R's. 72 animals. (Works Report)	Appendix. G.D.B.
"	12.6.17.	2.30 am.	Coy marched out of WANQUETIN at 3.30. A.M. arrived 6.16 to 2.3. Sh. 4:51.B. (Nth of ARRAS) at 2.15 p.m. Dismounted sections went forward by Railway factory. (N.9. ATHIES.) at 1. p.m. R. O.R's. evacuated. Strength. 6 officers 205. O.R's. 72 animals	G.D.B.
ARRAS.	13.6.17.		Maunsell Section at 6.16.6.2.3. Took out crew, making Mining Frames. Sections working on dugouts in Corps Line. 4. L.D. Horses evacuated. 2nd LIEUT. HAMPTON. joined unit. Strength 7 officers 205 O.R's. 76. animals.	G.D.B.
"	14.6.17.		As for 13.6.17.	G.D.B.
"	15.6.17.		As for 14.6.17. 1. O.R. joined unit. Strength. 7 officers 206. O.R's. 76. animals	G.D.B.
"	16.6.17.		As for 15.6.19.	G.D.B.
"	17.6.17.		As for 16.6.17. 3. O.R's. evacuated. Strength. 7 officers. 203. O.R's. 76 animals.	G.D.B.

Army Form C. 2118.

WAR DIARY
or
INTELLIGENCE SUMMARY.
(Erase heading not required.)

93rd Field Coy R.E.   SHEET No 2

Place	Date	Hour	Summary of Events and Information	Remarks and references to Appendices
ARRAS.	18.6.17		Manlet Section at G.16.b.2.3. Shaft S.I.B. Yiodical crew erecting mining frames. Section working on dugouts in Copse Line. —	G.D.B. —
"	19.6.17		Do to 18.6.17. (Works report)	Appendix B. G.D.B.
"	20.6.17		Do to 19.6.17.	G.D.B.
"	21.6.17		No. 2 Section returned to new H.Q. from Railway Cutting, erected Baraccas. C.S.M. returned to rear H.Q. No. 1, 3, 4 sections went from Railway cutting to forward billets in C.A.M. Trench. 2/Lt Lucas went to forward billets from rear H.Q. (Works Report)	Appendix 17.
"	22.6.17		Forward sections started work in the line. No. 2 Section started in Camp improvements.	G.D.B.
"	23.6.17		Do to 22.6.17. 1.O.R. accidentally injured (mule kick) Strength. 7 officers. 202 O.R's. 73 animals.	G.D.B.
"	24.6.17		Do to 23.6.17. 2 O.R's wounded. Strength. 7 officers. 200 O.R's. 76 animals. (Works reports)	G.D.B.
"	25.6.17		No. 2 Section went to forward billets at 9 h.m. No. 3 section returned to rear H.Q. arrived 4.30. A.m. (26.7) (Works report)	G.D.B. Appendix 12
"	26.6.17		No. 3 section worked on Camp improvements. 7 O.R's gassed work. R.O.R's. evacuated Strength 7 officers. 205 O.R's.	G.D.B. Appendix 12 G.D.B.
"	27.6.17		Do to 26.6.17 A.D.V.S. (Col.) inspected horses. 1.L.D. made evacuation Strength. 7 officers. 205 O.R's. 75 animals. (Works reports)	G.D.B. Appendix 13
"	28.6.17		Do to 27.6.17 Wet canteen opened at rear H.Q. (Works report)	G.D.B. Appendix 14
"	29.6.17		Do to 28.6.17. (Works report)	G.D.B. Appendix 15 & 16
"	30.6.17		Do to 29.6.17.	G.D.B. Appendix 17.

For Lt Col [signature] R.E.
O/C. 93rd Field Co. R.E.

Army Form C. 2118.

WAR DIARY
or
INTELLIGENCE SUMMARY.
(Erase heading not required.)

93rd (Field) Coy R.E.

Sheet No. 1

Place	Date	Hour	Summary of Events and Information	Remarks and references to Appendices
Sheet No. 51.b 6.16.b. 2.3.	1-7-17		No. 3 Section relieved No. 4 Section forward. 1 Rider evacuated. Strength. 7 Officers. 205 O.R. 74 Animals.	(Works Report.) Appendix 1.
	2-7-17		No. 4 Section had baths. 2.O.R. evacuated. Strength. 7 Officers - 203 O.R. 74 Animals.	(Works Report) Appendix 2.
	3-7-17		No. 4 Section at work in camp and dump. Strength. 7 Officers. 203. O.R. 74 Animals.	(Works Report) Appendix 3.
	4-7-17		As for 3rd. inst.	(Works Report) Appendix 4.
	5-7-17		As for 3rd. inst.	(Works Report.) Appendix 5.
	6-7-17		As for 3rd. inst. 1-O.R. Wounded slightly (at duty). No. 4 Section relieved No. 2 Section forward.	(Works Report.) Appendix 6.
	7-7-17		No. 2 Section had baths. Strength. 7 Officers. 203.O.R. 74 Animals.	(Works report and Progress Report.) Appendix 7. Appendix 8.

Army Form C. 2118.

Sheet N° 2.

WAR DIARY
~~INTELLIGENCE SUMMARY~~
(Erase heading not required.)

93rd (Field) Coy. R.E.

Place	Date	Hour	Summary of Events and Information	Remarks and references to Appendices
	8-7-17		N° 2 Section work in camp and dump. Strength. 7 Officers. 203 O.R. 74 Animals. (Works report)	Appendix 9
	9-7-17		As for above. 1.O.R. joined unit. Strength. 7 Officers. 204 O.R. 74 Animals. (Works report)	Appendix 10
	10-7-17		N° 2 Section relieved N° I Section forward. 2. O.R. joined unit. Strength. 7 Officers. 206 O.R. 74 Animals. (Works report)	Appendix 11
	11-7-17		N° I Section had baths. T/µ Lt. Lucas. admitted to Officers Rest Station Strength. 7 Officers. 206 O.R. 74 Animals. (Works report)	Appendix 12
	12-7-17		N° I Section work in camp and dump. 1.O.R. joined unit. Strength. 7 Officers. 207 O.R. 74 Animals. (Works report)	Appendix 13

Army Form C. 2118.

Sheet No 3.

WAR DIARY
INTELLIGENCE SUMMARY.
(Erase heading not required.)

93rd. (2nd) Coy. R.E.

Instructions regarding War Diaries and Intelligence Summaries are contained in F. S. Regs., Part II. and the Staff Manual respectively. Title pages will be prepared in manuscript.

Place	Date	Hour	Summary of Events and Information	Remarks and references to Appendices
	13-7-17		As for 12th inst. Received 1 Rider. Strength. 7 Officers 207.O.R. 75 Animals. A.D.V.S. inspected horse lines.	
	14-7-17		As for 13 th inst.	Appendix 14. (Works report.)
	15-7-17		No I Section relieved half of No 3 section forward. 1 Rider evacuated. 1. O.R. joined unit. Strength. 7 Officers. 208.O.R. 74 Animals.	Appendix 15. (Works report.)
	16-7-17		Half of No 3 Section had baths. 1 paid out. Received. 1. L.D. Horse. Strength. 7. Officers. 208.O.R. 75 Animals.	Appendix N. 16. Appendix N. 16A (Works report.) (Progress report.)
	17-7-17		Half of No 3 Section work in camp and dump. 2 O.R's evacuated. Strength. 7 Officers. 206.O.R. 75 Animals.	Appendix N. 17 (Works report.) Appendix N. 18 (Works report.)

Army Form C. 2118.

WAR DIARY
INTELLIGENCE SUMMARY.
(Erase heading not required.)

93rd (Field) Coy. R.E.   Sheet No 4

Instructions regarding War Diaries and Intelligence Summaries are contained in F. S. Regs., Part II. and the Staff Manual respectively. Title pages will be prepared in manuscript.

Place	Date	Hour	Summary of Events and Information	Remarks and references to Appendices
	18-7-17		Half of No 3 Section moved half of No 3 Section at QUARRY. I.13.a.1.3 Sheet 51.B.N.W. 3.O.R. joined unit. 1.O.R. evacuated. Strength. 7. Officers. 208.O.R. 75 Animals	Appendix A. 19. (Works report)
	19-7-17		Half of No 3 Section had baths and paid out. Strength. 7.Officers. 208.O.R. 75 Animals	Appendix A. 20. (Works report)
	20-7-17		Half of No.3 Section moved in camp and damp. 2.O.R. joined unit. Strength. 7. Officers. 210.O.R. 75 Animals. T/Lt. LUCAS rejoined unit from XVII Corps Rest Station	Appendix A. 21. (Works report)
	21-7-17		Half of No 3. Section went forward to QUARRY. I.13.a.1.3 Sheet 51.B.N.W 1.O.R. joined unit. 2.O.R. evacuated. 1.O.R. wounded Strength. 7.Officers. 208.O.R. 75 Animals.	Appendix A. 22. (Works report)
	22-7-17		No.4 Section came back to Rest Bd Gre from forward billets in evening Strength. 7. Officers. 208.O.R. 75 Animals	Appendix A. 23. (Works report)

Army Form C. 2118.

Sheet No 5

WAR DIARY
INTELLIGENCE SUMMARY
(Erase heading not required.)

93rd (Field) Coy. R.E.

Instructions regarding War Diaries and Intelligence Summaries are contained in F. S. Regs., Part II. and the Staff Manual respectively. Title pages will be prepared in manuscript.

Place	Date	Hour	Summary of Events and Information	Remarks and references to Appendices
	23.7.17		No. 4 Section had baths and were paid out. 1. O.R. wounded at duty. Strength. 7 Officers. 208. O.R. 75 Animals	Appendix 24. Appendix 25.
	24.7.17		No. 4 Section work in camp and dump (Works and Progress Reports) 1. L.D. horse shot. 1. O.R. evacuated 2. O.R. joined unit. Strength. 7 Officers. 209. O.R. 74 Animals.	Appendix 26.
	25.7.17		No. 4 Section work in camp and dump (Works report.) Strength. 7 Officers. 209. O.R. 74 Animals.	Appendix 27.
	26.7.17		No. 4 Section work in camp and dump. Received 1. Pony Strength. 7 Officers. 209. O.R. 75 Animals (Works report.)	Appendix 28.
	27.7.17		No. 4 Section work in camp and dump Strength. 7 Officers. 209. O.R. 75 Animals (Works report.)	Appendix 29.

Army Form C. 2118.

Sheet No. 6

WAR DIARY
INTELLIGENCE SUMMARY
(Erase heading not required.)

93rd (2nd/1st Cdn.) Coy. R.E.

Place	Date	Hour	Summary of Events and Information	Remarks and references to Appendices
	28-7-17		No. 4 Section went forward. Half of No. 2 Section came back to Rear Hd. Qrs. 1 O.R. evacuated. Strength 7 Officers. 208 O.R. 75 Animals	Appendix 30 (Works report.)
	29-7-17		Half of No. 2 Section had baths and were paid out. Strength 7 Officers. 208 O.R. 75 Animals	Appendix 31 (Works report.)
	30-7-17		Half of No. 2 Section came back to Rear Hd. Qrs. Strength 7 Officers. 208 O.R. 75 Animals	Appendix 32 (Works report.)
	31-7-17		Half of No. 2 Section had baths and were paid out. Strength 7 Officers. 208 O.R. 75 Animals	Appendix 33 (Works report.) Appendix 34 (Progress report.)

Zbelinger Jachmann Lt. R.E.
for O.C. 93rd (2nd/1st) Coy. R.E.

Army Form C. 2118.

WAR DIARY
INTELLIGENCE SUMMARY.
(Erase heading not required.)

93rd (Field) Coy. R.E.
Sheet No. 1.

Place	Date	Hour	Summary of Events and Information	Remarks and references to Appendices
Sheet 51 B. G.16 b.2.3	1-8-17		Strength 7 Officers 209 O.R's. and 45 Animals. One O.R. returned to duty. No. 2 Section at work on dump. (Works Report)	Appendix 1 W.R.
	2-8-17		Do. for above (Works Report)	Appendix 2 W.R.
	3-8-17		No.2 Section went forward. No.1 Section came back to Rear H.Q's. One O.R. admitted to Hospital. (Works Report) A.D.V.S. inspected Horses.	Appendix 3 W.R.
	4-8-17		No.1 Section had baths and was fed out. One O.R. admitted to Hospital. (Works & Progress Report)	Appendix 4 Progs. 5 W.R.
	5-8-17		No.1 Section at work on Camps and Dump. (Works Report) 3 O.R's. Wounded. Strength 7 Officers 206 O.R's. and 45 Animals.	Appendix 6 W.R.
	6-8-17		Do for above. One O.R. wounded. One O.R. evacuated. (Works Report) Strength 7 Officers 204 O.R's. and 45 Animals.	Appendix 7 W.R.
	7-8-17		Do. for above (Works Report)	Appendix 8 W.R.
	8-8-17		Do. for above. Lieut Beresford went to Divisional School for Instructional purposes. One O.R. admitted to Hospital. (Works Report)	Appendix 9 W.R.

Army Form C. 2118.

WAR DIARY
or
INTELLIGENCE SUMMARY. 93rd (Field) Coy. R.E. Sheet No 2

(Erase heading not required.)

Instructions regarding War Diaries and Intelligence Summaries are contained in F.S. Regs., Part II. and the Staff Manual respectively. Title pages will be prepared in manuscript.

Place	Date	Hour	Summary of Events and Information	Remarks and references to Appendices
Shot 51.B. 6.16.6.2.3	9-8-17		No 1 Section at work in Camp and Dumps. 1 N.C.O. and 6 Men from No 1 Section went to reinforce No 3 Section at the Quarry.	Appendix 10 (Works Report)
	10-8-17		Do for 9-8-17. Two O.R's admitted to Hospital. One O.R. returned to Duty. Strength 4 Officers 206 O.R's and 75 Animals.	Appendix 11 (Works Report)
	11-8-17		Do for 10-8-17.	Appendix 12 Aug 13 (Works Report and List)
	12-8-17		No 1 Section went to Quarry. No 3 Section came back from Quarry. Rear H.Q's in evening.	Appendix 14 (Works Report)
	13-8-17		No 3 Section had bath and was paid out.	Appendix 15 (Works Report)
	14-8-17		No 3 Section at work in Camp and Dumps. One O.R. evacuated. One O.R. joined unit. Strength 7 Officers 206 O.R's and 75 Animal. (Works Report and Progress Report)	Appendix 16,17,18
	15-8-17		Do for 14-8-17. 2 O.R's admitted to Hospital. (Works Report)	Appendix 18
	16-8-17		As for 15-8-17.	Appendix 19

A5834 Wt W.4973/M687 750,000 8/16 D.D. & L. Ltd. Forms/C.2118/13.

Army Form C. 2118.

Sheet No. 3

WAR DIARY
INTELLIGENCE SUMMARY. 93rd (Field) Coy. R.E.

(Erase heading not required.)

Place	Date	Hour	Summary of Events and Information	Remarks and references to Appendices
Sheet 51 B. G.16.b.2.3	17.8.17		As for 16.8.17. 1. O.R. Wounded at duty.	Appendix 20. (Works report.)
	18.8.17		Started work on new horse standings 1. O.R. returned to duty. Strength. 7 Officers. 206. O.R. 75 Animals.	Appendix 21. (Works report.)
	19.8.17		As for 18.8.17. 1. O.R. returned to duty.	Appendix 22. (Works report.)
	20.8.17		As for 19.8.17.	Appendix 23. (Works report.)
	21.8.17		As for 20.8.17.	Appendix 24. (Works report.)
	22.8.17		As for 21.8.17. 3. O.R. admitted to hospital. 1. O.R. evacuated.	Appendix 25. (Works report.)
	23.8.17		No.3 Section went forward. No.4 Section came back to Rear Hd. Qrs. Strength. 7 Officers. 205. O.R. 75 Animals.	Appendix 26. (Works report.)

Army Form C. 2118.

Sheet No. 4.

WAR DIARY
or
INTELLIGENCE SUMMARY

(Erase heading not required.)

93rd (Field) Coy. R.E.

Instructions regarding War Diaries and Intelligence Summaries are contained in F.S. Regs., Part II. and the Staff Manual respectively. Title pages will be prepared in manuscript.

Place	Date	Hour	Summary of Events and Information	Remarks and references to Appendices
Sheet 51.B.	24.8.17		No.4 Section had baths and were paid out.	Appendix 27
G.16.b.2.3	25.8.17		No.4 Section work in camp (winter accommodation) and drainage.	" 28 Appendix 29
	26.8.17		Do. for 25.8.17 3. O.R. evacuated.	Appendix 30
	27.8.17		Strength 7. Officers. 203. O.R. 75 Animals Do. for 26.8.17 3. O.R. evacuated	" 30 Appendix 30 "
	28.8.17		Do. for 27.8.17 Strength 7 Officers. 200. O.R. 75 Animals.	Appendix 32
	29.8.17		Do. for 28.8.17	Appendix 33
	30.8.17		Do. for 29.8.17	Appendix 34
	31.8.17		Do. for 30.8.17.	Appendix 35 " 36

(Works report)
(Progress report)
(Works report)
(Works report)
(Works report)
(Works report)
(Works report)
(Works report)
(Works report)
(Progress report)

For O.C. 93rd (Field) Coy. R.E.

Army Form C. 2118.

WAR DIARY
or
INTELLIGENCE SUMMARY.

(Erase heading not required.)

93rd Field Co. R.E.   Sheet No 1

Place	Date	Hour	Summary of Events and Information	Remarks and references to Appendices
G.16. b.2.5. Sheet 51.B. Rear Quarters:-	1.9.17.		Nos. 1, 2 and 3 Section working forward, in the line, No. 4 Section back at rear H.Q.	APPENDIX No 1 G.D.B. APPENDIX No 2
"	2.9.17.		As for 1.9.17. 3. O.R.'s joined unit. 2. O.R.'s evacuated. Strength 7 officers 234 O.R.'s 75 animals.	G.D.B. APPENDIX No 3
"	3.9.17.		No 4. Section went to forward billets. No. 2. Section returned to Rear H.Q. 3. O.R.'s joined unit. Strength 7 officers 207 O.R.'s 75 animals.	G.D.B.
"	4.9.17.		No 2. Section had baths, inspection and pay. 2. O.R.'s evacuated. Strength 7 officers 205 O.R.'s 75 animals.	APPENDIX No 4 G.D.B.
"	5.9.17.		No. 2 Section at work on winter accommodation at rear H.Q. Horse standings etc.	APPENDIX No 5 G.D.B.
"	6.9.17.		As for above. 1. O.R. Smith of Strength, on returning communicusion, 2. O.R.'s reported until after evacuation. Strength 7 officers 206 O.R.'s 75 animals	APPENDIX No 6 G.D.B.
"	7.9.17.		Do for abovt. 1. O.R. evacuated. Strength 7 officers 205 O.R.'s 75 animals.	APPENDIX No 7 G.D.B. and No 8
"	8.9.17.		As for above. 1. L.D. Horse evacuated. Strength 7 officers 205 O.R.'s 74 animals.	APPENDIX No 9 G.D.B.
"	9.9.17.		As for above.	G.D.B.
"	10.9.17		No 2. Section went up to forward billets after traffic and inspection. No 1. Section returned to home lines (Rear H.Q.)	APPENDIX No 10 G.D.B.
"	11.9.17.		No. 1. section had baths, inspection and pay.	APPENDIX No 11 G.D.B.
"	12.9.17.		No. 1. Section at work on winter accommodation at rear H.Q.	APPENDIX No 12 G.D.B.
"	13.9.17		Do for above	APPENDIX No 13 G.D.B.
"	14.9.17.		As for above. 1. L.D. Horse evacuated. Strength 7 officers 205 O.R.'s 73 animals.	APPENDIX No 14 G.D.B.
"	15.9.17.		Do for above.	APPENDIX No 15 G.D.B.
"	16.9.17.		Do for above.	APPENDIX No 16 G.D.B.
"	17.9.17.		As for above. No 1 Section had baths and inspection and went to forward billets. No 3. Section returned to Rear H.Q.	APPENDIX No 17 G.D.B.
"	18.9.17.		No 3. Section had baths, inspection and pay. 1. O.R. evacuated. 4. O.R.'s wounded (1 O.R. died of wounds) Strength 7 officers 201 O.R.s 73 animals. No 2 section who took part in said attained to Rear H.Q. APPENDIX	APPENDIX No 18 G.D.B. No 19
"	19.9.17.		No 3. and No 3 No 2 Section at work on winter accommodation at rear H.Q. Strength 7 officers 200 O.R.s 73 animals.	G.D.B. APPENDIX NO 20
"	20.9.17		Do for above. —	G.D.B. APPENDIX No 21

Army Form C. 2118.

WAR DIARY
~~INTELLIGENCE SUMMARY.~~
(Erase heading not required.)

93rd Field Co R.E. Sheet No 2

Instructions regarding War Diaries and Intelligence Summaries are contained in F. S. Regs., Part II. and the Staff Manual respectively. Title pages will be prepared in manuscript.

Place	Date	Hour	Summary of Events and Information	Remarks and references to Appendices
8.16 C.2.3 Sheet 51B	21.9.17		Parties went to French Funeral & either came back to our H.Q at 9 p.m.	app
Naulun	22.9.17		Company marched out of ST NICHOLAS at 1.45 p.m. arrived HAUTEVILLE at 6.30 p.m. went into billets then Church Parade for Company	app
Hauteville	23.9.17			app
"	24.9.17		Unit marched out of HAUTEVILLE at 2.30 p.m. arrived HERMAVILLE at 4.30 p.m went into billets then 2 L.D. horses received. Strength 7 officers 200. 5 R. 75 animals.	app APPENDIX No 23
Hermaville	25.9.17		At HERMAVILLE. 10 R wanted. Strength 7 officers 199 O.R. 75 animals	app
"	26.9.17		Company marched out of HERMAVILLE at 12.30 p.m. arrived BOUQUEMAISON 7 p.m. went into billets.	app APPENDIX No 24
Bouquemaison	27.9.17		At BOUQUEMAISON. Foot inspection.	app
"	28.9.17		At BOUQUEMAISON 8 am went did it.	app
"	29.9.17		Company marched out of BOUQUEMAISON at 11.30 a.m. 8 am billets drill in afternoon. at 9.30 a.m. arrived HUMBERCOURT at	app
Humbercourt	30.9.17		At HUMBERCOURT Company started training. to 5 officers 151 O.R 2 animals 11 pt. theuros surrounded M.C. Sergt Co annulled D.C.M.	app

A. P. Rua
11 Lt RE
for O.C. 93rd Field Co. R.E.

93rd FIELD COMPANY.

SHEET. N° 1.

Army Form C. 2118.

WAR DIARY
INTELLIGENCE SUMMARY.
(Erase heading not required.)

Instructions regarding War Diaries and Intelligence Summaries are contained in F. S. Regs., Part II. and the Staff Manual respectively. Title pages will be prepared in manuscript.

93 Fd Coy
1st Oct 25

Place	Date	Hour	Summary of Events and Information	Remarks and references to Appendices
HUMBERCOURT.	1.10.17.		Company training. 4. O.R's. joined unit. Strength. 7 officers, 205. O.R's. 75 animals. —	G. D. B. —
"	2.10.17		Company training	G. D. B. —
"	3.10.17.		Preparing for move on following day. —	G. D. B. —
PROVEN.	4.10.17.	4.30.a.m.	Entrained Lieutn Regt HUMBERCOURT. Detrained at MONDICOURT. Detrained Regt HUMBERCOURT 1.30. A.M.	G. D. B. —
		3. A.M.	at — 3. A.M. Entraining MONDICOURT. at 5-40. a.m. The whole arrived PROVEN. 4.30. P.M. Proceeded to PATAGONIA CAMP	
"	5.10.17.		at PATAGONIA CAMP. Reconnaissance & training.	G. D. B. —
"	6.10.17		Company training	G. D. B. —
"	7.10.17.		Base Refreshers Inspection.	G. D. B. —
"	8.10.17.		Company Training	G. D. B. —
"	9.10.17.		Pre/paring for move to forward area.	G. D. B. —
ELVERDINGHE.	10.10.17.	9.a.m.	Diamond Junction entrained at PROVEN. 8. A.M. arrived ELVERDINGHE. 9.a.m. Took over billets from W. RIDING 2. FIELD. Coy.	G. D. B. — App II
			At RED. HOUSE. ELVERDINGHE. Transport Section arrived at 7.30. a.m. arrived at Horse Lines. 11. 30. a.m. O. C. and Section Sergts: went to reconnoitre forward area. 1.O.R. joined unit. 2. O.R's evacuated. Strength. 7 officers 202. O.R's. 75 animals. 5 officers, 152 o.R.	Appx I G. D. B. —
"	11.10.17.		Company and Infantry parades 6. a.m. for forward work. Major J. Lundie rejoined unit Infantry attached to Coy for work.	
"	12.10.17.		N° 2. Section and Lance: Fusiliers attachment went to forward billets than Leart. —	
			at CANAL. BANK. BOESINGHE. at 6. p.m.	G. D. B. App II
"	13.10.17		N° 4. Section. Went to forward billets at Canal. Bank. 7.a.m. commander of Company and Infantry worked forward.	G. D. B. —
BOESINGHE.	14.10.17		N° 1 and 3. Sections attached Infantry and officer moved forward to Canal. Bank. 4. h.m.	G. D. B. App III
"	15.10.17.		Coy: worked at night on Dusborghs Track. 2. O.R's wounded. 1 sailor 1 stroke evacuated. Strength. 199. O.R's	G. D. B. App III
"	16.10.17.		Coy: worked on Canal. Bank billets. 1.O.R. evacuated. Strength 7 officers 198. O.R's. 73. animals. —	G. D. B. —
"	17.10.17.		Coy: paraded at 8.a.m. for forward work, 5. reorganising forward unit. Strength. 7 officers 203, O. R's. 73 animals.	G. D. B. —
"	18.10.17.		On fm. 17. 10. 17. —	II Lieut. SMIDDELLS. attached for work. G. D. B. —
"	19.10.17.		On fm 18. 10. 17. — 1. O. R. admitted to hospital. Strength 7 officers 202. O. R's. 73. animals.	G. D. B. —

Army Form C. 2118.

WAR DIARY
INTELLIGENCE SUMMARY.

93rd Fd. Coy. R.E.
~~November~~
OCTOBER. 1917

SHEET No 2.

(Erase heading not required.)

Place	Date	Hour	Summary of Events and Information	Remarks and references to Appendices
BOESINGHE	20.10.17		Coy working on Tramway Tracks for Left Artillery XIVth Corps near LANGEMARCK	R.C.L.
"	21.10.17		As above. 1 O.R. wounded at duty.	R.C.L.
"	22.10.17		As above. 50mm Northumberland Pleasion XIVth Corps Cavalry attached for work.	R.C.L.
"	23.10.17		As above. Cavalry working with Coy. 1 Cav. Officer attached for work	R.C.L.
"	24.10.17		Three Sections & Cav. as above by day. No 1 Section handed at 4 p.m. to assist batteries of 157th Bde. R.F.A. in removing guns but were not required on arrival. 1 O.R. wounded at duty	R.C.L.
"	25.10.17		Work as above. 1 L.D. Horse & 1 Mule evacuated.	R.C.L.
ELVERDINGHE	26.10.17		Strength 8 Officers 202 O.R.s 71 animals Work as above. Handed over billets & Z attd Geo to 92nd (3d) Coy R.E. on conclusion of work moved to GAS WORKS ELVERDINGHE.	R.C.L.
"	27.10.17		Forward Camp moved to (Sheet-28) B.8.a.7.0. (under canvas). B.C. went round work with CRE XIVth Corps Troops. 64th Sibunow Coy. attached for work	R.C.L.
"	28.10.17		Work commenced on Horse Standings for R.F.A. round ELVERDINGHE.	R.C.L.
"	29.10.17		Work as for 28.10.17. 1 O.R. killed. 1 O.R. evacuated. Strength 8 Off. 200 O.R.s	R.C.L.
"	30.10.17		Work as above. 1 L.D. horse joined unit. Strength 8 officers 200 O.R.s 71 animals	R.C.L.
"	31.10.17		Work as above. 72 animals	R.C.L.

R.C. Lambie, Major R.E.
O.C. 93rd (Fd) Coy R.E.

COPY. Appendix I

C.R.E 17th Division   CL.93

Work Report to 6am today.
One section repairing bridge at U.21.d.5.9
25% complete. 70 Sappers 112 infantry
working on mule track from
U.22 d 4.9 420 yds completed. 6 Sappers
making accommodation at Horse Lines.

(Sgn) R St L. Reid
Capt R.E
for O.C. 93rd Fld. Co R.E

12-10-17.

COPY   Appendix II

C.R.E 17th Division

Works Report for 12-10-17.
One section repairing TUFF'S FARM Bridge
60% complete. 50 Sappers & 110 Inf
working on Mule Track 250 yds
completed. 20 Sappers making
accomodation at CANAL BANK. 4
sappers on accomodation at Horse
Lines

(Sgn) R.C Lyndie Maj R.E
O.C. 93rd Coy R.E

13-10-17.

COPY   Appendix III

C.R.E 17th Division   CL.96

Work Report for this day.
Mule Track - 220 yds done - now complete to U.17.d.1.5. Three sections R.E. and 90 infantry employed.
CANAL BANK One section & 35 inf employed on duckwalking and accomodation
Horse Lines 6 sappers employed

14-10-17   (Sgn) R.E Lundie Mj RE
          O.C 93rd/Coy R.E.

COPY.   Appendix IV
CRE 17th Divn   C.L. 97

Works Report for today

Whole Coy and attached Inf worked
2½ hours on accomodation in
morning
Horse Lines. 6 sappers employed
Right Bn Track (Left Branch of "H"
track) 255 duckwalks laid. End of
Track now at U 18 d 2.7 (as far as
can be ascertained in darkness)
In error 46 duckboards were laid
in extension of the right branch
of "H" track in area of division
on our right.

     (Sgd) R.E. Lundie Maj RE
15-10-17.   O.C. 93rd (Fd) Co RE

Army Form C. 2118.

WAR DIARY or INTELLIGENCE SUMMARY

(Erase heading not required.)

93rd Field Company. R.E. Vol 26

Instructions regarding War Diaries and Intelligence Summaries are contained in F.S. Regs., Part II. and the Staff Manual respectively. Title pages will be prepared in manuscript.

Place	Date	Hour	Summary of Events and Information	Remarks and references to Appendices
SHEET 28. A.11.b.4.4.	1.11.17		Company Enemy under Command. Working on horse standings for R.A. under XIX Corps. 649th Labour Company attached for work. I.O.R. evacuated. Strength: 8 officers, 199 O.R's. 72 animals.	C.D.B.
"	2.11.17		As for 1.11.17. 3.O.R's. evacuated. Strength: 8 officers 196 O.R's. 72 animals.	C.D.B.
"	3.11.17		As for 2.11.17. Lieut. Beresford proceeded to PARIS on three days leave.	C.D.B.
"	4.11.17		As for 3.11.17. O.C. (Major R.C. Lumbu D.S.O) Proceeded on leave. Capt R.S.C. Reid (2nd in command) took command of Company.	C.D.B. APPENDIX I
"	5.11.17		As for 4.11.17. Works Report att'd	C.D.B. APPENDIX II
"	6.11.17		As for 5.11.17. O.C. 75 Field Coy; went round work with O.C. into a new 25 taking over. 3.O.R's joined unit. Strength	C.D.B. APPENDIX III
"	7.11.17		As for 6.11.17. 1.O.R. evacuated. Strength: 8 officers 198 O.R's. 72 animals. Lt. officers 199 O.R's. 72 animals.	C.D.B.
CANAL BANK	8.11.17	3.30 p.m.	Coy marched out of Camp at 1.45. p.m. Arrived CANAL BANK at 3.30 p.m. went into billets. Horse Lines annexed G.B. 20.b. 50.	Appendices IX C.D.B.
"	9.11.17		200 infantry attached as carrying party. Works Report att'd Coy. and infantry parade at 4 p.m. for forward work. I.O.R. evacuated. 2.O.R.s wounded. 2. mules lost. Strength 8 officers 196. O.R's. 72 animals. Works Report att'd	C.D.B. Appendices I
"	10.11.17		Coy. on forward work. 2.O.R.s joined unit. Strength 8 officers 198 O.R's. 72 animals.	Appendices II C.D.B. III
"	11.11.17		Took over HULL CAMP. for party working on narrow railway. 90 more infantry attached for work. Works Report att'd	C.D.B. IV
"	12.11.17		As for 11.11.17. 1.O.R. wounded. Strength 8 officers 197 O.R's. 72 animals. Works Report att'd	C.D.B. VII Appendices XIII
"	13.11.17		As for 12.11.17. 1.O.R. evacuated. Strength 8 officers 196 O.R's 72 animals. Works Report att'd	C.D.B. Appendices IX
"	14.11.17		As for 13.11.17. Works Report att'd	C.D.B. Appendices X
"	15.11.17		As for 14.11.17. 1.O.R. wounded. 2.L.D. heavy draws. Strength 8 officers 195 O.R's. 74 animals.	C.D.B.
"	16.11.17		As for 15.11.17. 1.O.R. joined unit. II. Lieut. Swindells returned to 75th Field Coy. R.E. Strength 7 officers 196 O.R's 74 animals. Works Report att'd	Appendices VII C.D.B.
"	17.11.17		As for 16.11.17. Works Report att'd	C.D.B. Appendices VIII
"	18.11.17		As for 17.11.17. 2.O.R.s evacuated. Strength 7 officers 194 O.R's 74 animals. Works Report att'd	C.D.B.
"	19.11.17		As for 18.11.17. Works Report att'd	Appendices XIV C.D.B.
"	20.11.17		As for 19.11.17. Works Report att'd	Appendices XV

Army Form C. 2118.

WAR DIARY
or
INTELLIGENCE SUMMARY.

93rd Field Company, R.E.

(Erase heading not required.)

Instructions regarding War Diaries and Intelligence Summaries are contained in F. S. Regs., Part II. and the Staff Manual respectively. Title pages will be prepared in manuscript.

Place	Date	Hour	Summary of Events and Information	Remarks and references to Appendices
CANAL BANK.	21.11.17		Coy: during forward work. (Duckwork Ventes, building camps, preparing wiring material) see Works Report att'd —	App. XIV-XVI
"	22.11.17		do for 21.11.17. Works Report att'd —	G.D.B. appendices XVII
	23.11.17		do for 22.11.17. Works Report att'd —	G.D.B. appendices XVIII
	24.11.17		do for 23.11.17. Works Report att'd —	G.D.B. appendices XIX
	25.11.17		do for 24.11.17. Works Report att'd —	G.D.B. appendices XX
	26.11.17		do for 25.11.17. Works Report att'd —	G.D.B. appendices XXI
	27.11.17		do for 26.11.17. Works Report att'd —	G.D.B. appendices XXII
	28.11.17		do for 27.11.17. 1.o.R. evacuated. Strength 7 o/June 191. O.R's. 74 animals. Works Report att'd —	G.D.B. appendices XXIII
	29.11.17		do for 28.11.17. 1.o.R. joined unit. Strength 7 o/June 192 O.R's 74 animals. Works Report att'd —	G.D.B. appendices XXIV
	30.11.17		do for 29.11.17. Works Report att'd —	G.D.B. appendices XXV

C.P. Crawford. Lt. R.E.
for O.C. 93rd (S.R.) Army R.E.

Army Form C. 2118.

WAR DIARY
or
INTELLIGENCE SUMMARY.
(Erase heading not required.)

93rd FIELD COY R.E. No 27

Place	Date	Hour	Summary of Events and Information	Remarks and references to Appendices
Canal Bank 1-12-17 C.19.a Sheet 28	1-12-17		Company on forward work (Works Report) Strength 7 Offrs 192 O.Rs 74 Reserve.	App I. p.1-4
"	2-12-17		As above (Works Report)	App II. p.1-4
"	3-12-17		As above (Works Report) 13 O.R. joined Unit.	App III. p.1-4
"	4-12-17		Strength 7 Offrs 205 O.Rs 74 Reserves As above (Works Report)	App IV. p.1
"	5-12-17		Officer from 204th Fd Co. R.E. came to take over. Attached Infantry reported Billets. As above.	p.1
Portland Camp 6-12-17	6-12-17		Dismounted portion entrained BOESINGHE at 12.30 P.M. arrived PORTLAND CAMP at 12.30 A.M. Mounted portion marched out at SIEGE CAMP at 12 noon arrived PORTLAND CAMP 3.30 P.M.	p.1
"	7-12-17		Mounted portion marched out PORTLAND CAMP 8 A.M. arrived LEDERZEELE 5 P.M. Dismounted stayed at PORTLAND.	p.1
"	8-12-17		Mounted portion marched from LEDERZEELE to LOUCHES Dismounted portion entrained at PROVEN STN 9.0 P.M. detrained AUDRUICQ 1.30 A.M.	p.1

R Ganely 2/Lt R.E.
for O.C. 93rd Field Coy R.E.

WAR DIARY

INTELLIGENCE SUMMARY

Army Form C. 2118.

Place	Date	Hour	Summary of Events and Information	Remarks and references to Appendices
LOUCHES	9/12/17		Marched to LOUCHES arrived 6 AM. Went into billets. Cleaning wagons &c.	J.T.G.
"	10/12/17		Cleaning wagons &c. 8 O.Rs joined Unit. 3 O.Rs evacuated. 2 L.D. Strength 7 Offrs, 210 ORs, 72 Decimals.	J.T.G.
"	11/12/17		Work as above. Lt BERESFORD met with accident (broken leg)	J.T.G.
MOULLE	12/12/17		Coy marched out of LOUCHES at 10 A.M. arrived at MOULLE at 3.15 P.M. Went into billets.	J.T.G.
"	13/12/17		General Fatigues	J.T.G.
"	14/12/17		Mounted portion marched out of MOULLE at 8 AM. Dismounted portion at 10 AM, for entraining at ARQUES. Train left ARQUES at 3 P.M. arrived MIRAUMONT at 11.30 P.M. Dismounted	J.T.G.
SAPPERS CAMP	15/12/17		Dismounted portion arrived ACHIET-LE-PETIT at 1.15 AM. Mounted portion arrived ACHIET-LE-PETIT (SAPPERS CAMP) at 3 AM. General improvements to CAMP.	J.T.G.
"	16/12/17		Coy marched out of ACHIET-LE-PETIT at 12.45 P.M. arrived ROCQUIGNY 7 PM	J.T.G.
LECHELLE	17/12/17		Coy marched out of ROCQUIGNY at 9.45 AM arrived RAILWAY WEST CAMP, LECHELLE, at 11.15 A.M. Work on Camp improvements	J.T.G.

R. Gaul 2/Lt R.E.
for O.C. 93rd Field Coy R.E.

Army Form C. 2118.

WAR DIARY
INTELLIGENCE SUMMARY.
(Erase heading not required.)

(3)

Place	Date	Hour	Summary of Events and Information	Remarks and references to Appendices
LECHELLE	17/12/17		O.C. went to V CORPS H.Q. to meet C.R.E., & went round work.	App 1
"	18/12/17		1 O.R. joined Unit. Strength 7 Offrs., 211 O.Rs, 72 animals. No. I Section went to patrol paths for advanced sect. No II, III, IV. Sections went to work on CORPS-RES-LINE at 8 P.M., in progress.	App 1
"	19/12/17		Wagons, 1 O.R. evacuated. 1 A.D. horse evacuated (temporarily). Strength 7 Offrs., 210 O.Rs, 71 animals.	App 1
"	20/12/17		Part of No. I Section on recce. Remainder as for 18-12-17.	App 1
"	21/12/17		Billeting party went to take over new billets from Hd Qrs. Sgt. DURHAM & 6 Sappers thro' Zoaus Camp & returned later. Remainder as for 19-12-17. (Works Report)	App V/VI etc
"	22/12/17		Coy preparing for move. Coy paid. (Work Report) Mounted portion & No. IV Section marched out of RAILWAY WEST CAMP at 10 A.M. arrived HORSE LINES at P.17.a at 12.30 P.M. Dismounted portion left at 1.45 P.M., arriving foot and billets at K.29.d.1.1 at 7 P.M. No. IV Section billeted at BROKEN HOUSE. Maj. LUNDIE admitted to 21 CCS (sick).	App VII App 1
GRAND RAVINE K.29.d.1.1.	23/12/17		Coy on forward work. T/Lt. J.F. GANDY, R.E. joined Unit. Signed 2/Lt R.E. for O/C. 93rd Field Coy, R.E.	App 1

A5834 Wt.W4973/M687 750,000 8/16 D.D. & L. Ltd. Forms/C.2118/13.

WAR DIARY
INTELLIGENCE SUMMARY

Army Form C. 2118.

Place	Date	Hour	Summary of Events and Information	Remarks and references to Appendices
GRAND RAVINE	24/12/17		Work as on 23-12-17. (Works Report) 150 Inf. attached for work	App.VIII/17
"	25/12/17		Work as on 24-12-17 (Works Report). 2/Lt R.H. HAMPTON, R.E. Transferred to R.F.C. (on probation).	App.VIII/17
"	26/12/17		Work as on 25-12-17. (Works Report)	
"	27/12/17		As above. (Works Report)	App.IX/17, App.X/17
"	28/12/17		Work as above. (Works Report). T/Lt G.D. BERESFORD, M.C. R.E. evacuated sick to ENGLAND. No. IV Section relieved No. III Section at forward billets. Strength 6 Offrs, 210 ORs, 71 animals.	App.XI/17
"	29/12/17		Work as above. (Works Report) Strength 6 Offrs, 209 ORs, 71 animals.	App.XII/17
"	30/12/17		Work as above. (Works Report) 1 L/D Horse evacuated. Strength 6 Offrs, 210 ORs, 70 animals.	App.XIII/17
"	31/12/17		Work as above. (Works Report) 1 OR joined Unit. 1 L/D Horse evacuated. Strength 6 Offrs, 210 ORs, 70 animals. 2 L/D Horses obtained.	App.XIV/17

K. Spence 2/Lt R.E.
for O.C. 193rd Field Coy, R.E.

WAR DIARY or INTELLIGENCE SUMMARY

Army Form C. 2118.

No. I Sheet

93rd Field Company R.E.

Vol 28

Place	Date	Hour	Summary of Events and Information	Remarks and references to Appendices
Horse Lines at P.17.a.1.1. K.29.d.1.1.	1-1-18		No. 2 Section at BROKEN HOUSE billets working at Horse Lines & Subterranean Tramlines. Nos. 1,3 & 4 Sections billeted at K.29.d.1.1. (Works Report). 1 O.R. joined unit. 2 O.Rs. transferred. (Trench to U.K. bonus) Strength 6 officers, 209 O.Rs. 72 animals.	App. I App. 2
	2-1-18		As for above (Work Report) 1 O.R. transferred. Strength 6 officers, 208 O.Rs. 72 animals.	App. II
	3-1-18		As for above (Work Report) No. 2 Section relieved No. 1 Section.	App. III
	4-1-18		Proceeded to BROKEN HOUSE billets. Started to take over near Divisional Front. (Work Report)	App. IV
	5-1-18		As for above. (Work Report) 4 O.Rs. joined Unit. 2 O.Rs. evacuated. Strength 6 officers, 210 O.Rs. 72 animals.	App. V App. VI
	6-1-18		As for above (Work Report) 2 L.D. horses evacuated.	App. VII
	7-1-18		As for 6th inst. (Work Report)	App. VIII
	8-1-18		Company moved from billets at K.29.d.11. to K.22.c.5.8. (Works Report) Lt MacQuarrie proceeded to 77 Field Coy R.E.	App. IX
	9-1-18		As for above (Work Report) 1 O.R. killed. Strength 5 officers, 209 O.Rs. 70 animals.	
	10-1-18		As for above (Work Report) No. 3 Section relieved by No. 1 Section.	App. X

WAR DIARY
INTELLIGENCE SUMMARY

No. II Sheet.   Army Form C. 2118.

93rd Field Coy R.E.

Place	Date	Hour	Summary of Events and Information	Remarks and references to Appendices
K.22.c.6.8.	11-1-18		As for 10th inst. (Works Report)	24/1/XI. 1/18
	12-1-18		As for above. (Works Report).	24/1/XII. 1/18
			1 O.R. wounded. 1 L.D. horse shot. 1 Officer joined Unit. Strength 6 Officers. 208 O.Rs. 69 Animals.	
	13-1-18		Work as usual (Works Report).	24/1/XIII. 1/18
	14-1-18		Work as usual (Works Report).	24/1/XIV. 1/18
	15-1-18		Work as usual (Works Report).	24/1/XV. 1/18
	16-1-18		Work as usual (Works Report).	24/1/XVI. 1/18
			1 O.R. evacuated. At Mine Quarries registered shot. Strength 7 Officers. 207 O.Rs. 69 animals.	
	17-1-18		Work as usual (Works Report).	24/1/XVII. 1/18
	18-1-18		Work as usual (Works Report).	24/1/XVIII. 1/18
			No. 3 Section relieved No. 4 Section. 1 O.R. wounded on duty.	
	19-1-18		Work as usual (Works Report).	24/1/XIX. 1/18
	20-1-18		Work as usual (Works Report).	24/1/XX. 1/18
			Forward Section moved from West at K.22.c.6.8. to K.27.a.1.8.	
K.27.a.1.8.	21-1-18		Work as usual (Works Report).	1/1/XXI. 1/18
	22-1-18		Work as usual (Works Report).	1/1/XXII. 1/18
	23-1-18		Work as usual (Works Report).	24/1/XXII. 1/18
			1 O.R. wounded on duty.	1/1/XXIII. 1/18

WAR DIARY or **INTELLIGENCE SUMMARY**

No. III Sheet
93rd Field Coy R.E.
Army Form C. 2118.

Place	Date	Hour	Summary of Events and Information	Remarks and references to Appendices
K.29.a.1.8.	24-1-18.		Work as usual (Works Report). 2 O.R. wounded. 2 O.R. joined Unit. Strength 7 Officers. 207 O.R. 69 animals.	24/I/XIV. 3/1/13
	25-1-18.		Work as usual (Works Report). No. 4 Section relieved No. 2 Section.	24/I/XXV. 1/1/13
	26-1-18.		Work as usual (Works Report). 1 O.R. evacuated sick. Strength 7 Officers. 206 O.R. 69 animals.	24/I/XXVI. 1/1/13
	27-1-18.		Work as usual (Works Report).	24/I/XXVII. 1/1/13
	28-1-18.		Work as usual (Works Report).	24/I/XXVIII. 1/1/13
	29-1-18.		Work as usual (Works Report).	24/I/XXIX. 1/1/13
	30-1-18.		Work as usual (Works Report). 2 L.D. horses evacuated. 4 Pack horses & 1 L.D. horse drawn to Strength 7 Officers. 206 O.R. 72 animals.	24/I/XXX. 1/1/13
	31-1-18.		Work as usual (Works Report). No night work on account of Batt'n Relief. 2 O.R. evacuated. Strength 7 Officers. 204 O.R. 72 animals.	24/I/XXXI. 1/1/13

J. Gantry 2/Lt R.E.
for O.C. 93 Field Coy R.E.

On His Majesty's Service.

WAR DIARY.

CONFIDENTIAL

The Officer i/c
A.G's Office at the Base

GENERAL STAFF.
XVII CORPS.
G.H.A./8.
9-3-18

93 Ja Cay. R.E.
J.J. 29

Army Form C. 2118.

WAR DIARY
or
INTELLIGENCE SUMMARY.

(Erase heading not required.)

Sheet No. 1. 93rd (3/22) Co. R.E.

Instructions regarding War Diaries and Intelligence Summaries are contained in F.S. Regs., Part II. and the Staff Manual respectively. Title pages will be prepared in manuscript.

Place	Date	Hour	Summary of Events and Information	Remarks and references to Appendices
In the Field Famars Bullet R.17 g.17 Hunt Line P.17.d.	1.2.18		Work as usual. 2 O.R.s wounded. No 2 Section sent 6 men on 14 hour's Rest L.F. Strength 7 officers 202 O.Rs. 72 animals	Appendix I & PSDs
	2.2.18		Work as usual. 40.R.s wounded. Strength 7 officers 198 O.Rs 72 animals	Appendix II O.P.O
	3.2.18		Work as usual. 2 O.R.s wounded. 10 R wounded. Sect. 7 officers 195 O.Rs 72 animals	Appendix III OPO
	4.2.18		Work as usual. 1 O.R wounded. Strength 7 officers 194 O.Rs 72 animals	Appendix IV
	5.2.18		Work as usual.	Appendix V OPO
	6.2.18		Work as usual.	Appendix VI OPO
	7.2.18		Work as usual. No night work on account of Brigade relief	Appendix VII OPO
	8.2.18		Work as usual. 1 O.R wounded. Strength 7 officers 193 O.Rs 72 animals	Appendix VIII OPO
	9.2.18		Work as usual.	Appendix IX OPO
	10.2.18		Work as usual.	Appendix X OPO
	11.2.18		Work as usual.	Appendix XI OPO
	12.2.18		Work as usual.	Appendix XII OPO
	13.2.18		Work as usual.	Appendix XIII OPO
	14.2.18		Work as usual. 2 O.R. joined unit. Strength 7 officers 195 O.Rs 72 animals	Appendix XIV OPO
	15.2.18		Work as usual.	Appendix XV OPO

Army Form C. 2118.

WAR DIARY
INTELLIGENCE SUMMARY.
(Erase heading not required.)

Sheet No. 1   93rd (3rd/3rd) Div. R.E.

Place	Date	Hour	Summary of Events and Information	Remarks and references to Appendices
Forward Billets K.27.a.1.7 Huns line P.17.d.	16.2.18		Work as usual. 15 O.R. evacuated sick. Str (9 aus) Strength 7 officers 180 O.R. + 72 animals	a/p/appx XVI
	17.2.18		Work as usual. (2 O.R. did pioneer duty for infantry.)	a/p/appx XVII
	18.2.18		Work as usual. Brigade Relief completed.	a/p/appx XIV
	19.2.18		Work as usual. 4 O.R. joined unit. 1 O.R. tr. rec'd Strength 7 officers 184 O.R. + 73 animals	a/p/appx XX
	20.2.18		Work as usual. 10 O.R. evacuated Strength 7 officers 183 O.R. + 73 animals	a/p/appx XXII
	21.2.18		Work as usual.	a/p/appx XXIII
	22.2.18		Work as usual. Battalion Relief.	a/p/appx XXIV
	23.2.18		Work as usual.	a/p/appx XXV
	24.2.18		Work as usual.	a/p/appx XXVI
	25.2.18		Work as usual. 2 O.R. evacuated. 1 R.D. home to H.V.S. Strength 7 officers 181 O.R. + 72 animals	a/p/appx XXVII
	26.2.18		Work as usual. Battalion Relief.	a/p/appx XXVIII
	27.2.18		Work as usual.	a/p/appx XXIX
	28.2.18		Work as usual.	

17th Div.

93rd FIELD COMPANY, R.E.

M A R C H

1 9 1 8

Attached:-

Appendices 1 to 28.

Army Form C. 2118.

WAR DIARY
INTELLIGENCE SUMMARY.
(Erase heading not required.)

93rd Field Coy R.E. Sheet No 1.

Place	Date	Hour	Summary of Events and Information	Remarks and references to Appendices
K.27.a.1.7	1·3·18		Horse Lines P.17.d. Forward billets K.27.a.1.7. All Sections marched forward (Works Report). Tank at K.11.b. blown up. 7 O.R. joined unit. Strength. 7 Officers 189 O.Rs. 72 Animals	Appendix 1
	2·3·18		As for above. (Works report.)	Appendix 2
	3·3·18		As for above. (Works report.) 2 O.R. joined unit Strength. 7 Officers 190 O.Rs. 72 Animals	Appendix 3
	4·3·18		As for above. (Works report.)	Appendix 4
	5·3·18		As for above. (Works report.)	Appendix 5
	6·3·18		As for above. (Works report.) 1 O.R. joined unit Strength. 7 Officers 191 O.Rs. 72 Animals	Appendix 6
	7·3·18		As for above. (Works report.) 3 O.R. evacuated. Strength. 7 Officers 188 O.Rs 72 Animals	Appendix 7

Army Form C. 2118.

Sheet No. 2.

WAR DIARY
INTELLIGENCE SUMMARY
(Erase heading not required.)

Instructions regarding War Diaries and Intelligence Summaries are contained in F. S. Regs., Part II. and the Staff Manual respectively. Title pages will be prepared in manuscript.

Place	Date	Hour	Summary of Events and Information	Remarks and references to Appendices
K.27.a.1.7.	8.3.18		As for above. (Works revnt.) 1. O.R. evacuated. 1 L.D. Horse evacuated Strength. 7 Officers. 187 O.Rs. 71 Animals	Appendix 8.
	9.3.18.		As for above. (Works report.) 1 O.R. evacuated. 1 O.R. Hospital. Strength. 7 Officers. 186 O.Rs. 71 Animals	Appendix 9.
	10.3.18.		As for above. (Works report.) not 2. L.D. Horses received Strength. 7 Officers. 186 O.Rs. 73 Animals	Appendix 10.
	11.3.18.		As for above. (Works report.) 3 O.R. admitted to hospital Strength. 7 Officers. 186 O.Rs. 73 Animals	Appendix 11.
	12.3.18		As for above. (Works report.) 4. O.R. joined unit Strength. 7 Officers 190 O.Rs. 73 Animals	Appendix 12.
	13.3.18		As for above. (Works report.)	Appendix 13.

Army Form C.

Sheet No 3

WAR DIARY
INTELLIGENCE SUMMARY
(Erase heading not required.)

Instructions regarding War Diaries and Intelligence Summaries are contained in F. S. Regs., Part II. and the Staff Manual respectively. Title pages will be prepared in manuscript.

Place	Date	Hour	Summary of Events and Information	Remarks and references to Appendices
K.27.a.17.	14.3.18		As for above (Works report) Strength. 7 Officers. 190 O.R.s 73 Animals.	Appendix 14
	15.3.18		As for above (Works report)	Appendix 15
	16.3.18		As for above (Works report) 1. O.R. joined unit Strength. 7 Officers. 191. O.R.s. 73 Animals	Appendix 16
	17.3.18		As for above (Works report) No night parties. Bn. relief.	Appendix 17
	18.3.18		As for above (Works report) and (52.G.875.)	Appendix 18, 19
	19.3.18		As for above (Works report) and (Works report) 3 O.R. evacuated 1 L.D. Horse evacuated Strength. 7 Officers. 188 O.R.s 72 Animals	Appendix 20, 21
	20.3.18		As for above. (Works report)	Appendix 22

Army Form C.
Sheet No. 4.

WAR DIARY
INTELLIGENCE SUMMARY
(Erase heading not required.)

Instructions regarding War Diaries and Intelligence Summaries are contained in F. S. Regs., Part II. and the Staff Manual respectively. Title pages will be prepared in manuscript.

Place	Date	Hour	Summary of Events and Information	Remarks and references to Appendices
K27.a.1.7.	21.3.18.	5:15.a.m.	R.E. and attacked bttn. standing by to occupy battle positions.	
		8:00 a.m.	Took up battle positions in LONDON TR. and JERMYN ST. Trenches. Worked on new fire steps and clearing trenches. Engaged low flying F.A. (R.L.15)	
			Transport withdrawn to BEAULENCOURT.	
			3. O.R. wounded. 1 O.R. wounded at duty.	
			Strength 7 Officers 195 O.Rs 72 Animals.	
	22.3.18.	2.a.m.	Orders received to hand over battle positions to WEST RIDING REGT. and MANCHESTER REGT. and withdraw to HEPBURN SPOILBANK.	
		4.15 a.m.	Withdrawal commenced via Railway and Canal Bank.	
		7:00 a.m.	Arrived HEPBURN SPOILBANK	
		30	Orders from C.R.E. to withdraw to GREEN LINE at BERTINCOURT	
		10 a.m.		
		15	Arrived BERTINCOURT.	
		11 a.m.		
		2:30 p.m.—6:15 p.m.	Destroying and firestepping GREEN LINE	
			2. O.R. rejoined unit from hospital.	
			Strength. 7 Officers. 187 O.R. 72 Animals.	

Army Form C.2118

Sheet No. 5

WAR DIARY
or
INTELLIGENCE SUMMARY

(Erase heading not required.)

Instructions regarding War Diaries and Intelligence Summaries are contained in F.S. Regs., Part II and the Staff Manual respectively. Title pages will be prepared in manuscript.

Place	Date	Hour	Summary of Events and Information	Remarks and references to Appendices
	23.3.18	6.45 am	Orders from C.R.E. to withdraw to horse lines at BEAULENCOURT	
		7.30 am	Marched out via BUS and ROCQUIGNY	
		11.00 am	Arrived BEAULENCOURT.	
		12.30 p.m.	Moved camp from N.12.c. to N.11.d.	
		5.00 p.m.	O.C. reconnoitred RED LINE in O.14.b with C.R.E.	
		7.30 p.m. to 11.30 p.m.	Company digging RED LINE 310 lin. yds. trench 3ft.–3ft. 6in. deep.	
			2. O.R. Killed. 1. O.R. wounded.	
			2 L.D. Horse killed. 1 L.D. Mule killed.	
			Strength 7 Officers. 184 O.Rs. 69 Animals.	
	24.3.18	7.30 am	Orders from C.R.E. for Transport to withdraw to COURCELETTE. Dismounted portion to dig in on line in N.16.d. facing SOUTH to cover retiring transport.	
		12.00 noon	Changed to line facing WEST in N.15.d. (not cing.)	
		4.00 p.m.	Orders from C.R.E. for Transport to withdraw to LAVIEVILLE	
		12.30 am (25.3.18)	Transport arrived LAVIEVILLE	

Army Form C.

Sheet No 6.

WAR DIARY
INTELLIGENCE SUMMARY
(Erase heading not required.)

Instructions regarding War Diaries and Intelligence Summaries are contained in F. S. Regs., Part II. and the Staff Manual respectively. Title pages will be prepared in manuscript.

Place	Date	Hour	Summary of Events and Information	Remarks and references to Appendices
	24.3.18	4.30 p.m.	Sections moved off to take up positions on opposite side of PILGRIMS WAY in N.31.c.	
		6.15 p.m.	Company posted covering flanks of withdrawing troops on crest of PILGRIMS WAY	
		8.00 p.m.	Company withdrawn to line of PILGRIMS WAY for the night	
		10.00 p.m.	Company marched to EAUCOURT L'ABBAYE bis N.19.C.b.1.	
			1 O.R. wounded. 1 O.R. missing	
			Strength. 7 Officers. 182 O.R's. 69 Animals	
	25.3.18	2.30 a.m.	OC reported to GOC 52nd Inf Bde in M.29 & reconnoitred line of road in M.29 with view to garrisoning it against reported enemy attack.	
		4.30 a.m.	Coy withdrawn from line with 52nd Inf Bde & marched to COURCELETTE via M.16. 6.8.9.	
		10.30 a.m.	Coy marched to POZIERES & took up position in X.5.C. on left of 52 Inf. Bde covering road from attack from E & 9 E.	
		12.30 p.m.	Coy proceeded to X.21.d.3.4 via CONTALMAISON.	
		2.30 p.m.	OC reported arrival to Bde H.Q. at FRICOURT CHATEAU.	
		5. p.m.	OC attended conference at Bde H.Q.	
		8. p.m.	Coy withdrawn overland to BECOURT SALVAGE DUMP F.1.d.9.5.	
		11 p.m.	Coy placed under 50th Bde.	
	26.3.19	2.30 a.m.	OC summoned to 50th Bde H.Q.	QMR
		4.30 a.m.	Coy marched from F.7.C.5.2. as part of rearguard covering withdrawal B.17th Div via MEAULTE	

WAR DIARY
INTELLIGENCE SUMMARY.
(Erase heading not required.)

Army Form C.

Instructions regarding War Diaries and Intelligence Summaries are contained in F. S. Regs., Part II. and the Staff Manual respectively. Title pages will be prepared in manuscript.

Place	Date	Hour	Summary of Events and Information	Remarks and references to Appendices
	26-3-18		9-DERNANCOURT to LAVIEVILLE. Attached Infantry reformed Battns.	Appendix 23
		11.30AM	Transport moved to VADENCOURT.	
		6 PM	Transport moved to FORCEVILLE.	
		11.30AM	Coy marched to HEMENCOURT.	
		5.30 PM	Coy marched to SENLIS	
		7.30 PM	Coy marched out of SENLIS in arty formations W.E 52nd Inf. Bde.	
		9 PM	Coy Ordered to return to billets at SENLIS	
	27.3.18	12.45AM	Transport moved to PUCHEVILLERS	
		2 PM	Transport moved 500 yds E.	
			Coy Commenced work on aerodrome (Works Reports) 1 OR rejoined Coy.	
			Strength 7 Officers 183 ORs 69 animals	
	28.3.18	7 PM	Transport moved to CONTAY	
			Coy (Works Report)	Appendix 24
	29.3.18		Coy (Works Report)	Appendix 25
	30.3.18		Coy (Works Report)	
	31.3.18		Coy (Works Report)	Appendix 26
			1 OR Killed 1 OR wounded. 2 OR wounded at duty.	
			Strength 7 Officers 181 ORs 69 animals	

APPENDICES

1 to 28.

-SECRET-   17th Divisional Engineers & Pioneers
Progress Report Ending 6 a.m 1-3-18
Appendix I

Unit	No of Men	Map Location	Nature of Work	Progress
93rd Fld Co RE	3 RE 4 RE 8 RAMC	P.17.d K.31.b.6.6	Accommodation Advanced Dressing Stn	Work continued. Partition completed. Shelving in Main chamber 50% completed. Sandbagging cook house 50% completed. 8 yds road made up and levelled. 240 ft of timber salvaged.
	4 RE	OWEN TRENCH	Revetting & Sandbagging	Supervising Infantry
	4 RE 25 Inf	GEORGE St. RYDER St.	Duckboarding	50 yds duckboards fixed. 80 yds trench cleared. Duckboards taken up cleaned & relaid
	1 RE 3 Inf	SHINGLER SUPPORT	S.2 POST.	Excavation for shelter completed. 60% of Shelter completed.
	2 RE	K.27.a.1.7.	Gas proof curtains	3 curtains completed.

-SECRET-   2.

Unit	No of Men	Map Location	Nature of Work	Progress
3rd Fld Co RE	2 RE	LONDON TRENCH K.21.c.9.4.	Repair of pump in Sap. 13.	Work continued
	2 RE	M.G. Hd. Qrs.	Gas proof curtains	3 curtains completed
	1 RE 6 Inf	SHIP TRENCH	Maintenance of trench	100 yds trench cleared. 20 yds duckboards repaired
	2 RE 14 Inf	DARWIN ALLEY	Duckboarding Deepening and Widening trench	31 yds trench deepened. 38 yds duckboards fixed on pickets. Inf made 3 journeys for duckboards.
	3 RE 6 Inf	K.28.a.5.5.	Water Supply	Work continued on Petrol pump. Brick revetment round well 20% completed. 250 yds pipe laid out.
	6 RE	FRONT & SUPPORT LINE	POSTS. Wiring firestepping revetting	Supervising Inf.
	1 RE 50 Inf	JERMYN STREET.	Digging out old trench	85 yds trench cleared 140 yds berm cleared.
	1 RE 60 Inf	K.16.b.5.3.	Digging	80 yds deepened to 5 ft 3 ft wide at bottom

SECRET 3.

Unit	No of Men	Map Location	Nature of Work	Progress
93rd Fld Co RE	3 RE / 19 Inf	SOAP TRENCH	Wiring	90 yds wire thickened / 75 yds wired & thickened
	4 RE / 15 Inf	Behind SHIP TRENCH	Clearing away German wire	360 yds taken up
	5 RE / 19 Inf	POST S 2	Carrying up material. Wiring & firestepping	Continued
	2 RE	K.11.b.	Patrol	
	2 RE / 50 Inf	DARWIN ALLEY	Deepening and widening	70 yds 6 ft deep 90% / 40 yds 4 ft deep
	10 Inf	GEORGE St	Clearing berm	180" completed

E. MacGregor MacQuarrie Lt RE
O.C. 93rd (Field) Coy RE

SECRET — 17th Divisional Engineers & Pioneers
Appendix 2
Progress Report Ending 6 A.M. 2-3-18

Unit	No of Men	Map Location	Nature of Work	Progress
93rd Fld Coy RE	4 RE	P 17 d	Accomodation	Work Continued
	4 RE / 8 RAMC	K 33 b 66	Advanced Dressing Station	Shelving in Main Chamber 90% completed / Sandbagging cookhouse 70% completed / Fixing and painting Red Crosses / 10% road levelled
	4 RE	OWEN TRENCH	Revetting & Sandbagging	Supervising Infantry

— SECRET — Progress Report (2)

Unit	No of Men	Map Location	Nature of Work	Progress
93rd Fld Coy RE.	4 RE 30 Inf	GEORGET Ryder St.	Duckboarding	40 ft duckboards fixed on pickets. 20 ft trench cleared. 60 ft duck boards taken up, cleaned & relaid
	1 RE 2 Inf	SHINGLER Support	S2 Post	1 Shelter completed. 15 ft trench cleared
	2 RE	Right Batt Bd Q'rs	Gas proof Curtains	3 Curtains completed
	2 RE	LONDON TRENCH Batt Hqrs	Gas proof Curtains	2 Curtains completed

— SECRET — Progress Report (3)

Unit	No of Men	Map Location	Nature of Work	Progress
93rd Fld Coy RE	2 RE	LONDON TRENCH K.21.c.9.4.	Repair of trench in Sap 13	Work continued
	1 RE 6 Inf	SHIP TRENCH	Maintenance of trench	50 ft trench cleared. 8 ft duck boards taken up, cleaned & relaid
	2 RE 14 Inf	DARWIN ALLEY	Duckboarding deepening & widening	40 ft trench deepened and cleared to complete. 26 ft duckboards fixed on pickets. Infantry made 1 journey for duckboards

— SECRET —   Progress Report   (4)

Unit	No of Men	Map Location	Nature of Work	Progress
93rd Fld Coy RE	2 RE 62 Inf	K26 a/5-8	Water Supply	600 ft piping laid out, 100 ft timber salvaged. Barricade around tank 10% completed
	1 RE 50 Inf	JESMYN ST	Cleaning trench and berm	50 ft cleaned 100 ft berm cleared 65 ft trench trimmed
	4 RE 15 Inf	SHIP TRENCH	cleaning old wire	100 sq ft completed
	3 RE 16 Inf	SOAP TRENCH	Wiring	50 ft wired
	1 RE 60 Inf	K.16. 6.5.3.	Digging	50 ft trench deepened 5' 4 ft & 3 ft wide at bottom, 200 ft berm cleared
	2 RE 50 Inf	DARWIN ALLEY	Digging	30 ft widened 6 ft deep & 4 ft 30 ft widened to 6 ft deep 90% 100 ft berm cleared

— SECRET —   Progress Report   (5)

Unit	No of Men	Map Location	Nature of Work	Progress
93rd Fld Coy RE	5 RE 19 Inf	S 2 post	Carry up Watering Firestepping & Wiring	Continued
	6 RE 7 Inf	K 11 6.2.1	demolishing old tank	Completed Infantry carrying & covering party
	19 Inf	GEORGE ST	Cleaning berm	250 ft Completed

C. MacGregor MacQuarrie Lt RE
a/O.C. 93rd (Field) Coy RE

—SECRET— 17th Divisional Engineers & Pioneers
Appendix 3

Progress Report Ending 6 AM. 3-3-18

Unit	No of Men	Map Location	Nature of Work	Progress
93rd Fld Coy RE	4 RE	P.17.d	Accommodation	Work continued
	4 RE 8 RAMC	K.33.b.6.6	Advanced dressing station	Shelving in main chamber completed. Sandbagging cookhouse 85% completed. 2 Red Crosses painted 6' road laid. 2' corduroy road laid 50' timber salvaged. Supervising Infantry
	4 RE	Gwen Trench	Revetting & Sandbagging	
	4 RE	George St	Duckboarding	100' duckboards fixed on pickets
	30 Inf	Ryder St		50 ft of trench cleared old boards taken up, cleaned and relaid
	1 RE	Shingler S.2 fort		Excavation for 1 shelter 70% completed
	2 Inf	Support		1 fire step cleared and revetted
	2 RE	Right Batt. H.Q.	Gas proof curtains	2 curtains completed
	2 RE	London Trench Batt H.Q.	Gas proof curtains	2 curtains completed

—SECRET— Progress Report

Unit	No of Men	Map Location	Nature of Work	Progress
93rd Fld Coy RE	2 RE	London Trench K.21.c.9.4	Repair of trench in Sep 17	Work continued
	1 RE 6 Inf	George St	Maintenance of trench	400 ft trench cleared. 200 " Duckboards repaired
	2 RE 14 Inf	Darwin Alley	Duckboarding. Deepening & Widening	45 ft trench cleared & templated 40 ft duckboards fixed on pickets. Infantry made 1 journey for duckboards
	6 RE 21 Inf	K.28.a.5.8	Water supply	Work continued 500 ft 2" pipes laid out along pipe line
	5 RE 19 Inf	posts 5-1, 5-2	Carrying up material. Wiring, Firestepping & Accommodation	Continued

No Infantry working parties on account of relief
L. MacGregor MacQuarrie Lieut
O.C. 93rd (Fld) Co R.E.

— SECRET — 17 Divisional Engineers & Pioneers Appendix 4

Progress Report ending 6AM 4-3-18

No & Unit	Unit Location	Nature of Work	Progress
4 RE	A 17 d.	accommodation	Work continued
93rd Fld Coy RE	5 RE K 33 b 6.6	advanced dressing station	Boxhouse 90% completed, waiting room 50% completed 300' timber salvaged 3' corduroy road laid
	8 RA/MC		
	4 RE OWEN TRENCH	Revetting	Supervising Infantry
	4 RE GEORGE ST		60' trench cleared 100% duckwalks fixed
	30 Inf RIDER ST	Duckboarding	on pickets 60 old duckboards taken up
	1RE 6 Inf SHIP TRENCH	& maintenance	cleaned and relaid
	2 RE " " B.H.2	Gas proof curtains	150 ft trench cleared 2 curtains completed
	1 RE		
	3 Inf Shingler SPT	S.2 Post	12' revetted. Excavation 1 Shelter completed
	1RE 10 Inf " "	S.1 Post	Firestep completed
	1 RE		31' duckboards laid 25' trench cleared
	14 Att DARWIN	duckboarding	& completed. Inf. carrying
	3 Inf ALLEY		duckwalks

— SECRET —

No & Unit	Unit Location	Nature of Work	Progress
	2 RE DARWIN		70 ft widened to 6 ft average depth 4 ft
	6 Inf ALLEN	digging	20 ft deepened to 6 ft 90% completed
93rd Fld Coy RE	2 RE LONDON TR. B.H.2	Gas proof Curtains	2 curtains completed
	8 RE		
	20 Att K 28 a 5.6	Water supply	Work continued
	1 RE	cleaning	
	50 Inf JERMYN ST	boring	640' completed
	3 RE SEAL		90' thickened 110' wired &
	16 Inf TRENCH	Wiring	thickened. Inf carried up 1 load
	1 RE SEAL		60' trench deepened 1 ft & sides
	25 Inf TRENCH	digging	trimmed. Inf working party arrived without tools of any sort. After 2 hrs 25 shovels were found remainder of party viz 35 men did no work
	4 RE Post S.2	wiring	250 ft 45% Completed
	4 Att		
	5 RE		
	15 Inf		

Unit	No. of Men	Map Location	Nature of Work	Progress
93rd Fld Coy RE	1 RE 3 Inf	Post S.2	Firestepping + Accommodation	Continued
	2 RE 5 Inf	Post S.1	Carrying up material Firestepping & accommodation	Continued
	5 RE 15 Inf	SEAL TRENCH	Digging Firesteps	5 firebays excavated

E. MacGregor MacQuarrie? Lt RE
O/C 93rd (Fld) Coy RE.

- SECRET -
Appendix 5

17 Divisional Engineers & Pioneers
Progress Report Ending 6 AM. 5-3-18

Unit	No. of Men	Map Location	Nature of Work	Progress
93rd FD Coy R.E.	4 RE 5 RE 6 RAMC	P.17.d K33 b.66	Accommodation advanced Dressing Station	Work continued. Cookhouse completed. Waiting room floor completed. Floor of Offrs cookhouse made up and levelled. 300 'ft timber salvaged
	4 RE	OWEN TRENCH	Revetting	Supervising Infantry
	4 RE 30 Inf	GEORGE ST	Duckboarding	20 ft trench cleared 150 ft berm cleared back 2½ft 100 ft duckboards fixed on pickets
	1 RE 6 2 Inf	SHIP TRENCH	Maintenance	trench cleared. duckboards repaired 100 ft
	2 RE	"	Gas proof curtains	2 curtains completed
	3 RE	SHINGLER		2 firesteps revetted
	10 Inf	Support	S.1 Post	2 excavations for shelters completed
	3 RE 8 Inf	"	S.2 Post	1 firestep revetted. excavation for 1 shelter completed + 30% erected
	1 RE 14 Inf	DARWIN ALLEY	Duckboarding	20 ft Duckboards fixed on pickets. 20 ft trench cleared. Inf made 1 journey for duckboards

Unit	Work Location	Nature of Work	Progress
93 Fd	2 RE DARWIN / 60 Fd ALLEY	Digging	75ft trench deepened to 5ft 6ins. Lower covered 2ft wide
96 Fd	2 RE LONDON TR	Yesterday's curtains & continuing	2 curtains completed
60 Fd RE 20 Dug	7 RE K2 & S.G	Water Supply	170ft tube jointed 50ft trench over 15 curtains. Half i bore for curves through trench with one piece in position. 3 shutter props transmission under shutter prob. advances to cellar.
	1 RE JERMYN ST	cleaning	completed. Work continued on hump. Over lower slopes leaks shown by July
	5 RE Fd SEAL TR.	firebathing	Revetting 510ft. 3ft cleared 3ft wide. 5 finished. 70% completed
	4 RE 7/6A S.2. Post	twinning	Revetting 70% completed
	3 RE 7/4(A) S.2 Post	FIRE STEPPING & ACCOMODATION	continued
	2 RE 3rd(B) S.1 Post		do
	1 RE Dug SEAL TRENCH	digging	10ft deepened to 6ft 6 16' wide at the bottom
	3 RE KING	twinning	200ft tunnel but no further
			Lt. Mac Bryan Mac Quaire 93 RE
			W.O. C.93 Fd full Co RE

— SECRET —

Appendix 6

17 DIVISIONAL ENGINEERS + PIONEERS
Progress Report Ending 6AM. 6-3-18

Units	No. of Men	Map Location	Nature of Work	Progress
		4 RE	P17 d	Accomodation	Work continued
93rd Fld Coy RE		5 RE 4 RAMC	K33. b.66	Advanced dressing station	5 Sq ft tiling laid 8 Sq yds cementing bookhow lined with C.I. and floor levelled
		4 RE	OWEN TR.	Revetting	Supervising Infantry
		3 REG 2nd	GEORGE ST.	Duckboarding	100 yds duckboards fixed on pickets electric revetted
		1 RE 2nd Dys	CLARGES AVENUE	"	80 yds trench cleared old duckboards taken up cleaned and relaid
		1 RE 6.2nf	SHIP TRENCH	Maintenance	50 yds trench cleared
			GEORGE ST		100 " "
		2 RE	MG Sap	Gas proof Curtains	4 Curtains completed
		3 RE	SHINGLER	S. 1. Post	1 firestep completed, excavation for 1 shelter 50% completed
		8Inf (a)	Support		1 " 90% " . 600 Sandbags filled
		3 RE	SHINGLER	S. 2 Post	1 Shelter completed 1 firestep 90%
		8Inf (a)	Support		completed 30 yds trench cleared

SECRET

Unit	Location	Nature of Work	Progress	Remarks / Progress
1 RE 11 Fd Coy (A)	DARWIN ALLEY	Duckboarding		Duckboards fixed to pickets 40 yds finished. Cleats to pickets 3'6" apart. 60 yds undercoat left deck
93rd 2 RE Fd Coy	"	"		"
2 RE LONDON TR.	Gastight Curtains	3 curtains completed	
50 Fd Coy RE, 5 RE				90% fife joists 1 through 90% completed through fife erected. Fife + lats
2 D Fd Coy (A)	K 28 a 5.8	Wooden Supply Box		for two through completed from F&A fife to through - finished through fife laid + covered 15 yds completed
1 RE		Clearing houses	206 yds	
48 Fd JERMYN ST.		Trench deepened	103 yds	
5 RE SEAL		"	5 ft depth 80% completed 45 yds	
15 Fd Coy (A) TRENCH		Supplypping tracks deepened + cleared		Sub works 1 tonnes for material 120 yds completed & chickened
4 RE SEAL		Wiring	110 "	
16 Fd TRENCH				
1 RE SEAL		Dugging	120 yds deepened 6 ft	
60 Fd TRENCH				

SECRET Progress Report

Unit	Nature of work	Location	Progress
6 R.E.	Front Support dowelling + TRENCHES Sandbagging	7D md	Supervising Infantry
93rd Fd Coy R.E.	3 R.E. SHINGLER 15 Ind Support	Trestleffung + Accommodation	1 trestle completed 2 shelters 65% completed 20 yds fence defened 1ft
603 R.E.			

L. MacGregor MacQuarn 2/Lt R.E.
a/o.c. 93rd Field Coy R.E.

— SECRET —

Appendix 7.   17 Divisional Engineers & Pioneers
              Progress Report ending 6AM 7-3-18

Unit	Task Location	Nature of Work	Progress
9/3 4 RE	P.17.a.	Consolidation	Work continued
4 RE	M.Mks K33 t/6		Leaving Adv O.P. fr cementing completed 8 yds curbing
1/3 4 RE	OWEN TR.	Station	on eastern road
2 RE		Gutting	Supervising Infantry
2/3 6 RE	GEORGE ST		20 Duckboards front on Fickets
3 RE	GLARGES	DUCK BOARDING	50 ft. french drains
25th AVENUE			100 Duckboards taken up
1 RE	GEORGE ST	Maintenance	cleaned and relaid
6 2/6	SHIP TR.	Tunnel	50 yds french cleared
2 RE	GEORGE ST. M.S.R. Geotreat Curtains		100 " "
1D RE		S.I. Post	2 curtains completed
3/2 Inf SHINGLER	S. 14 not-		1 Shelter Completed
25/b	Shithwort-	S.B. Post	30 ft french deepened, foot
Sub (A)			duckboards used 1 Dugout 25% revetted. Excavation for 1 Shelter Completed
			40 ft french cleared + duckboards laid

SECRET Progress Report

Unit	Inf. Unit	Location	Nature of Work	Progress
1 RE (A) 1(A)Fd 3rd Fd		DARWIN ALLEY	Duckboarding	36 yds duckboards fixed 20 yds trench cleared but made journey for material
2 RE 6th Fd 3rd Fd		"	"	35 yds widened out depth
2 RE Cay R/E		LONDON TR	Jagging Gasproof Curtains	60 yds deepened to 6'6" 90% completed 2 curtains completed
6 RE 1st Fd (ATT)			Water Supply	150 yds pipe jointed 2nd trough water connection to 2nd trough through Brigade Shelter floors concreted, some rubble moved trough 30% completed, doors salvaged for engine house door hung completed
10 RE ISAMM ST			Cleaning Repair + deepening trench	250' 1.5'
5 RE SEAL TRENCH 15 Fd (A)			Firesteps cleared Sub made 2 form ups material	5 firesteps completed 80 yds trench

SECRET — Progress Report

Unit	Men	Location	Nature of Work	Progress
1 RE	40?	SEAL		
	60?	TRENCH	Clearing Comm & deepening trench	300 yds 90"
93 FD Coy	6 RE	FRONT & Support Line	Revetting and sandbagging	Reinforcing Infantry 2 gaps
64 FD Coy	6 RE	SHIP TR	Clearing Fr	50 fds wide cleared
	60?	SEAL TR	German troze	

E. MacGregor Major
a/c O.C. 93rd Field Coy RE

SECRET - Progress Report, Engineers + Pioneers during 6 A.M. 6-3-18

Unit	Nature of Work	Progress
4 RE P17 a	accommodation	work continued
2 RE	covered dressing Station	excavation for oven completed 20% brickwork complete. BRICKS salvaged
9&10 TRAMC K33 G66	Revetting	Supervising Infantry
4 RE Owen TR	duckboarding	60/05 duckboards fixed on fireRets
7&8 2 RE George ST	duckboarding	100/05 trench cleaned duckboards taken up & cleaned
6&7 R&3 RE Clarges	Maintenance	underside 80/05 duckboards fixed on fireRets
30 NB Avenue	Yorkshire Burtons	150/05 trench cleaned + duckboards repaired
R&NB Ship. Trench	S 1 Post	2 geophone containers completed
2 RE Ship "	S 14 Post	excavation for one Shelter completed, 1 Shelter completed, 2 traverses repaired
7 RE	S 2 Post	and tunnel, 1 firebay 30% completed 25/05/06
2&3 NB Shiner support	S 3 Post	trench deepened and duckboarded, emergency firebay completed

SECRET

Unit	Sub Unit Location	Nature of Work	Progress Report
1 RE	DARWIN (LHS @) ALLEY	Duckboarding	40 yds duckboards (used 30 yds French trench material) cleared. Sub 1 journey for materials. French widened 6/ft Ave depth 3/ft 60 yds 90% completed. 6 ft deep.
9/3 - 5/3 &/or 6 Coy R.E. 2 RE	South trench	Floorboard curtains	3 curtains completed. 180 yds hips joisted 2'— clear floor to engine room and verge reverted. 2 no trenches with revetting completed.
8 RE	K 26 a 5.8 18 9/6 @	wire scaffolding	TONIGHT
5 RE	JERMYN ST SEAL	NO WORK	110 yds of trench deepened & cleared from sleeves for field of fire
15 Ju (4) 3 RE	TRENCH SEAL TRENCH 30 m	Digging trench	Completeds connecting for closing gap. Inf carrying
6 RE	FRONT + SUPPORT LINE	Revetting + sandbagging	Supervising Infantry

"SECRET"

Progress Report

Gallows O

Unit	Location	Nature of Work	Progress
15RE	SHIP-SEAL	hewing out 2 gaps 15'/25 each cut
82Ruf	TRENCH	German Wire	1 gap 50% cut
2RE	LOCK TRENCH	digging out	Completed
93rd 75Ruf	2 POSTS	Identifying	440 yds been cleared
9/6	IRE SEAL		
107,RE. 203rd	TRENCH	digging	16 yds trench deepened to 6ft

& Mac Gregor Mac Quarn & RE
V.O.C. 93rd & wld CoRE

SECRET — 17 Divisional Engineers + Pioneers
Progress Report Ending 6A.M 9-3-18

Unit	Map Location	Nature of Work	Progress
2ng 2nd			
9&12 2ReDoyle	4RE P17c K33.b.66	Accomodation Ad'Dressing Station	Work continued Over 75% completed
1/12	4RE OWEN TR.	Revetting	Sandbagging Infantry
4oyR.E.	2 REGEORGE ST	Duckboarding	60% duckboards fixed, duckboarding completed
	3 RE CLARGES		30% trench cleared Duckboards to be
	30&6 AVENUE		up cleared + repairs + refound
	1 RE	Duckboarding	50% trench cleared + duckboards
	6 2ng SHIP TRENCH	Manufacture	relaid Sub merced 3 hours
	2 RE "	Gaspass Curtains	2 Curtains completed
		S1A Post	1 Curtain completed
	7 RE SHINGLER	S1 Post	Shelter completed 40% duckboards fixed
	10 Fub Subtotal	S2 Post	2 Curtains cleaned and wired
		S3 Post	1 Curtain 75% completed
	1 RE DARWIN	Duckboarding	24 yds duckboards fixed 30 yds
	14 Punj ALLEY		trench cleaned
	2 RE	No working party	Turned up for nights party

— SECRET —

Unit	Map Location	Progress Last Report Work		Progress
93rd 7 RE K28&5.E Sub 18SubA Coy RE	2. RE LONDON TR.	apstrospeculine	Water Supply	3 centrios completed 250 yds fire trench 130 yds trench excavated for the depth 3ft fire trench blustieren cleared Button cleared out prototype cloor for everyone 100m 50% completed fire escape from (cont) to proposed trench another 100 yds laid out for jointing
6 R[E] 60 RE 18RE 80% (Tiighter) Traig IRE 15th CAREY 3. RE 5—6 1 RE Sub ALLEY 60 working Carico	JERMYN ST SEAL TR SHIP + SEAL TR	No wide No wide No wide Revetting + sandbagging + following old german wires 90 carrying stores wire + pickets Wiring Sheaving T.M. Batt relief		Supervising Infantry 300 sq yds wire cut 2 gels joined knocks 1 gab 70/80 wide 1 wire and 1 narrow gap cut 60 lb pickets 3 Double B. Wire 3 forwards 40 yds completed Work commenced G. MacGregor MacQuarrie Lt RE O.C. 93rd (Field) Co RE.

- SECRET -

17 Divisional Engineers + Pioneers
Progress Report evening 6 A.M. 10 = 3.16

Unit	Where Working	Nature of Work	Progress
93² 4.R.E.	P.17.a IRELAND K.33-A.66	Accommodation at Dressing Station	700 ft. constructed over revetted
93² 4.R.E.	OWEN TRENCH	Revetting	Behavioring Infantry
93² 4 RE CLARGES AVENUE	Deepening and Duckboarding	70 yds trench cleared & relaid both duckboards taken up
By R.E. 2/7 yds 5R2 yds SHIP TRENCH	Maintenance	60 yds duckboards relaid & the trench cleaned
2 R E	" "	Construction of Infantry Post	2 curtains completed excavation for 1 shelter completed excavation for 2nd shelter 75% completed
7. R.E.	SHINGLE R 8	1 POST	20 ft trench deepened 1 ft + duckboarded. 3 traverses cleaned & raised 4 of 8½
28 yds SUPPORT (ATT)		S.I.M. S 2 S 3	trench deepened + duckboarded. 1/fire bay completed / emergency firebay completed 40 yds duckboards laid 30 yds cleaned
I R E DARWIN 14.N.6.(d) ALLEY		Duckboarding	cleaned. 2 frames for duckboards

SECRET - PROGRESS REPORT

Unit	Nature of Work	Nature of Work (cont)	Progress
2RE 50 & DARWIN ALLEY, 2RE DRURY LANE	Digging Dugouts, Dugouts Continuing		8 Dugouts 6,6,9,9,10% completed 60% from cleared. 5 frames completed. 200 ft fule joined. Suction pipe salvaged & connected from cistern to pump. Wall & fire bricks cleanstone 6 cistern complete. Protection doors 75% completed. Timber Salvaged
93 & 7 RE, Fld 115 245, Coy RE	K2 & a 5-8	Water Supply	
1RE & 2 & 7 RE JERMYN ST FRONT & 4 RE SUPPORT LINE	Pushing, Renewing & Salvaging German wire		4 frames & bays excavation complete. Support wire infantry. 1000 sqft supports & fields cleared, 200 sqft Germ cleared. 384 " wire cut. Old McRuin pickets 32 roles barbed wire.
1 RE CAREY (7 Jul (b))	Carrying pickets wire & pickets		3 Journeys made.
3 RE POST 86	Running		500 ft 50% completed
4 RE ENGLANDER TRENCH	Fire Stepping		Excavations for fire bays completed.

Lt. MacGregor MacQuarrie 2 SCRE
40 C. 93 Fld. Coy RE.

SECRET

17 Divisional Engineers & Pioneers
Progress Report during 6 A.M. 11-3-15

Unit	Their Location	Nature of Works	Progress
93rd & 4 RE	RE HQ-a	Accomodation centring + sandbagging	work continued
Coy 27 MG	4 REOWEN TRENCH		Supervising Infantry
Sqd	RE CLARGES	Decking + duckboarding	100 ft trench cleared, duckboards taken up & relaid, 60 ft duckboards fixed
Coy RE MG	AVENUE		
	FLAGSHIP TRENCH	Various	40 ft duckboards taken up, cleaned & relaid
2 RE	"	Yastrad Curtains	2 works completed
	"	S/A Post	1 shelter completed + 1.56% completed
	TRESHINGLER	S 2 "	Traverses widened 50 ft trench cleared + duckboarded
	RMQ SUPPORT	S 3 "	30 ft trench deepened + trimmed
1 RE	DARWIN	Duckboarding	20 ft duckboards fixed 20 ft trench cleared
149(A)	ALLEY		Infantry were 1 journey
2 RE	"		60 ft deepened 64 ft + 120 ft × 3 ft
50th	"		drum cleared
2 RE	DRURY LANE	Jigging	2 Curtains completed
2 RE	"	Yastrad Curtains Duckboarding	30 ft trench cleared & duckboards fixed

SECRET - Progress Report

Unit	Map	Nature of Work	Progress
7 RE	R28 a 5-6	Water Supply	250 ft pipe laid out. Protective doors completed. 6 Areas for Ship cooks completed. Pump discharge Line out, and extra outer covers down.
032-020468 1 RE 2306 Coy RE	JERMYN ST	Sewerage	No 1 Recover 90% completed. 4 pick ups Cleaz, excavator completed
4 RE	FRONT to SUPPORT LINE	Sandbagging Remaining to be removed time	Supervising Infantry. 9105 Ya cut + Pickets cleared
Coy RE	SHIP + SEAL, TR		
HARE Coy	" "	Do	735 Sq ft cleared
	Post & 6	Wiring	150 ft completed
HARDON LONDON	TR	Investigating	12 pivotals, excavation completed

Lionel Siegel MacQuarrie Lt-RE
O.C. 93d Field Co RE

SECRET - 17th Divisional Engineers & Pioneers
Appendix 12. Progress Report ending 6 a.m. 12-3-18.

Unit	No. of Men	Map Location	Nature of Work	Progress
93rd (Aust) CoRE	4 RE	P.17.d	Accommodation	Work continued
	4 RE	OWEN M.TR.	Revetting and Sandbagging	Superintending Inf.
	4 RE 50 mJ (att 20J)	CLARGES AVENUE	Defences and floorboards	100 yds of trench deepened & cleaned. Duckboards taken up cleaned and relaid. 60 yds duckboards laid. 200 yds whitewashed trench 2'6"
	1 RE 6 mJ	SHIP TRENCH	Maintenance	30 yds trench cleaned. 20 yds duckboards cleaned and relaid
	2 RE "	SHINGLE POSTS	Gas projectors	2 cuttings completed
	6 RE isJ (att 10)	SUPPORT S.I.A		1 Shelter completed, 30 yds of trench deepened 1ft. 50 yds wiring 80% completed, 40 yds trench cleaned, camouflage repaired

SECRET:- 2

Unit	No of Men	Map Location	Nature of Work	Progress
93rd Field Co RE	2 RE} 60 Inf}	DARWIN ALLEY	Digging	70 yds trench deepened to 6 ft
	2 RE	DRURY LANE	Gasproof curtains	2 curtains completed
	1 RE	"	Duckboarding	20 yds duckboards fixed
	8 RE 20 Inf}	K.28 a 5.8	Water Supply	Timber salvaged & pipes bored from Well to cistern 25% completed. Pipe from Pump to Reservoir lowered in track. Outlet from No 1 Reservoir completed. Outlet from No 2 Reservoir 30% completed 200 yds pipe jointed. Approx total of pipe jointed 1100 yds
	1 RE} 18 Inf}	JERMYN STREET	Firebays	3 Firebays excavated 6 yds long
	1 RE} 13 Inf}	SEAL TRENCH	Duckboarding deepening	20 yds duckboards fixed 90 yds trench cleared

"SECRET"

3

Unit	No. of Men	Map Location	Nature of Work	Progress
93rd Field Co RE.	4 RE	Strand and Suffolk Ave	Revetting Sandbagging	Supervising Infantry
	7 RE carrying party	SHIP SEAL TRENCH	Clearing Shell Gun-emmine	600 yds wire cut and pickets drawn
	12 RE 70 Inf	"	"	500 yds wire removed
	1 RE 150 Inf	POSTS. 6.	Carrying party Wire & pickets Wiring	60 medium pickets. 30 coils barbed wire 65 yds completed 5% completed
	4 RE 4 Inf	LONDON TRENCH.	Firestepping	7 firebays completed Steps ete

E. MacGregor Major Quatrain SK RG
2/0 C 93rd Field Co RE.

SECRET — 17th Divisional Engineers & Pioneers
Progress Report ending 6 a.m. 13-3-18.
Appendix 13

Unit	No of Men	Map Location	Nature of Works	Progress
93rd Fld Coy RE	4 R.E.	P.17.d.	Accommodation	Work continued
	5 R.E. 31 Inf	CLARGES AVENUE	Deepening and duckboarding	100 yds duckboards faced. 100 yds cleared back 3'6". 40 yds trench deepened & cleared. Duckboards taken up, cleaned and relaid.
	1 R.E. 6 Inf	SHIP TRENCH GEORGE St.	Maintenance	60 yds trench cleaned. 50 yds duckboards repaired. 2 curtains completed.
	2 R.E.	SHIP.	Gas proof curtains	
	3 R.E. 9 Inf	SHINGLER SUPPORT POSTS. S.1. " S.3.		40 yds trench deepened and cleared. 30 yds duckboards faced. Doors 50% completed. 20 yds trench cleaned and duckboards faced.
	1 R.E. 55 Inf	DARWIN ALLEY	Rigging	450 yds been cleaned. No trickes with this party.
	2 R.E.	DRURY LANE Bde Hd Qrs	Gas proof curtains " "	3 frames faced. Refitting & curtains

-SECRET-   2/

Unit	No of Men	Map Location	Nature of Works	Progress
93rd Field Co R.E.	7 R.E. } 20 Inf }	K 28 a 5.8.	Water supply.	Pipe from Well to settling bund complete. Tank with R. Batt. 45% completed. Outlet from No. 2 Reservoir 6% completed.
	1 R.E. } 30 Inf }	JERMYN STREET.	Trenching.	Pipes joined 116 byds. 5 fine bays excavated
	1 R.E. } 7 Inf }	SEAL TRENCH.	Duckboarding	20 yds duck boards fixed
	9 R.E. } 60 Inf }	SHIP and SEAL	Deepening, clearing old German wire	20 yds trench cleared 350 sqyds wire cut
	1 R.E. } 4 Salvage Coy }	K 10. d. 4. 9. K 10. b. 3. 3.	Salvaging T.M's.	5 Wheels taken off. Spare parts removed.
	2 R.E. } 30 Inf }	SOAP.	Digging	120' dug 4'6" broad by 2' dup.
	18 R.E. } 64 Inf }	HAVRINCOURT defences.	Digging	Posts & front line entered.

& MacGregor MacQuannie Lt R.E.
4/O.C. 93rd (Field) Coy R.E.

SECRET.

17th Divisional Engineers & Pioneers Progress Report ending 6 a.m. 14-3-18.

Appendix 14.

Unit	No of Men	Map Location	Nature of Work	Progress
93rd (Fld) Co RE	4 RE. 3 RE } 30 Inf }	P.17.d. CLARGES AVENUE.	Accommodation Refining and duckboarding	Work continued. 60 yds duckboards lifted & cleaned out. 60 yds duckboards laid complete. 150 yds of trench cleaned.
	1 RE } 6 Inf }	SHIP TRENCH.	Maintenance	40 yds of trench cleaned
	2 RE. 3 RE } 10 Inf }	SHIP. SHINGLER SUPPORT.	Gas proof curtains POSTS.	2 curtains completed. 60 yds trench cleaned & widened. 5.6 yds duckwalks laid 10 yds been cleaned
	2 RE } 7 Inf }	DARWIN ALLEY.	Draining	20 yds been cleared. 50 yds duckwalks laid. 70 yds trench cleaned & widened. 80 yds trench dug out. 160 yds been cleaned
	3 RE. 7 RE } 20 Inf }	Batt Hd Q.M. K.28.a.5.8.	Gas proof curtains Water supply.	1 New Gas Curtain complete. 1 Repaired. Pipe joints 200 yds. Outlet No 2 Reservoir complete. Track excavation 100 yds average 5 ft. No 1 Tank (R.E) excavation complete. Tank R.E.M.E. fixed. R Batt.

4.O.C. 93

SECRET -

2.

Unit	No of Men	Map Location	Nature of Work	Progress
1 RE	30 Inf	JERMYN STREET.	Continued	No 2 Tank exit excavation 6/6 complete. 1 RE: 9 Inf carrying fight from dump to fight tank. 6 Inf trays excavated.
1 RE	3 Inf	SEAL TRENCH.	Shieldfying	
7 RE.		SHIP & SEAL TRENCH.	Duckboarding	26 yds duckboards fixed on pickets.
			Cleaning old German wire	800 sq yds wire cut. Pickets drawn. 500 sq yds cleared.
6 RE	75 Inf			
2 RE	49 Inf	SOAP TRENCH.	Digging	70' × 4'6" broad by 2' deep. 30' completed from last night.
14 RE	50 Inf	HAVRINCOURT	Digging	180 yds trench deepened & widened. 50 yds berm cleaned. Stovelifs improved
1 RE	56 Inf	do	do	90 yds trench dug 6' wide × 3 ft. & man Great Mail Queens St RE. O.C. 93 Fd (H+) wid Co RE

SECRET - 17th Divisional Engineer & Pioneer Progress Report. ending 6 a.m 15-3-18.

Appendix 15

Unit	No of Men	Map Location	Nature of Work	Progress
93rd (Field) Co RE	4 RE	P.17.d	Accommodation	Work continued
	3 RE	CHARGES	Deepening and	60yds trench cleared, duckboards
	20 Inf	AVENUE (a.K.22.9.2.1)	Widening	taken up cleaned & relaid.
			Duckboarding	20 yds berm cleared.
	1 RE	SHIP TRENCH	Maintenance	30 yds trench cleaned
	6 Inf	DARWIN ALLEY	"	60 yds trench cleaned
	2 RE	SHIP TRENCH	Gas proof curtains	2 curtains completed.
	3 RE	SHINGLER	POSTS.	180 yds berm cleaned. 24 yds trench
	10 Inf	SUPPORT		widened and cleared. 20 yds XPM duckboards faced. Bombstop/muttholds
	2 RE	DARWIN	Duckboarding	40 yds duckboards faced
	9 Inf	ALLEY.(G.K.17.a.33)		20 " berm cleared
	2 RE	LONDON TR.	Gas proof curtains	3 curtains completed
	7 RE	K.28.a 5.8	Water Supply	Pipe jointed 85 yds (to Res Batt)
	20 Inf att			HAVRINCOURT. MOEUVRES.ROAD. Pipe found and recovered.

SECRET. 2

Unit	No of Men	Map Location	Nature of Work	Progress
93rd (Field) Co RE		K.21.d.8.4.		No.1. Tank R. Batt. H.Qrs. WHITE HALL fixed & ready for water, pipe connected to same.
		K.27.b.9.9.		Stop cocks on Reservoir boxed.
		K.21.d.9.2.		100 yds track excavated forward reservoir
1. RE } 30 Inf }		JERMYN STREET.	Firestepping	Excavation for 3 Firebays completed. 12 Firebays cleared.
1. RE } 9 Inf }		SEAL TRENCH.	Duckboarding	16 yds duckboards fixed. 180 yds berm cleared
7 RE Days Party		SHIP & SEAL TRENCH.	Clearing old German Wire.	760 sq yds wire cut and pickets drawn.
7 RE 80 Inf }		"	"	800 sq yds cleared.
3 RE } 50 Inf }		SOAP. TRENCH. K.10.d.7.8.	Digging	150 yds 4' 6" wide 2' deep.
14 RE } 58 Inf } art		K.22.C.8.3 HAVRINCOURT defences K.21.d.61 – K.22.C.32.	Digging	100 yds of trench deepened and widened. 100 yds of trench and firesteps completed. 1. M.G. emplacement completed.

SECRET—

3.

Unit	No. of Men	Map Location	Nature of Work	Progress
93rd (Field) Co RE.	3 R.E. 150 Inf	EASTERN END LOCK TRENCH	Digging	270 yds trench deepened 6'8" and berm cleared.

E. MacGregor Major 93rd Field Co RE
9/0/c 93rd Field Co RE

SECRET — 17th Divisional Engineers & Pioneers
Progress Report Ending 6. a. m. 16-3-18

Appendix 16

Unit	No of Men.	Map Location	Nature of Work	Progress
93rd (Field) Co RE.	4 RE	P. 17. d.	Accommodation	Work continued
	3 RE } 30 Inf }	CLARGES AVENUE	Deepening widening Duckboarding	60 yds trench cleared, 60 yds duckwalks fixed. 150 yds Berm cleared.
	2 RE } 4 Inf }	LOCK. TRENCH. (Day Party)	Firestepping	1 Firestep 10 yds long completed 1 Firestep 50% completed
	2 RE	SHIP. TRENCH.	Gas proof curtains	2 curtains completed.
	2 RE	SHINGLER SUPPORT.	POSTS.	Bomb stop cleared and prepared for rebuilding
	2 RE } 2 Inf }	DARWIN. ALLEY	Duckboarding	35 yds duck boards fixed. 35 yds trench cleared. 150 yds Berm cleared.
	2 RE	T.M.B's LONDON. SUP	Gas proof curtains	2 curtains completed.
	7 RE 20 Inf } att	K 21. b. K 28. a. 5. 8.	Water Supply	190 yds piping jointed. 450 yds piping carried from pipe dump to proposed track.

2

Unit.	No. of Men	Map Location	Nature of Work	Progress
93rd (Field) CoRE		K.15.d & S. K.28.a.5.8.		Braziers completed. No.2 Tank hilt excavation of Bibcock. Pump & engine overhauled. No.1 Tank 'WHITEHALL' Tank cover 7'×3'6" completed. Duck boards fixed for Diesies & Petrol cans. No.2 Tank WHITEHALL. Excavation 60% completed. Jumber along for tank cover.
2 R.E.		SEAL TRENCH.	Defensive widening	28 yds trench cleaned.
7 R.E. Day party		SHIPSEAL TRENCH.	Clearing old German mine	600 yds wire cut. 6 pickets drawn
5 R.E. 709		"	"	600 rg yds wire cleaned
2 R.E. 50		SOAR TRENCH. K.10.d 7 S.	Rigging	100' 4' deep. 56' × 2' deep.
14 R.E. 57		HAVRINCOURT. K.21.d.	Digging	180 yds trench deepened & widened. 5 firebays excavated. 50 yds then cleaned

3

Unit	No. of Men	Nat. Duration	Nature of Work	Progress
93rd (Field) Co RE	1 RE 50 mf	SUPPORT POST K.22.c	Digging	70 yds trench excavated 7' wide 2'6" deep
	1 RE 12 mf	K.22.c.5.3.	"	18 yds trench excavated 7 ft wide 3 ft deep
	2 RE 100 mf	LOCK TRENCH	Digging	295 yds trench deepened widened and berm cleaned back 2 ft

E. MacGregor. MacQuarrie 2/Lt RE.
O.C. 93rd (Field) Co RE

SECRET — 17th Divisional Engineers & Pioneer
Progress Report Ending 6 a.m. 17-3-18.
Appendix 17

Unit	No of Men	Map Location	Nature of Work	Progress
93rd (Field) Co RE	4 RE	P.17.d.	Accommodation	Work continued
	3 RE 30 Inf	CHARGES AVENUE	Ride-way widening Duckboarding	50 yds duckboards laid. 50 yds trench cleared. 180 yds benchland. 2 Bridges demolished
	2 RE 6 Inf	LOCK TRENCH	Trench lifting	1 Shrislif completed, 1 Shrislif 75% completed, 1 Shrislif 50% completed
	2 RE	SHIP TRENCH	Gas proof curtains	3 Curtains completed
	2 RE	SHINGLER SUPPORT	POSTS. S.3.	Bomb stop 50% completed. 6 yds trench widened 2 ft.
	2 RE	T.M.B. Hd. Qrs LONDON SUP	Gas proof curtains	2 Curtains completed
	8 RE 20 Inf	K.21.b.0.5. K.15.d.6.4.	Water Supply	190 yds piping jointed. No. 2 Tank R. Batt Hd Qrs WHITEHALL. Platform made & tank fixed

SECRET:-

2/

Unit- No of Men	Map Location	Nature of Work	Progress
	K.28.a.5.8.	Water Supply	Protective barricade from Well to cistern 60% completed. Exhaust pipe fixed on engine. No.1 Tank shed 50% emplied
	K.15.d.8.4.		80× Pipe carried from dump to proposed track
3 RE 10 Inf.	K.21.b. SEAL TRENCH	Deepening, widening, duckboarding	50 yds trench cleared. 30 yds berm cleared 50 yds duckboards faced.
7 RE Day Party	SHIP & SEAL TRENCH	Clearing old German wire	900 yds wire cut & pickets drawn
6 RE 80 Inf.		"	900 sq yds wire cleared
3 RE 45 Inf.	SOAR. TRENCH K.10.d.7.9	Digging	80 yards to 4 ft deep.
14 RE 57 Inf. Aust.	HAVRINCOURT. Defences. K.21.d.4.1.- K.21.d.8.3.-	Digging	200 yds trench deepened & widened. Excavation for 2 firebays 18 ft long. 1 firebay 15 ft long. 75% completed. 50 yds of berm cleared

SECRET-

3

Unit	No of Men	Nat. Location	Nature of Work	Progress
93rd (Field) Co R.E.	2 R.E. 180 Inf	LOCK TRENCH. BILHEM.	Digging	180 yds trench deepened, widened & berm cleared.
	1 R.E. 60 Inf	CHAPEL WOOD SWITCH. K 2 b.	Investigating	3 dimity's byds long excavated. 150 yds trench cleared.

E. MacGregor Maan Quarier Lt R.E.
 %O.C. 93rd (Field) Co R.E.

SECRET 17th Divisional Engineers & Pioneers

52 G.S.19 Div. 18/19 Progress Report ending 6 a.m 18.3.18.

Unit	No of Offrs, men	Map Location	Nature of Work	Progress
93rd (Field) Co RE	4 RE 3 RE 30 Inf	P 17.d CHARGES AVENUE	Accommodation Deepening, Widening Duckboarding	Work continued 20 yds trench cleared. 58 yds duckwalks fixed in pickets 40 yds trench cleared
	1 RE 2 Inf	SHIP. TRENCH "	Maintenance "	4" duckboards relaid 2 curtains completed
	2 RE		Gas proof curtains	Bomb stop completed
	2 RE	SHINGLER SUP S.3 POSTS.		4 frames completed
	2 RE	T.M.B. H.Q.rs LONDON. SUP.	Gas proof curtains	
	6 RE 20 Inf	K.21.d.8.5	Water Supply	Pipe jointed to support Bat's. Tank sites reconnoitred. No 7 Tank R. Batt.WHITEHALL Shed completed & hole for fifth cut in moved No. 2 Tank R. Batt. WHITEHALL frames ready for water Protective camouflage from Well to Cistern 90% completed. begun & hung taken up for transfer to 559 A.T. Coy
		K.21.a.4.5.		

SECRET

2

Unit	No of Men	Map Location	Nature of Work	Progress
93rd (Still) Co RE	3 RE 2 Inf	SEAL TRENCH	Deepening/widening Duckwalking	40 yds trench cleaned 40 yds duckboards fixed
	7 RE Day Party	SHIP & SEAL TRENCH	Cleaning old German mine	860 sq yds wire cut & firebas drawn
	14 RE 579 Inf (pts)	HAVRINCOURT DEFENCES. K21d	Digging	3 firebays completed. 1 firebay 75%. 1 firebay 50%. 300yds trench deepened and widened
	1 RE 2 Inf	LOCK TRENCH	Stocklifting	1 stretch completed 1 " 50%

No night parties on account of relief.

E. Mac Brys Mac Quintin Lt RE.
O.C. 93rd Still Co. RE

SECRET 17th Divisional Engineer 9 Provost

Appendix 20 Progress Report ending 6 a.m. 19-3-18.

Unit	No of Men	Map Location	Nature of Work	Progress
93rd (Field) Co RE	4 RE	P.17.d	Accommodation	Works continued
	3 RE	CLARGES.	Refuting, Widening	60yds trench cleared, 80yds been cleared
	30 Inf	AVENUE. K.22.d.95	Duckboarding	45yds duckboards fixed. 45tps resetted
	1 RE	SHIP TRENCH	Maintenance	50 yds trench cleared
	4 Inf			
	2 RE	"	Gas proof curtains	2 curtains completed
	2 RE	T.M.B. Hd Qr. LONDON. SUP.	" "	4 curtains completed
	7 RE	K.28.a.5.8.	Water Supply	Protective bank made from well to cistern completed. Pump cellar thoroughly cleaned out.
	20 Inf Ad	K.15.d.2.4.		R. Bat Ad Q.r. WHITEHALL 70 yds trench excavated and pipe covered. No.1 Tank 200 Sandbags filled for apheleful proof wall. No. 2 Tank trench deepened and steps made. Hole for pipe cut in cover. Shelt 50% completed

SECRET-

2

Unit	No of Men	Map Location	Nature of Work	Progress
93rd (Field) Co R.E.		K.21.a.8.5	Water Supply	Support Batt. LONDON TRENCH. 50 yds track excavated and pipe lowered. Tanks 1 & 2 Excavation for tanks completed and stands fixed.
	2 RE 29 Inf	SEAL TRENCH	Deepening & widening	50 yds trench cleared
	7 RE Day Party	SHIP & SEAL K.16.d	Clearing old German Wire	900 sq yds wire cut and pickets drawn
	6 RE 80 Inf	" "	Clearing wire and Spreading at BILHEM CHAPEL SWITCH.	1100 sq yds.
	13 RE 57 Infantry Day Party	HAVRINCOURT Defences. K.21.b.4.1.— K.22.c.8.2.	Digging	3 Firesteps 8 yds long 60% completed. 3 Firesteps 7 yds long completed 200 yds trench deepened & widened 80 yds berm cleared.
	1 RE 50 Inf	K.22.c.5.1.		38 yds trench dug 6 ft wide 3 ft deep. 14 yds 6 ft wide 2 ft deep.

SECRET.   3.

Unit	No of Men	Mof. Location	Nature of Work	Progress
93rd (Fld) Co RE	6 RE Day Party	LOCK TRENCH	Firestep	1 Firestep 9 yds long. 1 " 11 " " Deepened & widened, completed for revetting. 1 Firestep 25 yds long deepened, widened & 50% revetted
	2 RE 140 Inf	LOCK TRENCH	Digging	120 yds to depth of 5 feet 130 yds to depth of 6 feet and berm cleared
	3 RE 802 Inf	BILHEM. CHAPEL-SWITCH K 2 1 b	Clearing trench	220 yards clearing

R.C. Lundie, Major. R.E.
O.C. 93rd (Fld) Coy R.E.

SECRET — 17th Divisional Engineer and Pioneer
Weekly Progress Report ending 6 a.m 19-3-18.

Unit	Map Jerusalem	Nature of Work	Progress
93rd (Field) Co R.E.	P.17.d.	Accommodation	Work continued
	CLARGES AVENUE	Deepening, widening Duckboarding	330yds trench deepened & widened. 433yds duckboards fixed. 680yds berm cleared
	SHIP TRENCH	Maintenance	160 yds trench cleared
	GEORGE STREET	Maintenance	54 yds duckboards repaired 50 yds duckboards repaired
	SHIP TRENCH	Gas proof curtains	14 Curtains completed
	SHINGLER SUPPORT	POSTS.	S.1.A) S.1. } Completed S.11. S.111
	DARWIN ALLEY.	Deepening widening duckboarding	345 yds deepened & widened 125 yds duckboards fixed 700 yds berm cleared DARWIN completed to STAFFORD AVENUE

SECRET

Unit	No. of Men	Map Reference	Nature of Work	Progress
93rd (Field) Co RE		DRURY LANE LONDON SUPP. K.28.a.5.8.	Gun emp. cut and lined	13 completed
			Water Supply	The whole pipe line is connected with necessary stop cocks. R.Batt. H.Q. WHITEHALL 2 tanks fixed and ready for water, complete with inlet cocks and can fillers. 2 Reservoirs complete & ready for water. SUPPORT Batt. R.21.a.6.5. 2 Tanks fixed in position and ready for water. 14. Completed. Work completed
		JERMYN STREET SEAL TRENCH	Drainage Refixing unshipped duckboarding	188 yds distance deepened & widened 210 yds berm cleared
		SHIP & SEAL TRENCH	Clearing Wire	150 yds duckboards fixed 5,170 sq yds cut and cleared

SECRET.
3.

Unit.	No of Men	Map Reference	Nature of Work	Progress.
93rd (Field) Co R.E.		K.10.d.4.9	Salvaging	Spare parts and 5 wheels taken off. Work completed.
		K.10.b.3.3.	3. T.M.'s	370yds trench excavated 4'6" broad 4' deep. 880 yds deepened & widened
		60 A.P. TRENCH.	Digging	1,160 yds trench deepened & widened
		HAVRINCOURT DEFENCES.	Digging	230 yds berm cleaned. 558 yds trench excavated 6' wide 3' deep. 18 firebays excavated. 1. M.G. emplacement excavated.
		— LOCK TRENCH.	Digging	995 yds trench deepened to 6 ft & widened 875yds trench cleaned. 3 firebays completed.
		BILHEM CHAPEL SWITCH	Digging	3 firebays excavated 370 yds trench cleaned.

R.C. Sandie, Major R.E.
O.C. 93rd (Field) Co. R.E.

SECRET – 17th Divisional Engineer & Pioneer
Appendix 2.2. Progress Report ending 6 a.m. 20-3-18.

Unit	No of Men	Map Location	Nature of Work	Progress
93rd (Field) Co RE.	4 RE	P.17.d.	Accommodation	Work continued
	3 RE	CLARGES	Deepening, Widening	25 yds trench cleared
	30 Inf	AVENUE	Duckboarding	50 " " cleared
	1 RE	K.22.b.05.S.	Maintenance	40 yds duckboards placed
	6 Inf	SHIP TRENCH		70 yds trench cleared
	2 RE	" "	Gas proof curtains	1 curtain completed
		SUN ALLEY – Coy Hd Qrs.		1 " 50% completed
	2 RE	LONDON SUPP	Gas proof curtains	3 frames completed
	1 RE 20 Inf	K.28.a.5-8.	Water Supply	Borehole pump returned from 559 Coy and refixed. Reservoir damaged by shell fire taken out & replaced by new one

SECRET.—

Unit	No of Men	Map Location	Nature of Work	Progress
		K.15.d.7.4	Water Supply	R.Batt. Hd Qrs WHITEHALL No 1. Tank Sand bag & splinter proof wall 30% completed. No. 2 Tank 6 yds trench deepened & duck boarded. Shed completed.
		K.21.a.8.5.	"	SUPPORT. Batt. LONDON TRENCH. Tanks. No. 1. & 2. Stands altered and tank fixed. Excavation for petrol cans & discus completed. 8. duckboards salvaged.
2 RE) 2 Inf)		SEAL.TRENCH.	Deepening, Widening Duckboarding	25 yds trench cleared. 75 yds berm cleared. 25 yds duckboards fixed.
7 RE Day Party		SHIP & SEAL K.27.b.	Clearing old German Wire	960 sq yds wire cut and pickets drawn.
6 RE 80 Inf		K.22 b.	-do-	900 yds cleared & handed to BILHEM. CHAPEL SWITCH

SECRET-

3.

Unit	No of Men	Map Location	Nature of Work	Progress.
93rd (Field) Co RE	14 RE 56 Inf	HAVRINCOURT DEFENCES	Digging	3 firebays 8 yds long 90% excavated 150 yds trench deepened & widened 150 yds berm cleaned.
2/2 Div			No anight party	
	6 RE 15 Inf Day Party	LOCK TRENCH	"	1 firebay 11 yds long 50% revetted 1 trench 25 yds long 70% revetted 1 " 5 " " Revetted complete
	2 RE 10 Inf	LOCK TRENCH	Digging	13 yds trench cleaned 130 yds trench deepened & widened to 6' & berm cleaned. 250 yds berm cleaned.
	2 RE 65 Inf	BILHEM CHAPEL SWITCH	Digging	75 yds cleaned 5 firebays completed
	1 RE 50 Inf	K.15.d.7.4 – K.15.d.7.4	Digging in fire line.	150 yds trench excavated 2'6" deep. 18" wide

R.C. Lumsden major RE.
O.C. 93rd (Field) Co RE

C.R.E. 17th Division   Appendix 23

Senders Number	Date	In reply to No.
E 64.	26	C. 700

Fighting strength at present in village of HÉNENCOURT.

4 OFFICERS
75. O.R.s

R.C. Lunde Major R.E
O C 93rd Field Co R E

C.R.E. 17th Division   Appendix 24.

Works Reports Ending 28-3-18.

11 posts totalling 420 yds wire dug last night in V.23.b. and V.24.c. and d.

R.C. Lunchey Major RE
O.C. 93rd Field Co RE

C.R.E. 17th Division   Appendix 25.

Works Report ending 6 a.m. 29-3-18.

Two Support posts totalling 128 yds
dug in V.23.b & d.
One new suppt post 27 yds and one
old post repaired and extended at
Cross Roads in V.24.c.
220 additional yds front line dug.

                    R.C. Lunder Major RE
            O.C. 93rd Field Co R.E.

C.R.E. 17th Division Appendix 26

Works Report Ending 6.a.m. 30-3-18

390 yds Strand barbed wire fence carried and erected.
170 yds Support line and 60 yds front line dug.
20 yds old trench cleared.

R.C. Lundie Major R.E.
O.C. 93rd Field Co R.E.

CRE 17th Division Appendix 27

Works Reports ending 6 a.m. 31-3-18

One Front line post in V.23.b.
36 yards of New Trench dug.
88 yards of Trench deepened and widened
330 yards of single strand wire carried and erected

Note
    No Pioneers available last night

        R.C. Lundee Major RE
        OC 93 Field Co RE

C.R.E 17th Division Appendix C 28

E 86.   1-4-18.
Reference attached report the late
hour at which orders arrived and the
fact that I had to proceed to
MILLENCOURT to arrange details
with G.O.C Right Brigade made
any satisfactory reconnaissance
of the work impossible. Under the
circs, all I could do was to send
a Subaltern and some guides up to
Left Bn H Q ahead of the Coy.
The work done was what the
Bn Commander considered most
urgent for the defence of his sector.

                        R.C. Lundie Major R.E
1-4-18   O.C 93rd Field Co R E

17th Divisional Engineers

WAR DIARY

93rd FIELD COMPANY R. E.

APRIL 1918

CONFIDENTIAL

WAR DIARY

of

93rd Field Company, R.E.

From 1-4-18 to 30-4-18

93RD FIELD COMPANY, R.E.
No. —
Date 1-5-13

Army Form C. 2118.

WAR DIARY
of
INTELLIGENCE SUMMARY.
(Erase heading not required.)

23rd Field Coy R.E.

Sheet I

Place	Date	Hour	Summary of Events and Information	Remarks and references to Appendices
SENLIS	1st		Coy at SENLIS. Horse Lines at CONTAY. 1 O.R. rejoined unit. Strength 7 Officers 182 O.R's 69 animals.	
CONTAY	2nd	5 P.M.	Coy arrived at CONTAY. 1 L.D. evacuated. Strength 7 Officers 182 O.R's 68 animals. Orders received to carry out work, awaiting further orders.	
	3			
VILLERS-BOCAGE	4th	8:20 AM 12:30 PM	Coy with transport moved off. Coy arrived VILLERS-BOCAGE.	
	5th	11:50 AM	Received orders from 3rd Inf Bde to move from VILLERS-BOCAGE.	
FIEFFES	6th	4:10 PM	Arrived FIEFFES. Cleaning transport waggons. 1 O.R. evacuated. Strength 7 Officers 181 O.R's 68 animals.	
	7th		Coy had baths & clean clothes	
	8th		Coy training.	
	9th		Brig Gen Carpenter DSO RE addressed Coy on leaving for IV Corps. Coy training. Coy dinners held in evening.	
	10th		Packing waggons for move.	
TOTENCOURT	11th	10 AM 4:45 PM	Coy marched out. Arrived TOUTENCOURT. In reserve at 2 hours notice to move forward.	

9:30 July by RE

Army Form C. 2118.

Sheet No 5

WAR DIARY
of
INTELLIGENCE SUMMARY.
(Erase heading not required.)

Place	Date	Hour	Summary of Events and Information	Remarks and references to Appendices
TOUTENCOURT	12th		Coy Training	
			2 Officers & 110 infantry attached	
	13th		Coy training	
			3 LD mules received	
			Strength 7 Officers 181 ORs 71 Animals	
	14th		Coy training	
			4 ORs evacuated	
			Strength 7 Officers 177 ORs 71 Animals	
RUBEMPRÉ	15th	2 PM	Coy & attached infantry marched out	
		4 PM	Coy arrived at billets in FORCEVILLE	
		4 PM	Transport marched out	
		5.15 PM	Transport arrived CLAIREFAYE FARM	
	16th		Coy at work on reserve line	
			6 ORs evacuated	
			24 ORs joined unit	
			Strength 7 Officers 195 ORs 71 Animals	
	17th		Coy work as above	
			3 LD mules received	
			2 ORs evacuated	
			Strength 7 Officers 193 ORs 74 Animals	
	18th		Coy work as above	
			1 OR killed 6 ORs wounded 2 ORs wounded at duty	
			Strength 7 Officers 186 ORs 74 Animals	

Army Form C. 2118.

WAR DIARY
INTELLIGENCE SUMMARY.
(Erase heading not required.)

Sheet no 3

Place	Date	Hour	Summary of Events and Information	Remarks and references to Appendices
FORCEVILLE	19		Coy work on Reserve Line. 1 O.R evacuated	Appendix no 1
	20		Strength 7 Officers 185 O.R's 74 animals. Coy work as before	Appendix 2
	21		Coy work as before	Appendix 3
	22		1 Officer wounded 1 O.R killed 2 O.R's wounded. attached appendix	Appendix 4
	23		Coy work as before 2 O.R's evacuated Strength 7 Officers 183 O.R's 70 animals. Coy work as before 2 O.R's joined unit Strength 7 Officers 185 O.R's 74 animals	Appendix 5 & 6
	24		Coy work as before 1 O.R. evacuated Strength 7 Officers 184 O.R's 74 animals	Appendix 7
	25		Coy work as before	Appendix 8
	26		Coy work as before	Appendix 9
	27		Coy work as before 4 O.R's joined unit Strength 7 Officers 188 O.R's 74 animals	Appendix 10
	28		Coy work as before 1 O.R Evacuated Strength 7 Officers 187 O.R's 74 animals	Appendix 11

Army Form C. 2118.

93rd Field Coy R.E.

WAR DIARY
INTELLIGENCE SUMMARY.

(Erase heading not required.)

Instructions regarding War Diaries and Intelligence Summaries are contained in F. S. Regs., Part II. and the Staff Manual respectively. Title pages will be prepared in manuscript.

Sheet No. 1

Place	Date	Hour	Summary of Events and Information	Remarks and references to Appendices
FORCEVILLE	29		Coy Work on Reserve line. 1 O.R Evacuated. Strength 7 Officers 186 O.Rs 74 animals	Appendix 12
	30		Coy work as above. 1 O.R Evacuated. Strength 7 Officers 185 O.Rs 74 animals	Appendix 13, D14

M.M.M.
Capt. R.E.
for O.C. 93rd (Field) Co. R.E.

SECRET. Progress Report ending 6 a.m. 19-4-18.

Unit	No. of men	Map Location	Nature of work	Progress
93rd Field Co. R.E. (Say) O.C. 93rd (Field) Co. R.E.	3. R.E. 8 att. Inf.	P.21.d.4.0.	Divisional Baths	Bathroom ready for cementing. 15' cement skirting completed. 21 yds Pathway cleared and bricked ready for cementing. 10ˣ drain for waste water bricked ready for cementing. 40ˣ trench excavated for water pipe and filled in on top of pipe. Waiting and changing rooms cleaned. Sump hole deepened. Bricks collected in village & carried to job.
	16. R.E. 16. Inf.	Q.31.C	Drainage Digging	3 bays drained. 40ˣ trench dug to 4' deep 6' wide. 12ˣ trench completed 6'x6' Berms cleared. Parapets dressed.
	4. R.E. 12. Inf.		Wiring	50ˣ low wire entanglement completed.
	5.R.E 13.9	No 5 post	Digging	35ˣ completed to 6' deep.
	9.S.14.9	No 6 post	Digging	48ˣ 85% completed.
	19.S.20.9	No 7 post	Digging	70ˣ trench completed to 6'. 6ˣ 90% completed.
	60 Inf	Q.31.b.3.7	Digging	60ˣ trench dug 6' wide at top 4' at bottom 3' deep, parapet levelled berm cleared.
	5 Inf	Q.32.a.1.6	Digging	60ˣ trench dug 4' wide 3' deep parapet levelled berm cleared.
	45. Inf	Q.26.c.3.1	Digging	62ˣ trench dug 4' wide 3' deep. Parapet levelled berm cleared.
	36 Inf	Q.26.c.7.2	Digging	64ˣ trench dug 4' wide 3' deep. Parapet levelled berm cleared.
	16. R.E 20. Inf	Q.32.a.2.3	Wiring etc	320ˣ double apron fence completed. 25ˣ old trench filled in by 9.Inf 11.Inf. carrying

SECRET. Progress Report ending 6 a.m. 20-4-18.

Unit	No of men	Map Location	Nature of Work	Progress
93rd Field Co R.E.	4. R.E. 4. att Inf.	P.21.d.4.0	Divisional Baths	6' of drain for waste water bricked ready for cementing. Sump hole completed, capable of holding 3,544 galls. of waste water. Bricks collected from village for paths leading to bath house.
	3. R.E.	ENGLEBELMER	Wells	Preparing and fixing charges for demolition
	4. R.E.	FORCEVILLE HEDAUVILLE	Wells and Water Points	Preparing and fixing charges for demolition
	20. R.E.	Q.25.C.3.5 Q.25.C.7.2. Q.25.C.7.5. Q.25.C.5.1	Bridging trenches for R.A.	4 trench bridges completed. 2 gaps in wire
	10. R.E. 20. Inf	Q.32.a.0.5.	Wiring	280ˣ double apron fence completed. Inf carrying materials
	15. R.E. 67. Inf	No 37 Post	Digging	3 - 33' firebays widened from 6' to 8' 3' deep. 48ˣ traverse widened from 4' to 6' 4½' deep. 4ˣ traverse deepened from 3' to 4½'. 500ˣ berm cleared. All firebays in this post can be manned. 60ˣ trench trimmed
	25. Inf 5. R.E.	No 36 Post	Digging	2 firebays widened from 6' to 8' & completed. 3. 30' firebays (4 firebays in post) can be manned. 70ˣ trench trimmed
	25. Inf	No 35. Post	Digging	1. 30' firebay widened from 6' to 8' & completed. All firebays in this Post can be manned.
	56. Inf	No 34 Post	Digging	Post completed
	47. Inf	No 42 Post	"	56ˣ 6' top 4' bottom 3' deep
	40. Inf	No 41 Post	"	46ˣ "
	16.S.169	No 39 Post	"	75ˣ trench completed. 2 firebays dug
	4. Strs	Q.31.c.5.6		Completing previous night's work

(Sgn) R. B. Lundie Maj R.E.

O.C. 93rd (Field) Co R.E.

Army Form C. 2118.

WAR DIARY
or
INTELLIGENCE SUMMARY.

(Erase heading not required.)

Instructions regarding War Diaries and Intelligence Summaries are contained in F. S. Regs., Part II. and the Staff Manual respectively. Title pages will be prepared in manuscript.

Place	Date	Hour	Summary of Events and Information	Remarks and references to Appendices

A.5834 Wt.W4973/M687 730,000 8/16 D. D. & L. Ltd. Forms/C.2118/13.

SECRET   Progress Report ending 6 a.m. 21-4-18   3

Unit	No of men	That Location	Nature of Work	Progress
93rd Field Coy R.E	4. R.E 4 att. Inf	P.21.d.4.0.	Divisional Baths	Storage tanks in village dismantled and taken to site of Baths, tanks cleaned and holes plugged. Pit excavated and tanks lowered in 17" brick drain. Steps erected leading to waiting room. Bricks collected in village for pathways. Material sifted for grouting.
	3. R.E	ENGLEBELMER	Wells	Preparing and fixing charges for demolition
	4. R.E	FORCEVILLE HEDAUVILLE	Wells and Water Points	Preparing and fixing charges for demolition
	14. R.E 15 Inf	Post 42	Digging	68" widened to 6' 8 Firesteps cut
	40 Inf	Post 39	Digging	28" completed to 6' deep. Firebays dug
	6 Inf	Post 38	Digging	2 Firebays dug
	12. R.E	Post 38 Post 34		2 parapets reduced all parapets reduced
	16. R.E 55 Inf	Post 37	Digging etc	Post completed and all parapets reduced
	20 Inf	Post 36	Digging	2 Firebays completed from 6' wide to 8'. deepened to 6'. all parapets reduced & berms cleared
	50 Inf	Post 35	Digging	60" completed 2 parapets reduced
	14. R.E 15 Inf	Q.31.d.5.9	Wiring	320 yds double apron fence completed. Inf carrying materials
	20. R.E 20 Inf	Q.32.a.5.5.	Wiring	380" double apron fence completed. Inf carrying materials 35 coils of wire salved and carried to jot.

(Sgd) P.E. Lundie Maj. R.E.
O.C. 93rd (Field) Coy R.E.

SECRET   Progress Report ending 6 am 23-4-18   5

Unit	No. of men	Map Location	Nature of Work	Progress
93rd (Field) Coy R.E	3. R.E. 4 att. Inf.	P.21.d.4.0	Divisional Baths	Cement floor laid in bathroom. Excavation for 2,400 galls tanks completed and 1 tank placed in position. Making & fixing cover for 200 gall storage tank. Making & fixing seating in one changing room. 18' of duckboards made. Inf digging & carrying materials.
	3. R.E.	ENGLEBELMER	Wells and barbed wire concertinas	Standing by for demolitions. 6 barbed wire concertinas completed.
	18. R.E. 27. Inf	Q.31.&	Wiring	300ˣ double apron fence completed.
	2. R.E. 15. Inf	Post 35	Digging	20ˣ deepened to 6'. Firesteps completed & parapet levelled.
	1. R.E. 50. Inf	Post 35. & " 34.	Digging & joining up	60ˣ depth 2'-9" x 8'-0'
	6. R.E. 5 att Inf 22 Inf	Post 40	Digging	3. Firesteps completed. 50ˣ trench 90% complete deepened to 6'
	5. R.E. 3 att Inf	Post 41	Digging	Post completed
	6. R.E. 8 att Inf	Post 42	Digging	Post completed
	21. R.E. 2R att Inf	Q.31.c & d	Wiring	350ˣ double apron fence erected

(Sgn) R.E. Lundie Maj. R.E.
O.C. 93rd (Field) Co. R.E

SECRET 6.

C.R.E. 17th Divn.   (L.4)

Herewith Report of State of Defences
& other Work of this unit to 6 p.m
this evenning, in accordance
with your M.340 of today —

(1) <u>Trenches</u>

Post	42	95%	complete
"	41	100%	complete
"	40	75%	complete
"	39	100%	complete
"	38	100%	complete
"	37	95%	complete
"	36	80%	complete
"	35	80%	complete
"	34	100%	complete
Worked "	33	90%	complete
on "	32	100%	complete
by "	31	100%	complete
Pnrs "	? (Q.31.a.9.5)	100%	compl.
"	? (Q.31.a.8.7)	90%	

Trench connecting Posts 34 & 35.
                                      45% complete

<u>Note</u>. All above trenches require steps up to
firesteps and all (except 42) steps down
into trench from ground level. 39 is
the only post with drainage

- Add to above list
Post ? (Q.31.c.8.6.) 100% complete
Started by R.E. & finished by
Pioneers. Above note applies also
to this post.

(ii) Wire

Single belt of double apron fence from
Q.31.c.5.3 in front of Suitab. Line
to Q.26.c.8.2
There is a second belt from same point
to Q.31.a.3.5 & from Q.31.b.7.1 to
Q.32.a.3.7 & a third belt from
Q.31.b.7.1 to road at Q.32.a.0.4
Single belt joins wire of ENGLEBELMER
- MILLENCOURT Line at Q.31.c.5.3
Concertinas have been provided for
blocking road in Q.32.a & old "Boyau"
beside road has been blocked both
by filling in & with wire

(iii) Demolitions

Wells & water supply arrangements
in HEDAUVILLE, ENGLEBELMER &
FORCEVILLE are prepared for
demolition as already reported

(iv) Baths
Open FORCEVILLE 8am 24-4-18

(Sgn) R.B. Lundie, Maj RE
O.C. 93rd Fd. Co R.E

S.E.C.R.E.T.   Progress Report ending 6 a.m. 24-4-18

Unit	No of men	Map Location	Nature of Work	Progress
93rd Field Co. R.E.	8. R.E. 4 att Inf	P.21.d.4.0.	Divisional Baths	Bathroom floor completed. Step erected to changing room. 10ˣ drain boxed in. 30ˣ brick pathway grouted. Lowering 2nd 400 galls storage tank into ground, and connecting water from mains (making 1,000 galls storage in all). 42' of duckboards made for No.I changing room. Repairing & rehanging door. 2 seats 8ft & 10ft long made for No.2 changing room. Timber salvaged from village. Standing by for demolitions.
	3. R.E.	ENGLEBELMER	Wells & barbed wire concertinas	3 concertinas made. Salvaging wire in village
	26. R.E. 20 att Inf	Q.32.a.	Wiring	402ˣ double apron fence completed
	3. R.E. 60 Inf	Post 34 & 35	Joining up Digging	37ˣ deepened to 6' & parapet levelled. 24ˣ depth 3' width 8'.
	1. R.E. 24 att Inf	Post 36	Digging	30ˣ trench deepened to 6'. All firebays complete. 15ˣ trench widened to 6' depth 3'.
	1 Sapper	Post 39	Cutting steps up to firesteps	5 steps completed
	7. R.E. 15 att Inf	Post 40	Completing previous nights work	60ˣ trench completed
	25 Inf	Post 40	Digging	30ˣ completed.
	1. R.E. 20 att Inf	Post 41	Digging	Steps cut in firesteps ends of post.
	7. R.E.	Post 42	Digging	Steps cut in firesteps. Parapets etc. finished
	22. R.E. 10 Inf	Q.31.c & d	Wiring	450ˣ double apron completed.

(Sgd) R.B. Lundie Maj. R.E.
O.C. 93rd (Fd). Co. R.E.

SECRET. Progress Report ending 6 a.m. 25-4-18.   7

Unit	No. of men	Map Location	Nature of Work	Progress
93rd Field Co. R.E.	8 R.E. 4 att Inf	P.21.d.4.0	Divisional Baths	16^x brick pathway laid & gravelled. Sump hole deepened. Duckboard 8' by 6' made & fitted under sprayers. 2 notice boards (BATHS) made. Rooms for No. 2 changing room each 7' 6" long made. 30' duckboards made. Bricks collected in village for pathways. Baths have been working 9 hrs. No. of men bathed 700.
	3 R.E.	ENGLEBELMER	Wells & B. wire concertinas	Standing by for demolitions. 4 concertinas made. Salvaging wire.
	2 R.E.	Bde Hd Qrs P.24.c.2.2	Accomodation	Office for signals 20' x 12'. 40% completed.
R.E.	28 R.E. 30 att Inf	Q.31.d.3.4.to Q.32.a.1.1.	Wiring	610^x double apron completed.
	2 R.E. 30 att Inf	Post 35	Digging	Post completed.
	27 R.E. 22 att Inf	Q.31.a	Wiring	595^x double apron completed.
	5 R.E. 275 Inf	ENGLEBELMER - MILLENCOURT Line	Digging	Post at Q.25.a.8.1. 53^x of trench widened to 8'. 50^x of drain deepened & widened. Post at Q.25.c.9.8. 60^x of trench widened to 8'. 24^x of drain widened and deepened. Post at Q.25.c.9.2. 48^x of trench widened to 6'. 23^x of new trench dug 6' wide 3' deep. C.T at Q.31.c.5.8 130^x of trench dug 4' wide 3' deep.

Signed R.S. Lundie Maj R.E.
O.C 93rd (Field) Co. R.E.

SECRET   Progress Report ending 6 am 26-4-18.   8

Unit	No. of men	Map Location	Nature of Work	Progress
93rd Field Co R.E	6 R.E 4 att Inf	P.21.d.4.0	Divisional Baths	Wood blocks cemented in No 2 changing room for fixing forms. 9" brick pathway laid. Excavating 2nd Sump hole. 32' Duckboards made for passage & No 2 changing room. Salvaging timber. Standing by for demolitions.
	3 R.E	ENGLEBELMER	Wells & B. wire concertinas	5. B wire concertinas made.
	2 R.E	P.30.c.9.2	Battn Hd Qrs Accomodation	Officers mess 10'x5'x8' completed. material sal. from ENGLEBELMER
	11 R.E 10 att Inf	Q.31.c – Q.31.d	Wiring	260ˣ apron fence completed.
	2 R.E 4 att Inf	Q.31.c.6.6	Digging & sandbagging	Box drain (17') placed in position and covered in.
	2 R.E 3 Inf	Q.31.a.2.2	Cutting pickets	30 long 100 short cut.
	16 R.E	Q.31.c.5.3	Digging	3 firebays completed. 10ˣ drain deepened & widened.
	2 R.E 80 Inf	Q.31.c.5.8	Digging	32ˣ new C.T dug 6' wide 3' deep. 124ˣ widened to 6'.
	2 R.E 95 Inf	Q.25.c.4.1	Digging	95ˣ new C.T dug 6' wide 3' deep.
	1 R.E 80 Inf	Q.25	Digging	350ˣ trench widened to 8'.
	22 R.E 20 att Inf	Q.32.a	Wiring	385ˣ double apron fence completed.
	5 R.E 54 att Inf	Post 34 35	Gaming up	Completed.

(Sgd) R.E Lundie. Maj R.E
O.C. 93rd (Field) Co R.E

-SECRET-   Progress Report ending 6 a.m. 27-4-18   Appendix to 9

Unit	No. of men	That Location	Nature of Work	Progress
93rd (Field) Co. R.E.	6. R.E. 4. Inf (attached)	P.21.d.4.0.	Divisional Baths	Brick floor 3yds x 2yds laid and cemented, outside bathroom. Excavation of 2nd Sump hole continued. 75' of 5"x2" & 25' of 4"x2" salvaged. Forms fixed around No 2 changing room & 15' of duckboards made. 2 forms 11' long each made. Bricks collected for floor.
	3. R.E.	ENGLEBELMER	Wells and B. wire concertinas	Standing by for demolitions 5 concertinas made.
(Sqn) O.C. 93rd (Field) Co. R.E.	2. R.E.	P.30..c.q.2.	Battn. Hd. Qts accommodation	Cook house 10'x5'x8' completed Aid Post 30% excav. completed
	1. R.E.	Q.28.a.q.5.	Battn. Hd. Qts accommodation	Entrance to dugout repaired
	2. R.E. 4. att Inf.	Q.31.c.2.7.	Cutting short pickets	100 pickets cut
	12. R.E. 12. Inf.	Q.31.B.	Wiring. Carrying materials	270ˣ apron fence complete
	12. R.E. 51 att Inf	Post 33	Digging C.T. leading from Post 33	65ˣ. 6' x 3'. 75ˣ. 6' x 9"
	18. R.E. 20 att Inf	Q.32.a.	Wiring	390ˣ double apron fence completed
	11. R.E. 80. Inf.	Q.31.c.5.3.	Digging	2 firebays completed 30ˣ of drain widened & deepened. 60ˣ trench deepened to 6'.
	2. R.E. 100 Inf.	Q.31.c.5.8	Digging	134ˣ trench deepened to 6'. 34ˣ widened to 6'. 70ˣ trench dug 6' wide 3' deep.
	1. R.E 70 Inf.	Q.25.c.q.2.	Digging	75ˣ trench deepened, 3 firebays cut 75% completed.
	1. R.E 30 Inf.	Q.25.c.7.2	Digging	45ˣ widened to 8'

S.E.C.R.E.T. Progress Report ending 6am 28-4-18   10.

Unit	No of men	Map Location	Nature of Work	Progress
93rd Field Co R.E.	6 R.E. 4 att. Inf	P.31.d.4.0	Divisional Baths	Brick floor 3 sq. yds laid. Manure in yard cleared up. Ground levelled & covered with fresh coal. Drain dug & sump hole deepened. 3 forms made & fixed in officers dressing room. Shelf 6'6"x 6' made and fixed in store room. 22' duckboards made. Timber salvaged.
	3. R.E	ENGLEBELMER	Wells & Bruce concertinas	Standing by for demolitions. 4 concertinas made.
	2. R.E.	P.30.c.9.2	Battn H.Q accomodation	Assisting inf clearing dugout.
	10. R.E. 13 att Inf	Q.31.c.9.1.	Wiring	240^x completed apron fence.
	9 R.E 2att Inf			Making large bobbins for plain wire. & winding same
	2. R.E 13. R. E.	Q.31.c.5.5. Post 39	Digging	Preparing post for duckboards & draining etc.
	13. R. E. 12 att Inf	Q.32.a	Wiring	280^x double apron fence completed
	17 R.E. 37 att Inf	Post 33.	C.T. from Post 33 digging	42^x deepened to 6'. 19^x deepened to 5'.6"
	4. R.E. 6att Inf 75 Inf	Q.31.c.5.3	Digging	120^x trench deepened to 6'. 40^x widened to 6'. Berm cleared & batter of trench corrected
	4. R.E 14 Inf. A 25 Inf	Q.31.c.5.8	Digging	35^x trench deepened to 6'. Batter of trench 134^x corrected & berm cleared
	2. R.E. 92 Inf	Q.25.c.4.1.	Digging	20^x trench dug 6' wide 3' deep. 150^x trench deepened to 6'.
	5. R.E. 50 Inf	Q.25.c.9.2	Digging	70^x trench in post completed. 6' deep & 6' wide with firebays
	3. R.E 50 Inf	Q.25.c.7.2.	Digging	50^x trench deepened to 6' with firestep
	4. R.E. 75 Inf	Q.25.a	Digging	30^x trench deepened to 6' with firestep. 20^x widened to 8'. 20^x drain deepened & widened

(Sgn) P.L Lundie Major R.E
O.C 93rd (Fld) Co R.E

SECRET. Progress Report ending 6 a.m. 29-11-18.

Unit	No. of Men	Map Location	Nature of Work	Progress
93rd Field R.E.	6 R.E. 40 Inf.	P.21.d.4.0	Divisional Baths	Digging trench 26ˣ long. Laying 26ˣ of 4" pipes for draining water from No.1 Sump hole & filling in trench. Deepening No.2 Sump hole. Duckboard 6' long made for No.2 changing room. Making & fixing 3 soap boxes 2' long 6"x 6". Making & fixing 6 brackets for officers changing room. Fixing fence in front of bathroom 14'x 4'6"
	3 R.E.	ENGLEBELMER	Wells	Salvaging timber
60 R.E.				Standing by for demolitions
	2 R.E.	P.30.c.9.2	Battn. H.Q. Accomodation	Aid Post completed.
	1 R.E.	Q.28.a.9.5	Battn. H.Q. Accomodation	Assisting Inf.
	4 R.E. 4 Inf.	Post 39	Duckboarding Draining	32ˣ deepened 18" for drainage purposes. 25ˣ duckboards laid
	1 R.E. 3 Inf.	Q.31.d	Cutting gaps	5 gaps
	6 R.E. 8 Inf.	Q.31.d.9.9	Wiring	120ˣ apron fence completed
	6 R.E. 4 att. Inf.	Q.32.a	Wiring	Cutting gaps & repairing wire damaged by shell fire
	27 R.E. 70 Inf.	Post 33	C.T. from Post 33 digging	78ˣ trench to 3'. 30ˣ trench from 2'-9" – 5'-9" & berm cleared
	3 R.E. 30 Inf.	Q.25.c.9.2	Digging	Post completed.
	3 R.E. 68 Inf.	Q.20.a.5.7	Digging	70ˣ trench dug 6' wide 3' deep
	4 R.E. 62 Inf.	Q.25.c.4.1	Digging	110ˣ deepened to 6'. 90ˣ completed. 120ˣ trench finished off.
	7 R.E. 100 Inf.	Q.25.c.8.9	Digging	94ˣ trench deepened to 6' with firesteps. 18ˣ 50% complete. Drain deepened.
	6 R.E. 40 Inf.	W.1.a	Digging	185ˣ trench widened to 6'. 25ˣ deepened to 6'. 3 firebays cut

Sgn. R.E. Lundie. Maj. R.E.
O.C. 93rd (Fd) Co R.E.

S.E.C.R.E.T.   Progress Report ending 6 am 30-4-18.   12

Unit	No of men	Map Location	Nature of Work	Progress
93rd Field Co. R.E.	3. R.E. 4 atts Inf	P.21.d.40	Divisional Baths	Yard cleared & levelled. Wire fence round Sump holes erected. Preparing material for extra sprayers, making 2 forms 8' long each & fixing outside baths. 1 duckboard 5'6" long made & fixed from under sprayers to officers changing room. 3 doors taken off & stored in loft. Standing by for demolition.
	3. R.E.	ENGLEBELMER	Wells	
	1. R.E.	P.30.c.q.2	Accomodation	Digging in charges assisting Inf.
	20 R.E.	P.22.d.30	Accomodation	2 Bivouacs 11'x 8' complete.
	10. R.E.	Q.20.a.5.b & Q.20.a.9.9	Artillery Bridges	2 bridges completed.
	23 R.E. 26 atts Inf	Q.31.C	Wiring	320ˣ double apron fence completed 60ˣ 25% completed
	50 Inf. 3. R.E.	C.T. from Post 33	Digging	54ˣ trench 6'x 3'. 6 cub yds earth moved where C.T. joins post.
	5. R.E. 4 att Inf	Post 39	Duckboarding	42ˣ duckboards laid. 50ˣ deepened 1' for drainage purposes

Sgn. R. P. Lundie Maj. R.E.
O.C. 93rd (Field) Co. R.E.

-SECRET- 13

C.R.E 17th Div   (L.S.)

Herewith Weekly Progress Report of this unit to 6 p.m. today

(i) Trenches
Post 35 completed and joined to Post 34. Junction 80% complete.
* C.T. from Post 35 to front line of MILLENCOURT - ENGLEBELMER System 85% complete
* Trench joining Posts 35 & 36 - 30% complete.
* Trench connecting Post 37 to front line of ENGLEBELMER System 15% complete
C.T. back from Post 33 75% complete
C.T. back from Post 30 15% complete
Post 39 duckboarded

ENGLEBELMER System
C.T.'s from front to support line
Q.31.c   85%
Q.31.a   85%
Q.20.a   10%
Six front line posts average 75% complete
* Post 39 duckboarded
* Post 33 completed

Note. Items marked * have been worked on by Pioneers.

(ii) Wire as on attached Progress map

Sgd. R.B. Lundie Maj RE
O.C 93rd Field Co RE

30-4-18

SECRET. Progress Report ending 1-5-18.   14

Unit	No. of men	Map Location	Nature of Work	Progress
93rd Field Co RE	3 R.E	ENGLEBELMER	Wells	Standing by for demolitions. Digging in charges
	1 R.E	P.30.c.9.2	Accomodation	Assisting Inf.
	17 R.E	P.22.d.3.0	Accomodation	14 sq. yds. excavated for bivouacs
	3 R.E 120 Inf	Q.20.a.5.7	Digging	90ˣ trench deepened to 6'. 25ˣ trench dug 6' wide 3' deep
	5 R.E 100 Inf	W.1.a	Digging	100ˣ trench deepened to 6'. 2 firebays dug.
	3 R.E 64 Inf	Q.25.a.8.1	Digging	60ˣ trench dug 8' wide & 6' deep with firestep. 50ˣ drain dug 4'.6' deep.
	4 R.E	Q.25.c.8.9	Digging	60ˣ trench walls perfectly levelled & berm cut
	3 R.E 100 Inf	Q.31.9.4.8	Digging	110ˣ trench deepened. 25ˣ drain deepened
	8 R.E	Q.25.a.9.3	Bridging	1 Art. Bridge completed. 1 Trench crossing repaired
	26 R.E	Q.31.d.9.9	Wiring	550ˣ completed
	31 Inf	Q.31.d	Carrying	Wire etc.
	2 R.E 55 Inf	Post 37	Digging	76ˣ C.T. 6'x 3' completed

Sgd. R. E. Lundie Maj. R.E.
O.C. 93rd (Field) Co. R.E.

CONFIDENTIAL

WAR DIARY

— of —

93rd Field Coy. R.E.

From 1-5-18 to 31-5-18

Army Form C. 2118.

WAR DIARY

INTELLIGENCE SUMMARY.

(Erase heading not required.) 93rd (field) Co R.E. Sheet No. 1

Place	Date	Hour	Summary of Events and Information	Remarks and references to Appendices
FORCEVILLE	1st		Forward billets FORCEVILLE. Hors Lines CLAIRFAYE FARM. Strength 7 Offrs 185 O.R's 74 animals	Appendix 1
	2nd		As above. 1 O.R evacuated sick. Strength 7.0pm 184 O.R's 74 animals	Appx
	3rd		As above. 1 Rider evacuated debility. Strength 7.0 pm 184 O.R's 73 animals	Appendix 2 Appx
	4th		As above. 1 OR evacuated sick. Strength 7.0 pm 183 O.R's 73 animals	Appendix 3 Appx
	5th		As above. 1 OR evacuated. Strength 7.0/pm 182 O.R's 73 animals	Appendix 4 Appx
	6th		As for above.	Appendix 5 Appx
	7th		As for above.	Appendix 6 Appx
	8th		Dismounted portion marched out of FORCEVILLE 12.30pm arrived O.12.d.75. at 1.30pm. Mounted portion marched out of CLAIRFAYE FARM at 7pm arrived O.12.d.7.5 2am/pm	Appendix 7 Appx
ACHEUX	9th		Coy at work on Purple System at MAILLY-MAILLET & BEAUSART Switch.	Appx
	10th		1 Section training each day. Workers.	
	11th		As above.	Appx

WAR DIARY
INTELLIGENCE SUMMARY

Army Form C. 2118.

93rd (F.28d.) Fos R.E. S2a3. no 2

May 1918

Place	Date	Hour	Summary of Events and Information	Remarks and references to Appendices
ACHEUX	12		Coy at work on Purple System. 1 Section tramway.	
	13		22 O R S found	
	14		Strength 7 Officers, 204 ORs. 73 animals	
	15		As above	
	16		As above	
	17		As above	
			As above	
			1 O R joined unit	
			Strength 7 Officers 205 ORs 73 animals	
	18		As above	
	19		As above	
	20		As above	
	21		As above	
	22		As above	
			Sector completion C R E inspected section	

Army Form C. 2118.

WAR DIARY
INTELLIGENCE SUMMARY.

(Erase heading not required.)

93rd (3rd/Fd) Co. R.E.   Sheet No. 3

May 1918.

Place	Date	Hour	Summary of Events and Information	Remarks and references to Appendices
ACHEUX	23		Work on Purple System. 6. O R's joined. 2. O R's evacuated. Strength 7 Officers 209 O R's 73 animals	A/1
	24		As above. 1 Rider evacuated. Strength 7 Officers 209 O R's 72 animals. Pack run of for more	A/2
	25		Packing up for move	A/3
MAILLY	26	5.0AM	Coy marched at 5 AM arriving P.17.A.4.4. 5.30am. /Serlin Killed v. MAILLY-MAILLET. Mounted Portion marched & 30am arrived LOUVENCOURT WOOD 8.0 AM.	A/4
	27		Work as Works Report. 2. O R's wounded. Strength 7 Officers 207 O R's 72 animals	A/5
	28		As above. 10 R Killed. Strength 7 Officers 206. O R's 72 animals	A/6
	29		As above. 1 O R wounded. Strength 7 Officers 205. O R's 72 animals	A/7
	30		As above. 2 O R's joined. Strength 7 Officers 207. O R's 72 animals	A/8 Appdx 12

Army Form C. 2118.

WAR DIARY
INTELLIGENCE SUMMARY.

(Erase heading not required.)

of 93rd (Fd.) Co. R.E. Sheet No 6

May 1918

Place	Date	Hour	Summary of Events and Information	Remarks and references to Appendices
ACHEUX	31st		Work as Works Report.	

McNeid Capt. R.E.
for O.C. 93rd (Field) Co. R.E.

- SECRET -

17th Divisional Engineers & Pioneers

Progress Report ending 6 a.m. 2-5-18

APPENDIX 1.

Unit	No. of men	Map Location	Nature of Work	Progress
93rd Field Coy R.E.	3. R.E.	ENGLEBELMER	Wells	Standing by for demolitions. Digging in, charges.
	1. R.E.	P.30.c.9.2	Accomodation	Assisting infantry
	12. R.E.	P.22.d.3.0	"	Work continued
	5. R.E. 4 att. Inf	Post 39	Digging & Duckboarding	20ˣ trench deepened 2' & widened 2'. 24ˣ duckboards fixed on pickets. Clearing trade in Sunken Rd. 30ˣ duckboard track laid & fixed on pickets
	6 R.E. 210 Inf	Q.31.a.5.5	Digging C.T.	200ˣ 6ft wide 3ft deep 4 ft wide at bottom dug.
	3. R.E. 80 Inf	Q.31.a.1.7	Digging C.T.	75ˣ 6ft wide 3ft deep 4ft wide at bottom dug.
	3. R.E. 90 Inf	Q.20.a.4.7	Digging C.T.	85ˣ 6ft wide 3ft deep 4ft wide at bottom dug. 10ˣ trench deepened and widened.
	13. R.E.	Post 24	Digging	40ˣ of parapet levelled ready for manning. 20ˣ trench firestepped. 8ˣ trench deepened to 6ft.
	13. R.E. 14 att. Inf	Q.20.c.	Wiring	320ˣ double apron fence completed
	35 att. Inf	C.T. from Post 30	Digging	36ˣ trench dug 6' x 3'.
	19 R.E. 6 att. Inf	ENGLEBELMER LINE	Wiring	400ˣ apron fence completed
	1. R.E. 20 att. Inf	Post 39	Digging	C.T. from Post to road 30ˣ completed.

(2)

Unit	No. of men	Location	Nature of Work	Progress
93rd R.E.	1 R.E. 5 att. Sgt.	C.T. from P.35 - P.36	Digging	10' apx. connected up. 3' x 3'
Field Co R.E.	1 R.E. 5 att. Sgt.	Post 33.	Digging	7' X. Loosened to 2' 8" for onedroy

(Sgn) R.E. Dundas Maj RE.

O.C. 93rd (Id) Coy RE

SECRET

17th Divisional Engineers and Pioneers
Progress Report ending 6 a.m. 3-5-18.

APPENDIX 2.

Unit	No of men	Map Location	Nature of Work	Progress
	3. R.E	ENGLEBELMER	Wells	Standing by for demolitions. Digging in charges
93rd Field Co. R.E.	1. R.E	P.30.c.9.2	Accomodation	Work continued. Wiring T.P.
	12.R.E	P.22.d.3.0.	"	Work continued
	4.R.E 4 att Inf	Q.31.c.	Cleaning road & Duckboarding	40ˣ duckboard track fixed
	22 R.E 15 att Inf	Q.25.c	Wiring	400ˣ double apron fence completed
	6 att Inf	Q.25.a	Camouflaging	4 double screens height 10' 50ˣ single
	15 R.E 15 att Inf	Q.19.d 9. Q.20.c	Wiring	360ˣ double apron completed
	9. R.E 40 att Inf	C.T. from Post 31.	Digging	45ˣ 6'X3' dug
	7. R.E 200 Inf	Q.31.a.5.5.	Digging C.T	200ˣ completed 6ft deep 6ft wide at bottom
	4 R.E 85 Inf	Q.31.a.1.7	"	75ˣ — ditto —
	4 R.E 75 Inf	Q.31.a.4.4.	"	75ˣ — ditto —
	10 R.E	Q.25.c.7.7.	"	35ˣ 6ft wide 3ft deep, 4ft wide at bottom dug. Knocked off work at 9.30 p.m

(Sgd) R.C. Lundie Maj R.E
O.C 93rd (Fld) Co. R.E

SECRET

17th Divisional Engineers and Pioneers
Progress Report ending 6 a.m. 4-5-18.

APPENDIX 3

Unit	No. of Men	Map Location	Nature of Work	Progress
	3. R.E.	ENGLEBELMER	Wells	Standing by for demolitions. Digging in charges.
	12 R.E. 8 att. Inf.	P.22.d.3.0.	Accommodation	Work continued
93rd Field Co. R.E.	4 R.E. 4 att. Inf.	Q.31.c.6.5.	Cleaning road duckboarding	Road cleaned & 54x of duckboards fixed on pickets
	20. R.E. 15 att. Inf.	Q.25.c.	Wiring Carrying	450x double apron fence completed
	6 att. Inf.	Q.25.a.	Camouflaging	8x double screen complete. 10x raised 2'
	10. R.E. 28 att. Inf.	Q.31.c.2.a to Q.31.c.2.b.	Digging	290x of Support Line dug. 4 ft wide 3 ft deep. 2 ft wide at bottom
	4. R.E. 91. Inf.	Q.31.a.4.4	Digging C.T.	75x 5½ ft deep. 2 ft at bottom
	1. R.E. 44 att. Inf.	Q.31.a.4.8 (C.T)	Digging	3 firebays completed ready for manning. 6x widened to 9½ ft. 10x widened to 7½ ft. all 2 ft at bottom
	19 R.E. 14 att. Inf.	Q.20.c.	Wiring	405 yds. double apron completed

(Sgn) R. C. Lundie
Maj. R.E.
O.C. 93rd (Field) Co. R.E.

SECRET.

17th Divisional Engineers & Pioneers

Progress Report ending 6.a.m 5-4-18.

APPENDIX. 4.

Unit	No of men	Map Location	Nature of Work	Progress
93rd Field Co R.E.	3. R.E.	ENGLEBELMER	Wells	Standing by for demolitions. Salvaging Timber.
	40. R.E. 60 att Inf	P.22.d.3.0.	Accomodation	Bivouacs for 2 sections completed and occupied.
	4. R.E. 4 att Inf	P.39.Q.31.C.	Cleaning & duckboarding	Road cleaned & 20' duckboard track. Pured on pickets. Trench cleaned & 20' duckboards on pickets
	30. R.E. 13 att Inf	Q.20.B.	Wiring carrying	500' apron fence completed

(Sgd) R. E. Lumsdie Maj. R.E.
O.C. 93rd (Field) Coy. R.E.

— SECRET —

17th Divisional Engineers and Pioneers.

Progress Report ending 6 a.m 6-4-18.

APPENDIX 5.

Unit.	No. of men.	Map Location.	Nature of Work.	Progress.
93rd Field Coy R.E.	3 R.E.	ENGLEBELMER	Wells	Standing by for demolitions
	6 R.E. 8 att. Inf.	P.22.d.3.0.	Accomodation	Work continued
	4 R.E. 4 att. Inf.	Post 39.	Clearing trench & duckboarding	Trench deepened & widened. 32ˣ duckboards fixed on pickets
	15 R.E.	Q.21 & S.S.	Wiring	100ˣ of partly finished double apron fence completed
	24 R.E	Q.22.a.8.8	Wiring	200ˣ L iron pickets placed in position
	90 inf	S.P.12	Digging	35ˣ trench 6ft wide 3ft deep 4ft at bottom. 45ˣ trench 6ft wide 2½ft deep 4ft at bottom.
	10 R.E 10 att. Inf.	Q.20.b.	Wiring Carrying	270ˣ apron fence completed. Also gathered all available material to central dump.
	12 R.E 15 Inf	Q.22.d	Wiring Support Line	200ˣ double apron
	1 R.E 12 Inf	Q.22.d 4.3 to 7.3	Firestepping CHARLES AV. to five South	4 Fire Bays completed
	2 R.E 7 Inf	Q.22.d	Digging out Support Line N. of CHARLES AV.	200 yds widened & deepened

Note. Owing to two wagon loads of wiring materials going astray work on Div. N. Boundary and Intermediate System was very greatly hampered.

(Sgn) R C Lundie, Maj RE.

O.C. 93rd (Field) Co R.E

— SECRET —

17th Divisional Engineers and Pioneers.
Progress Report ending 6am 7-5-18

APPENDIX 6.

Unit	No. of men	Map Location	Nature of Work	Progress
93rd Field Coy. R.E.	3.R.E.	ENGLEBELMER	Wells	Standing by for demolitions. Salvaging timber.
	6 R.E. 8 att. Inf.	P.22.d.3.0	Accomodation	Work continued.
	2 R.E. 140 Inf.		Digging	180ˣ trench excavated 4'-6" wide 0'3" deep.
	16 R.E. 15 att. Inf.	Q.21.b.7.5	Wiring	200ˣ double apron fence completed.
	21 R.E. 21 att. Inf.	Q.16.c.4.4	Wiring	190ˣ double apron fence 90% completed.
	82 Inf.	S.P.12 to S.P.13	Digging	40ˣ C.T. 6'x4'x3' 40ˣ " " " 50%.
	12 R.E. 15 att. Inf.	Q.20.b	Wiring	250ˣ apron fence completed. 150ˣ 75% completed.

(Sgn) R.C. Lundie, Maj. R.E.
O.C. 93rd (Field) Coy R.E.

SECRET:-

17th Divisional Engineers and Pioneers.
Progress Report, ending 6.a.m. 8-5-18.

APPENDIX 7.

Unit	No. of men.	Location	Nature of Work	Progress
93rd Field Coy	3 R.E. 4 R.E. 8 att. Inf.	ENGLEBELMER. P.22.&.30.	Wells. Accommodation	Standing by for demolitions. Work continued.
R.E.	38 R.E. 40 att Inf	RIDGE SUPPORT S. of CHARLES.	Wiring	550× double apron fence complete erected.
	32 R.E. 44 att Inf	RIDGE SUPPORT N. of CHARLES.	Wiring	570× double apron fence.

(Sgn) R.E. Dundas Maj. R.E.
O.C. 93rd (Field) Coy. R.E.

17th Division R.E. and Pioneers Progress Report.

93rd (Field) Coy R.E. 24 hours ending 6 a.m. 27-5-18.

APPENDIX 8

No. of hours worked	O.R. Inf.	O.R. Inf.	Location	Nature of Work	Progress	Present State of Work
20	29	-	Q.14.d.1.4.	Revetting C.T.	32½ pacing S 28 " N	} completed
18	30	-	Q.15.a.	Wiring S. of C.T.	350' double apron	Complete from outer Posts of Arc System Restaurants
24	30	-	Q.15.d.	Investigating C.T.	3 new trench steps & 6 old ones cleaned	} completed & camouflaged
30	0		R	Working with Pioneer Brigade	Detailed report not yet to hand	

(Sgd) R.E. Rundle Maj R.E.
O.C. 93rd (Field) Co. R.E.

17th Divisional R.E. and Pioneers
Daily Progress Report for 24 hours
ending 6 a.m. 28-5-18

APPENDIX 9

Unit 93rd (Field) Co. R.E.

No. of men			Location	Nature of Work	Progress	Present state of Work
Sapr NCOs	Other Rks	Inf				
22	30	-	Q.15.d	Wiring C.T. S. side	410' double apron	770x now complete E of the System
22	30	-	Q.15.d & 16.c	Finishing C.T.	12 new firesteps dug	Trench finished from Sunken rd about Q.16.c.3.6 here as in progress
22	21	-	Q.15.c.9d	Wiring C.T. S. side	220' double apron complete 90' 50%	from Q.15.d.2.2 to Q.15.c.7.1.
4	8	-	Q.16.B.3.5	Cutting Shelters	3ft deep for 2 shelters	as under Progress
4	-	-	Q.12.B & 5.0	Xroads Progress Dugouts	—	—
4	-	60	Q.17 & 5.0	Digging	220' cleared to 6ft deep 9ft at bottom	Rockwork Sgt. Major Refs R.W. as under Progress.

(Sgd) R. E. Lunde Major R.E.
O.C. 93rd (Fld) Co. R.E.

-SECRET-

17th Division R.E. and Pioneers
Progress Report for 24 hours ending
Unit 93rd (Field) Co. R.E.   6 a.m 29-5-18

APPENDIX 10

No. of men			Location	Nature of Work	Progress	Present State of Work
Sap-pers	att Inf.	Inf.				
22	30	-	Q.15.d	Wiring C.T. S. Side	400^x double apron	1,170^x now complete. E. of Int. System
22	30	-	Q.15.d & 16.c	Firestepping C.T.	16 new firebays dug N. & S. sides of C.T.	Trench firestepped from Int. Line to about Q.16.c.5.6
18	20	-	Q.14.a.1.7. Q.21.a.2.8. Q.15.c.6.1.	Wiring C.T. S. Side	490^x double apron of which 90^x was 50% completed the night.	710^x now complete W. of Int. System
1	4	-	Q.16.b.3.4	Digging	Previous 2 excavations 6'x12' to 6' deep	
1	5	-	Q.16.b.3.5			
2	-	-	Q.7.a.1.0	Salvage	Timber salvaged suitable for accommodation	
2	-	20	Q.23.a.3.8	Wiring	400 Bucket	
2	-	-	Q.17.c.5.0	-do-	low entanglement	
2	-	7	Q.16.b.4.6	-do-	200^x -do- -do- pickets	
2	-	35	Q.17.b.5.9.4 Q.16.a.5.9	Digging -do-	21^x deepened 1', 28^x deepened 1½'	
3	-	-	Q.7.a.1.0	Gas proofing dugout	1 entrance completed & framework for 1 prepared	
2	under 52nd Bde			Gas N.C.O		

(Sgd) J. F. Handy Lt R.E.
for O.C 93rd (Fd) Co. R.E.

SECRET

17th Division R.E. and Pioneers

Progress Report for 24 hours
ending 6 a.m. 30-5-18

From 93rd (Field) Co. R.E.

APPENDIX II

No. of men		Location	Nature of Work	Progress	Present state of Work
Batt.	Sap.				
	11	Q.15.c.	constructing	11 new knife rests / 330 x double apron	Completion of N.S.T.W. of N.E. System (front line)
	5	—	"	325 x double apron	Completed Q.14 & 13.5 to Q.10 B00
50		Q.16.c.	"		S. Div. Boundary, one belt completed from this System to about Q.16.04.8.
Section 9.10 oth S.B.			clearing	forward	

(Sgd.) R. & Division hay R.E.
O.C. 93rd (Fd.) Co. R.E.

SECRET.

17th Division R.E. and Pioneers

Progress Report for 24 hours ending 6.a.m 31-5-18
Unit 93rd (Field) Coy R.E.

APPENDIX 13.

No of men Sap. att. Pnrs.	Sp	Location	Nature of Work	Progress	Present State of Work
20	11	Q.14.d	Wiring	280 x double apron	Single Belt complete from Q.14.a.9.6. to Q.14.d.4.8.
21	23	Q.15.d	Wiring	380 x double apron	Second Belt for most localities in Q.15 & d complete from Q.15.d.2.3 to Q.15.d.5.7.

No I Section + attd S.P. Resting
No V Section forward work with 52nd Bde.

(Sgd) R.B. Dundas Maj. R.E.
O.C. 93rd (Field) Coy R.E.

SECRET

APPENDIX 13

17th Division R.E. and Pioneers.

Progress Report for 24 hours ending 6.a.m 1-6-18.

Unit: 93rd. (82d) Co. RE.

No of men			Location	Nature of Work	Progress	Present State of Work
Sap att 82	Pnr					
30	-		Q.15.C	Digging	6. Junctions completed. 240 x double apron	
19	29		Q.15.C	Wiring	8. Junctions completed	
21	15		Q.9.c.9.3	Digging	380 x double apron	Unfinished but not owing to failure of supply of material
	30		Q.15 & 9d	Wiring		new locality from Q.15.d.1.2. to Q.15 & 8.1
1 Section with Box (52nd) 1 Coy Pioneers working on locality in Q.15. & 9d						

(Sgd)
R. E. Bundie Maj RE
OC 93rd Coy RE

WO 95/33

CONFIDENTIAL

WAR DIARY

of

93rd (Field) Coy. R.E.

From 1-6-18 to 30-6-18

93RD
FIELD COMPANY,
R.E.
No.
date 2-7-18

WAR DIARY or INTELLIGENCE SUMMARY

Army Form C. 2118.
Sheet No 1

Place	Date	Hour	Summary of Events and Information	Remarks and references to Appendices
P17a47	1/8/18		4 Sections on work in Forward Area	appendix 1
	2/8/18		Strength: 7 officers, 205 OR, 72 Animals (Works Report) 2 OR evacuated	appendix 2
	3rd		Work as usual (Works Report)	appendix 3
	4th		Work as usual (Works Report) 1 OR wounded	appendix 4 Works Cas
	5th		Strength: 7 officers 204 OR 72 Animals	appendix 5
	6		Work as usual (Works Report) 2nd Lieut C. Carolin RE Temporarily attached to unit. 4 OR evacuated	appendix 6 cas
	7		Strength 8 officers 200 OR, 72 Animals. Work as usual (Works Report) 1 OR evacuated	appendix 7 cas
	8		Strength 8 officers 199 OR 72 Animals Work as usual (Works report) No 1 Section returned No 3 at MAILLY-MAILLET	appendix 8 cas
	9		Work as usual (Works report)	appendix 9
	10		Work as usual (Works report)	appendix 10
	11		Work as usual (Works report)	appendix 11 cas
	12		Work as usual (Works report)	appendix 12 cas

Army Form C. 2118.

WAR DIARY
or
INTELLIGENCE SUMMARY.
(Erase heading not required.)

Sheet 2

Place	Date	Hour	Summary of Events and Information	Remarks and references to Appendices
P17a 47	13/6/18		Work as usual (works report)	appendix 13
	14		Work as usual (works report) 1 OR wounded	appendix 14
			8 officers 197 OR 72 animals	
	15		Work as usual (works report) 2 OR found unfit: 1 officers charger	appendix 15
			drawn. Strength 8 officers 199 OR 73 animals	
	16		Work as usual (works report)	appendix 16
	17		Work as usual (works report) 1 OR evacuated	appendix 17
			Strength 8 officers 198 OR 73 animals	
	18		Work as usual (works report) 1 OR wounded	appendix 18
			8 officers 197 OR 73 animals	
	19		Work as usual (works report) 7 OR joined unit	appendix 19
			8 officers 204 OR 73 animals	
	20		Work as usual (works report) No 4 Sect relieved No 1 at MAILLY-MAILLET	appendix 20
			1 officers charger drawn. Strength 8 officers 204 OR 74 animals	
	21		Work as usual (works report) OC 248 Coy RE recounnoitred work with OC 93 by us	appendix 21
			1 OR evacuated. Strength 8 officers 203 OR 74 animals	

Army Form C. 2118.

WAR DIARY
or
INTELLIGENCE SUMMARY.

Sheet 3

(Erase heading not required.)

Place	Date	Hour	Summary of Events and Information	Remarks and references to Appendices
217 a 47	22/8/18		Work as usual (Works report) 1 OR evacuated	appendix 22
			8 Officers 202 OR 74 animals	CC
	23/8/18		Dismounted personnel marched out at billets at 7.17 a 47	CC
			at 2 pm and arrived P.O.W. camp TOUTENCOURT at 5 pm	
			Mounted personnel marched out of camp in LOUVENCOURT wood at 1 PM	
			and arrived P.O.W. camp TOUTENCOURT at 3 pm	
T60.2.5.	24		Sections resting; Kit inspection 1 OR joined unit.	
			Strength 8 Officers 203 OR 74 animals	
	25		Coy Training	CC
	26		Coy Training	CC
	27		Coy Training 1 rider evacuated	
			Strength 8 Officers 203 OR 73 animals	CC
	28		Coy Training 1 OR evacuated	
			Strength 8 Officers 202 OR 73 animals	CC
	29		Coy Training 3 OR joined unit, Strength 8 Officers 205 OR 73 animals	CC
	30		Physical drill and Church parade	CC

F.F. Lewis Lieut for Maj R.E.
T/O R.E.
O.C. 93rd (92a) 2o. R.E.

17th Division R.E. and Pioneers
Progress Report for 24 hours ending 6.a.m. 2-6-18.
Unit 93rd (Field) Co RE.

No. of Men

Sap pers	att Inf	Inf	Location	Nature of Work	Progress	Present state of Work
8	9	-	Q.16.C	Wiring	180 yds Double Apron	Q.16.C.8.7. to Q.16.C.7.4.
10	12	-	Q.16.C cent	Dug out	-	Site for Dug Out cleared and first shift commenced.
22	20	-	Q.15.C.	Wiring and Firestepping	230 yds Double apron. 6. Firesteps Dug.	Complete Belt of Wire all round. S.P.
19	17	-	(S.P) Q.9.C.9.3.	Wiring	370 yds Double Apron	Wired round except on N. Side.
3	-	-	"	Camouflaging fire steps etc.	-	-

Sgn. R.C. Lundie Major R.E.
O.C. 93rd (Field) Coy RE.

17th Division RE and Pioneers
Progress Report for 24 hours
ending 6 am 3-6-18

Unit 93rd (Field) Co. R.E.

No. of Sap. hrs	No. of att. Sap.	No. of Inf.	Location	Nature of Work	Progress	Present state of Work
12	12	-	S.P. Q.9.c.2.3.	Wiring	230x double apron	Wire to join to that of front at Q.9.c.8.5.
10	7	-	"	Knotsteppung & improving French	2 new knotsteps	60% complete
14	14	-	Q.16.c.2.4.	Dugout	23ft. 3½ft deep 6¼ft wide	Both shafts commenced, top frames set in position
7	10	-	Q.16.c.2.4.	Bearing French		—
16	20	-	Q.14.d.8.3	Knotsteppung Dug? TRIGGER AV Knotsteps	150 x (posts only)	Joining all around line of S.P. to wire round S.P. at Q.14.d.9.8
6	9	-	Q.15.c.o.4.	Wiring		

(Sgn) R.E. Lundie Maj R.E.
O.C. 93rd (Field) Co R.E.

17th Division R.E. and Pioneers
Daily Progress Report for 24 hours
Unit 93rd (Fld) Co. R.E.   ending 6.a.m. 4-6-18   3

No. of Men			Location	Nature of Work	Progress	Present state of Work
Sap-pers	att. Inf.	Inf.				
22	29	–	(S.P) Q.15.C.	Wiring	350 yds 200 "	Complete. Pickets only.
14	14	–	Q.16.C.2.3.	Deep Dugout	Both entrances commenced	7 Frames in position 5'0" earth over first one.
7	10	24	Q.16.C.2.5.	Digging	24 yds 25 "	deepened to 6'0" 5 ft wide x 3 ft deep.

No. 3 Section & 10 attd Inf. under Bde.
No. 4 Section Baths & night off.

R C Lundie Major R.E.
O.C 93rd (Fld) Co R.E.

17th Division. R.E and Pioneers.
Daily Progress Report for 24 hours ending
6 am 5-6-18   Unit 93rd (Field) Co RE.

4.

No. of men			Location	Nature of Work	Progress	Present State of Work
Sap-pers	att. 32	3?				
14	12	-	Q.15.c.2.3	Deep dugout	12 frames fixed	10 frames & 9 frames now in each shaft. (about 14 ft cover).
1	12	-	"	Carrying	16 frames carried up.	
2	-	-	"	Digging	6 yds trench	Dug to depth.
15	12	-	S.P. at Q.q.d.0.3	Wiring	150ˣ double apron fence	from Q.q.d.1.4 to Q.q.c.8.3. Q.q.c.q.1 to Q.q.d.1.2
1	3	-	"	Digging	140ˣ -do- 1. turnbay in	N of NEWBURY AV.
2	-	-	"	"	Turning	W BOVET TR
2	-	-	-	"	Cleaning	BOVET. TR
				Wiring	Filling in gaps.	
3	3	-	Q.q.d.q.1	Removing trees	3 trees felled & removed	
			No.1 Section	Baths & Rest.		
			No.3 "	with Bde.		

Sgn R.L. Lundie. Maj. R.E
O C 93rd (Field) Roy. R.E

17th Division R.E. and Pioneers
Daily Progress Report for 24 hours ending
6am 6-6-18.
Unit 93rd Field Co: R.E.

5″.

No of men Sap-pers	att. Inf.	N.P.	Location	Nature of Work	Progress	Present state of Work
12	13	-	S.P Q.9.d.0.3	Wiring	230x double apron fence	50x at Q.9.d.1.4. 75x at Q.9.c.7b.35. 65x at Q.9.c.9.1.
9	-	-	-do-	Digging	60x BOYETTR trimmed & widened	on both sides of NEWBURY AVENUE
22	19	-	Q.15.c.	Wiring	430x double apron	Belt all round 80% double.
14	14	-	Q.16.c.2.3.	Dugout	13 frames	13 frames in each shaft.
3	15	-	-do-	Digging	22x Trench 3 deep x 6 ft	
1	10	-	-do-	Carrying	12 frames & other mat'l carried up	

(Sgn) R.L. Lindie Maj RE.
O.C. 93d (Fd) Co RE.

17th Division R.E. and Pioneers
Daily Progress Report for 24 hours

Unit. 93rd Field Co. R.E.   ending 6 a.m. 7-6-18   6.

No. of Men			Location	Nature of Work	Progress	Present state of Work
Sap-pers	att. Inf.	Inf.				
21	13	-	(S.P.) Q.9.d.0.3.	Wiring	360 yds double apron fence.	Three belts of wire from Q.9.d.1.4. to Q.9.c.1.1. Two belts of wire from Q.9.c.1.1 to Q.9.c.2.4. One belt of wire from Q.9.c.2.4 to Q.9.d.1.4.
22	16	-	(S.P.) Q.15.c.	Wiring and Firestepping Dep Dugout	240 yds 6 Firesteps 12 Frames.	22 frames in each shaft (@ 0'-9" Covers).
15	15	-	Q.6.c.2.3	Carrying Digging out Trench.	-	-
1	12	-				
3	15	-				

R. C. Lundie. Major R.E.
O.C. 93rd (Fld) Co R.E.

17th Divisional Engineers and Pioneers
Daily Progress Report for 24 hrs

Unit 93rd (Fld) Co. R.E.   ending 6 A.M. 8-6-18

No. of Men Sappers	Att Infy	Inf Infy	Map Location	Nature of Work	Progress	Present state of Work
31	11	—	S.P.Q.9.d.o.3.	Digging & Wiring	2 new fire bays completed. Trenches turfaced, deepened & widened. 40 Jds. double apron fence completed. 55 Jds rows strengthened with loose wire. Gaps cut	Strong Point completed except concertinas for blocking trenches & boards for marking gaps.
15	15	—	Q.16.C.2.3.	Deep Dugout	7 ft in each Shaft.	Gallery at foot of stairway advanced 7 ft in each case. Last shift curtailed owing to operations.

No other Parties owing to operations
No. I. Section relieved No. 3. Section in advanced Billets.

(Sgd) R. E. Lundie. Maj. R.E.
O.C 93rd (Field) Co. R.E.

17th Division R.E. and Pioneers.
Daily Progress Report for 24 hours.
93rd (Fd) Co. R.E.   ending 6am 9-6-18

Sap. last	att. SN	SN	Location	Nature of Work	Progress	Present state of work
22	29	-	ST Q.15.c	Wiring	200 x 200 x	complete Pickets only
14	14	-	Q.16.c.23	Deep dugout		Work continued
7	10	24	Q.16.c.2.5	Digging	49 yds	5ft wide x 3ft deep

No 1 Section working under Bde.
No 4 Section Baths & rest.

(Sgn) R.E. Lundie. Maj. R.E.
O.C. 93rd (field) Co. R.E.

17th Divisional Engineers & Pioneers
Daily Progress Report for 24 hours
ending 6 A.M. 10-6-18

Unit. 93rd (Fld) Co. R.E.

No of Men Sappers	Att Inf.	Inf.	Map Location	Nature of Work	Progress	Present state of Work
2	4	—	S.P.Q.94.0.3.	Wiring	16. B.W. concertinas for blocking trenches	corner of M.G. Shelter removed.
2	9	—	S.P.Q.9C.2.3.	Wiring	405 fds double apron fence completed	
8	—	—	S.P.Q.16C.8.2	Wiring	140 fds double apron 75% completed	work was continually interrupted by enemy shell fire.
10	13	—		carrying wire etc.		
15	18	—	Q.16.C.2.3.	Deep dugout		
1	8	—	do do	do "	carrying	
6	16	25	Q.16.C.2.4	S.P.	Deepening + Firestepping	

Sgn. R.E. Lundie Maj R.E.
O.C 93rd (Field) Co R.E.

17th Divisional Engineers & Pioneers
Daily Progress Report for 24 hrs
ending 6. A.M. 11-6-18.

Unit 93rd (Fld) Co. R.E.

Sappers	No of Men ATT Inf	Inf	Map Location	Nature of Work	Progress	Present state of Work
1	2	—	S.P.Q.9.d.0.3	Wiring and marking Gaps for blocking	3.B.W. concertinas fixed ready, 6 gaps marked	Post Complete
19	11	—	S.P.Q.9.c.2.2.	Wiring	385 yds double apron fence completed	Post wired round and 100 yds second belt completed
2	—	—	Mailly Maillet	Salving wiring materials		
16	—	—	S.P.Q.16.c.5.2	Wiring	320 yds apron fence completed. 140 yds 35% completed	460 yds of Southern belt of post completed.
1	23	—		Carrying wire etc.		
17	18	—	Q.16.c.	Deep Dugout	8ft of Chamber	Chamber 9ft wide & 7ft long at foot of each shaft
2	—	—	Do	Cleaning	—	—
1	12	—	Do	Carrying	—	—

(Sgd) R. E. Lundie. Maj RE.
O.C 93rd (Field) Co R.E.

17th Division R.E and Pioneers
Daily Progress Report for 24 hours
Unit 93rd Field Co: R.E.   ending 6 a.m. 12-6-18

No of men Sap. pers	att. Inf.	Inf.	Location	Nature of Work	Progress	Present state of Work
22	16	1	S.P) Q.9.c.2.2.	Wiring	425 yds double apron fence completed	Second belt round S.P. completed except for 130 yds.
2			-do-	-do-	Fastening apron wires on thick plain wire (210 yds)	(The diagonals were thick plain wire, & owing to the number of corners the apron wires had slipped)
1	-	-	Wire dump on road.	Straightening up dump.	—	—
17	-	-	S.P) Q.16.c.82.	Wiring	320ˣ Double Apron Completed	780ˣ Fence Completed. Work is much hindered by low wire, long grass; shell holes & trenches.
1				guide		
1	22			Carrying Wire etc		
18	24	-	Q.16.c.2.3.	Deep Dugout	—	Chamber 10'-6" long at each end.
1	10	-	-do-	-do-	Carrying	
3	-	-	-do-	-do-	Timbering & Sandbagging Trench	

Sgn. R. C. Lundie Major R.E
O.C. 93rd (Field) Co. R.E.

17th Division R.E. and Pioneers
Daily Progress Report for 24 hours
Unit 93rd (Fld) Co R.E.   Ending 6.a.m. 13-6-18.   12.

No. of men			Location	Nature of Work	Progress	Present state of work
Sap. prs.	att. Inf.	Inf.				
22	16		(SP) Q.9.c.2.2.	Wiring	420 yds double apron fence completed	Second belt round S.P. completed. Third belt from Q.9.c.2.1 to Q.9.c.2.3 completed.
17	22		(SP) Q.16.c.8.2.	Wiring	340 yds double apron fence completed	1120 yds completed
18	24		Q.16.c.3.2.	Def. Dugout	— —	Chamber 13' 6" long at each end.
1	7		"	"	Carrying	
2			"	"	Trimming & Sandbagging Trench	
1	—	38	Q.16.c.3.4.	S.P.	Deepening & Firestepping	

Sgn. R.C. Lundie Major R.E.
O.C. 93rd Field Co. R.E.

17th Division R.E. and Pioneers
Daily Progress Report for 24 hours
Unit - 93rd (Fld) Co R.E.   ending 6 a.m. 14-6-18.   13.

No of men Sappers	att. Inf.	Inf.	Location	Nature of Work	Progress	Present state of work
19	26	-	Q.16.C.3.2.	Deep Dugout S.P. (17)	- - -	16' 6" Chamber driven from either end.
3			" " "		Trimming and Sandbagging Trench	
4			Q.16.C.3.6.	Wiring S.P. (17)	275x double apron Camp	75% first belt completed
	21		" " "	Carrying wire etc.		
1	-	40	Q.16.C.4.3.	S.P. (17)	8 Firebays Completed	
20	14		Q.9.C.2.2.	Wiring S.P.	385 yds double apron fence	Third belt 75% completed.
4	8		-do-	Digging firebays	3-10x firebays completed	

Sgn. R.C. Lindie Major R.E.
O.C. 93rd (Fld) Co R.E.

17th Division R.E. and Pioneers.
Daily Progress Report for 24 hours
Unit 93rd (Fld) Co RE   ending 6 a.m. 15-6-18.   14.

No of Men Sappers	at Inf.	Inf	Location	Nature of Work	Progress	Present State of Work
13	20	-	Q.16.C.5.7	Wiring (17) Inf Carrying	260' Apron Fence Comp.	1st Belt 85% Completed.
2	2		Q.16.C.	Making gaps in Wire	8 gaps completed	
18	28	-	Q.16.C.3.2	Deep Dugout S.P. (17)	-	19' 6" Chamber driven from one end. 20' 0" Chamber driven from the other end.
3	-		" " "	" "	Trimming & Sandbagging Trench	-
1	8		" " "	" "	Carrying Mining material	-
14	12		Q.9.C.2.2	Wiring S.P.	275 yds double apron fence completed	Third belt round S.P. completed.
3	4		Q.9.C.2.2	Digging firebays	2 firebays completed	5 firebays completed.
6	2		Q.9.C.3.3	Filling in old trench & camouflaging firebay etc.	6 yds old trench filled in. 1 firebay camouflaged. 1 Firebay deepened 4 inches	
25	-		-	-	-	Working with 50th Bde

Sgn. R. C. Lundie Major R.E.
O C 93rd (Fld) Co. RE.

17th Division R.E and Pioneers
Daily Progress Report for 24 hours

Unit 93rd (Fld) Co. RE   ending 6.a.m. 16-6-18.   15.

No of men Sap-pers	att. Inf.	Inf.	Location	Nature of Work	Progress	Present state of work
23	26		Q.9.C.45.10 to Q.15.a.3.7.	Wiring	450 yds double apron fence completed	Two belts completed & gaps marked.
2	-	-	Q.9.C.15.00	With Pioneers cutting wire etc	—	—
1	4		Q.9.C.2.2.	Salving wiring material	—	—
18	22	-	Q.16.C.3.2	Deep Dugout S.P. (17)	—	Excavation for Chamber Completed
4	6	-	Q.16.C.3.2	S.P.	Deepening & firestepping Trench.	—
1	-	40	Q.16.C.3.2.	Digging S.P. (17)	50ʸ widened 2 to 3 ft 1 Fire Step in TRIBBER AVENUE	
17	26	-	—	Resting	—	No. 3 Section
18	-	-	—	With 50th Bde	—	No. 1 Section

Sgn. J Algaindy Lieut R.E.
for O.C. 93rd Field Co. RE

17th Division RE and Pioneers
Daily Progress Report for 24 hours
Unit 93rd (Fld) Co. RE   ending 6 a.m. 17-6-18.   16

No of men Sappers	att Inf	Inf	Location	Nature of Work	Progress	Present state of work
18	3	-	Q.16.C.3.2	Deep Dugout S.P. ⑰		Stairs 75% Completed Lagging 35% " " & accomodation Commenced
3	17	-	Q.16.C.3.2.	S.P.	Deepening & Firestepping Trench	— —
1	6	-	" "	"	Carrying up Material	— —
14	35	-	Q.16.C.5.5.	Wiring & Carrying S.P. ⑰	280ˣ apron fence comp.	First Belt of Wire Completed
19	32	-	Q.9.d.8.2.	Wiring	350ˣ double apron fence completed	
2	-	80	Q.9.d.8.2.	Digging	120ˣ fire trench & C.T. 80% completed 4 ft at top 2 ft at bottom & 3 ft deep	
8	6	-	P.11.b.3.4	New right Bde Hd Qrs.		Accomodation 35% finished
3			" "	Gas proof curtains		

Sgn R. C. Lundie Major RE
O C 93rd Field Co RE

17th Division R.E. and Pioneers
Daily Progress Report for 24 hours
ending 6 a.m. 18-6-18

Unit 93rd (Fld) Co. R.E.

Sappers	No of men att. pnr.	Inf.	Location	Nature of Work	Progress	Present state of Work
5	-	-	P.11.b.3.4	New R.E. Bde. H.Q. Dugouts	—	Accommodation 40% complete
18	3		Q.16.C.3.2	Deep Dugout S.P. ⑰		Stairs Completed Accommodation "
4	17		Q.16.C.3.2	" "	Excavating for Shelters etc.	70% Complete
1	9		" "	" "	Carrying up Shelters etc	
21	28		Q.15.b.6.5	Wiring	350 yds double apron fence comp	—
1	4		Q.9.c.40.15	Clearing dump	—	
2		80	Q.9.d.8.2	Digging S.P.	120° completed 100 yds dug 1st Task	220 yds on S. Side dug
26	-	-	—	Working with 50th Bde	—	Includes 4 O.R.'s attending for work on T.M.B. dugouts
3	-	-	—	Gas curtains 50th Bde	—	—
4	-	-	—	Gas Guard		
8	8	-	Q.15.d.	Deep Dugout	—	Both Stairway excavation complete
8	20	-	—	—	Resting	

18 (P) Sappers under establishment
This figure will be verified to-morrow but I think is approx. correct.

Sgn. R.C. Lundie Major R.E.
O.C. 93rd Field Co. R.E.

17th Division R E and Pioneers
Daily Progress Report for 24 hours
Unit 93rd Field Co RE   ending 19-6-18.   18

No of men						
Sap -pers	att Inf	Inf	Location	Nature of Work	Progress	Present state of Work
20	22	—	Q.15.d.4.6.	Def Dugout	2 Frames in each entrance	Excavation for trench cleared.
5	—	—	Q.16.c.3.2.	Dug out S.P. ⑦	—	Revetment round head of dugout & stairs 50% Complete.
20	32	—	Q.16.c.3.7 to Q.16.a.2.2. Q.16.c.3.8 to Q.16.c.0.9.	Wiring	—	350 yds double apron fence completed. 6 yds double apron fence completed.
7	5	—	—	—	Resting	—
2	24	60	Q.9.d.8.2	Digging	110ˣ trench 45ˣ old trench cleaned up and made serviceable	4' top 2' bottom 3' deep. 100% complete
4			P.11.b.3.4.		New Rt Bde H.Q.	Dugout accomodation 65% complete
3	—	—		Gas curtains 50TD Bde.	—	
30			50TD Bde			No. 1 Section forward (includes 4 on T.M.B.

Sgn. R. C. Lundie Major R.E.
O.C. 93rd Field Co R.E.

17th Division R.E. and Pioneers
Daily Progress Report for 24 hours ending 6 a.m. 20.6.18

Unit 93rd (Fld) Co R.E.

No. of men Sappers	Att. Inf.	Inf.	Location	Nature of Work	Progress	Present state of Work
17	30	–	Q.16.a.2.2 to Q.16.a.1.5	Wiring	–	350 yds double apron fence complete
4			Q.16.c.3.2	Dug. Out S.P. ⑰	–	Revetment round dugout & head of stairs 60% completed
2			Bde HdQrs	Accommodation	–	–
4	28	60	Q.9.d.8.2	Digging	100% complete 90% "	86 yds trench 4' top 2' bottom x 3' deep. 120 yds old trench improved and deepened
20	28	–	Q.15.d.4.6	Deep Dugout ㉚	Frames in each shaft	4 Frames in each shaft (Much delayed by flooding)
26	–	–	–	With 50th Bde includes 4 with T.M.B	–	–
4	–	–	–	Gas Guard	–	–
12	–	–	–	Resting owing to change over	–	–
1	–	–	–	Coy draughtsman	–	–
2	–	–	–	Orderlies	–	–
1	3	–	–	Coy Dugout	–	–
3	–	–	–	Gas curtains 50th Inf Bde	–	–

Sgn. R. C. Lundie Major R.E.
O.C. 93rd Field Co. R.E.

17th Division R.E. & Pioneers
Daily Progress for 24 hours
Unit 93rd (Fld) Co R.E.   ending 6 a.m 21-6-18   20.

No of Sappers	No of Inf Att	Men Inf	Map Location	Nature of Work	Progress	Present state of Work
21	24	–	Q.15.d.4.5.	Deep Dugout (30)	6 frames in each shaft	10 Frames in North Shaft / 11 " " South "
4	–	–	Q.16.c.3.2.	Dug out S.P. (17)		Revettment round dugout 75% complete
21	30	–	Q.16.a.1-6.6 / Q.15.b.9.5.6 / Q.15.b.7.4.	Wiring		420 yds double apron fence completed
1	1	90	Q.9.c.9.2	Deepening & repairing old trench		240 yds 80% complete
–	29	–	Q.14.d	Draining and Pumping out Trigger Av.	80 yds drained / 300 yds	Still almost impossible
20	–	–		Resting owing to change over		
4	–	–		Gas Guard		
3	–	–		Gas Curtains 50th Bde.		
26	–	–		50th Bde includes T.M.B		
1	3	–		Coy Dugout		

(Sgn) R.P. Lundie Maj R.E
O.C 93rd. (Fld) Co. R.E.

17th Divisional Engineers + Pioneers
Daily Progress Report for 24 hours
Unit. 93rd (Fld) Co R.E.   Ending 6 A.M. 22-6-18

Officers	No of men Att Sub	men Sub	Map Location	Nature of Work	Progress	Present State of Works
19	30	-	Q.15.b.7.4 to Q.15.6.7.2	Wiring	-	90 yds double apron fence completed
4	-	-	Q.16.a. Q.16.c.3.2	" Dugout S.P.17		700 yds single fence completed. Revetment round Dugout 90% completed.
-	29	-	Q.14.d. Q.15.d.	draining & cleaning out Trigger Av.		150 yds cleaned and 2 large sump holes dug
2	-	60	Q.9.c.9.2. Q.15.d.4.6.	Digging Dugout		200 yds old trench cleaned up.
4	-	-		Gas Guard		
1	3	-		Co Dugout		
3	-	-		Gas Curtains		
14	-	-		Resting		
32	-	-		50th Bde includes T.M.B		

(Sgd) R.E. Lundie Maj R.E.
O.C. 93rd (Field) Co R.E.

1st Division R.E.
Daily Progress Report for 24 hours ending 6am 23.6.18   93rd (Field) Co R.E. 22

No Employed	O.R. at Dy	Nemi- No	Location	Nature of Work	Progress	Present State of Work
19	20	-	Q.10 & 7.4 to Q.15 & 7.2	Wiring	-	90ᵗ double apron fence completed
14			Q.16.c Q.16.c.3.2	Dugout S.P. 17		700ˣ jungle fence completed. Revetment round dugout 90% completed
	29		Q.14.d Q.15.c	Draining & cleaning out TRIGGER AVE		150ᵗ cleaned out. Large sump hole dug
2	60		Q.9.c.9.2 Q.15.a.4.6	Digging Dugout		200ᵗ Cd. trench cleaned up

(Sgd) R.E. Lundie. Maj. R.E.
O.C. 93rd (Field) Coy. R.E.

Vol 34

CONFIDENTIAL.

WAR DIARY
— of —
93rd Field Coy RE
From 1-7-18 to 31-7-18.

93RD FIELD COMPANY. R.E.
Date 2-2-18

WAR DIARY

INTELLIGENCE SUMMARY

(Erase heading not required.)

Army Form C. 2118.

93rd (3D) Coy. R.E.
July 1918.   Sheet I

Place	Date	Hour	Summary of Events and Information	Remarks and references to Appendices
Sheet 57.D. T.G.b.2.5.	1/7/18	—	Coy in Camp. Training. Strength 7 off. 205 O.R. 73 animals	R.C.L.
do.	2/7/18	—	Training. 2 O.R. evacuated. Strength 7 off. 203 O.R. 73 animals	R.C.L.
do.	3/7/18	—	Training	R.C.L.
do.	4/7/18	11.45 P.M.	Practice "Stand to" for taking up position as part of R.S.L.R. Div. V.t. Coys.	R.C.L.
do.	5/7/18	—	Training	R.C.L.
do.	6/7/18	—	do. 1 O.R. joined unit. Strength 7 off. 204 O.R. 73 animals	R.C.L.
do.	7/7/18	—	Training	R.C.L.
do.	8/7/18	—	do. 1 O.R. joined unit. Strength 7 off. 205 O.R. 73 animals	R.C.L.
do.	9/7/18	—	do. O.C. went round lines with O.C. 70th (3D) Coy. R.E. who was taking over. 1 O.R. evacuated. Strength 7 off. 204 O.R. 73 animals	R.C.L.
do.	10/7/18	—	Training. Coy marched out of Camp at 8.30 A.M. H.Q. & Nos. 1 & 3 Sections to V.7.b.6.2. Nos. 2 & 4 Sections to V.17 central. Above lines to U.10 cent. forward work commenced.	App. I. R.C.L. Works Report.
V.7.b.6.2.	11/7/18	—	Forward work continued.	App. II. Works Report
do.	12/7/18	—	do. 1 O.R. wounded. Strength 7 off. 203 O.R. 73 animals	App. III. Works Report
do.	13/7/18	—	do.	do. App. IV. R.C.L.
do.	14/7/18	—	do. 1 O.R. wounded (at Duty)	do. App. V. R.C.L.
do.	15/7/18	—	do.	do. App. VI. R.C.L.

WAR DIARY
INTELLIGENCE SUMMARY

93rd (Fd.) Coy. R.E. Army Form C. 2118.
JULY 1918   Sheet. II

Place	Date	Hour	Summary of Events and Information	Remarks and references to Appendices
Sheet 57.D. V.7.b.6.2.	16/7/18	—	Forward Work Continued.	A/h. VII RCE
	17/7/18	—	1 O.R. evacuated. Strength 7 Off. 202 O.R. 73 animals. (Works Report)	
do	18/7/18	—	Forward Work Continued. Strength 7 Off. 203 O.R. 73 animals. Works Report.	A/h. VIII RCE
do	19/7/18	—	1 O.R. joined unit. Strength 7 Off. 203 O.R. 73 animals. Works Report. No. 1 & 3 Sects & H.Q. marched out of billets in V.7.b. at 11h. in 3 moved to the CEMETERY at SENLIS V.10.d.	A/h. IX RCE
V.10.d.	20/7/18	—	Forward Work Continued. H.Q. Nos. 1 & 3 Sections moved to V.17 cent. Strength 7 Off. 202 O.R. 73 animals. Works Report.	A/h. X RCE
V.17 cent.	21/7/18	—	Forward Work Continued. 1 O.R. joined unit. Strength 7 Off. 203 O.R. 73 animals. (Works Report)	A/h. XI RCE
do	22/7/18	—	do. 1 O.R. evacuated. Strength 7 Off. 202 O.R. 73 animals.	A/h. XII RCE
do	23/7/18	—	do. Works Report.	A/h. XIII
do	24/7/18	—	Forward Work Continued. 1 O.R. wounded. 3 O.R. evacuated. Strength 7 Off. 198 O.R. 73 animals. Works Report.	A/h. XIV RCE A/h. XV RCE A/h. XVI RCE
do	25/7/18	—	Forward Work Continued.	do
do	26/7/18	—	do.	do
do	27/7/18	—	do.	A/h. XVII RCE
do	28/7/18	—	Forward Work Continued. 2 Platoons B. Coy. 1st Bn. 305th Engineer Regt. U.S.A & the Pioneer Platoon of 319th Inf. Regt. U.S.A attached to unit for training & work.	A/h. XVIII RCE
do	29/7/18	—	Work Continued.	RCE A/h. XIX
do	30/7/18	—	do. 1 O.R. wounded. Strength 7 Off. 197 O.R. 73 animals. Works Report.	A/h. XX RCE A/h. XXI RCE
do	31/7/18	—	do. 1 R.E. (Lieut) 1 R.E. (O/R) struck off strength, sent to CRE's autumn Strength 5 off. 197 O.R. 74 animals. Works Report.	A/h. XXI RCE A/h. XXII RCE

R.C. Lumb. Maj. R.E.
O.C. 93rd (Fd) Coy R.E.

17th Divl.
Engineers.

93rd FIELD CO.,

ROYAL ENGINEERS,

AUGUST 1918.

WR 35

Confidential

War Diary

93rd F'd Coy R.E.

From 1-8-18 —————— To 31-8-18

93RD FIELD COMPANY R.E.
No. ✓
Date 9-9-18

Army Form C. 2118.

WAR DIARY
or
INTELLIGENCE SUMMARY.
(*Erase heading not required.*)

Instructions regarding War Diaries and Intelligence Summaries are contained in F. S. Regs., Part II. and the Staff Manual respectively. Title pages will be prepared in manuscript.

Place	Date	Hour	Summary of Events and Information	Remarks and references to Appendices

WAR DIARY
INTELLIGENCE SUMMARY

(Erase heading not required.)

93rd (31) Coy. R.E. AUGUST. 1918. Army Form C. 2118. SHEET I.

Place	Date	Hour	Summary of Events and Information	Remarks and references to Appendices
V.17 cent. SHEET.57.D	1/8/18	–	Horse Lines U.10. central. Strength. 7 Off. 197 O.R. 72 animals etc. Work as usual on Reserve Lines.	App. I App.
"	2/8/18	–	Work as usual.	Works Report. App II RCL
"	3/8/18	–	Work as usual. Pioneer Platoon 319th Regt. U.S.A. rejoined their unit.	Works Report. App III RCL
"	4/8/18	–	Work as usual.	Works Report. App IV RCL
"	5/8/18	–	Work as usual.	Works Report. App V RCL
HERISSART	6/8/18	9.30 AM	Dismounted Section marched to HERISSART. } arrived 12 noon. Mounted " " " "	Works Report. RCL
"	7/8/18	–	Coy at Horse going to home. Coy resting & General fatigues. 2 O.R. joined unit. Strength 7 Off. 199 OR. 72 animals.	RCL.
"	8/8/18	–	Morning Coy Training. Orders to march received at 1.30 p.m.	RCL.
"	"	2.20 P.M.	Coy marched off. Arrived Bois L'ABBAYE at 3.40 p.m.	RCL.
BOIS L'ABBAYE	9/8/18	10. PM	Coy moved out with 504 Bde Group	RCL.
CORBIE	10/8/18	2 A.M	Coy arrived at CORBIE & bivouaced there for the night.	RCL
"	"	–	Coy awaiting orders. Bathing Parades	RCL.
"	11/8/18	–	" "	RCL.
"	12/8/18	1.30 P.M.	Received Orders from CRE (Verbal) to take over from 11th Cav.(?) Fd. Coy. Advance Party dispatched Coy. marched at CORBIE with 504 Bde Group at 4.50 p.m. & marched to Q.13 cent. 51.b. 62.D. Fed on the bivouac scheme near the marched in H.Q. at 9.21.b.2.6 arriving 11.15 p.m. 1 O.R. joined unit. Strength 7 Off. 200. O.R. 72 animals. Took over "Battery Zone" and O.C. 93rd Coy Sections 1,2,3 & 4	Rcl.
Q.21.b. SHEET 62.b.S.E.	13/8/18	9.30 A.M.	CRE went round "Battery Zone" and O.C. 93rd Coy Sections 1,2,3 & 4 night work No 3 Section making forward wire with 504 Bde.	Works Report. App VI B.

Army Form C. 2118.

WAR DIARY
or
INTELLIGENCE SUMMARY.
(Erase heading not required.)

93rd (31) Coy. R.E.
AUGUST 1918.
SHEET II

Place	Date	Hour	Summary of Events and Information	Remarks and references to Appendices
SHEET 62.D. Q.21.b.2.8.	14/8/18	—	No. 3 Section moved to Q.30.c.7.5. Other Sections as for 13.9.18	App VII R.C.L.
"	15/8/18	—	1.O.R. killed. 1.O.R. wounded. 1.O.R. evacuated. Strength 7.Off. 197 O.R. 72 animals. Works Report as for 13.9.18.	App VIII R.C.L. Works Report
"	16/8/18	7.55 AM	1.O.R. evacuated. Strength 7.Off. 196 O.R. 72 animals during day. Operation Order rec'd Coy to be relieved by 14th Aust. Fd Coy.	
"	"	10 A.M	O.C. 14th Aust. Fd Coy went round work etc with O.C. 93rd (31) Coy. Handing over completed by 2 p.m.	
"	"	3.30 P.M.	Dismounted portion marched out to DAOURS & went into billets there at 6.30 p.m.	R.C.L.
"	"	4.30 P.M.	Mounted portion arrived at DAOURS	
DAOURS.	17/8/18	—	Fatigue Parades Baths & Rest. 2.O.R. evacuated. 1.O.R. joined unit - 2nd Lieut. R.L. CLAY R.M.R.E. joined unit. Strength 8.Off. 195 O.R. 72 animals.	R.C.L.
"	"	10 P.M.	Marched out of DAOURS. Reached HERRISSART at 2.30 A.M. Went into Billets	
HERRISSART.	18/8/18	—	Resting. With 52nd Bde Group	R.C.L.
"	"	9.30 P.M.	Marched out anyway at BEAUQUESNE at 10 A.M. Went into Billets	
BEAUQUESNE.	19/8/18	—	Kit & Equipment inspected. 3.O.R. evacuated. 1 L.D. horse evacuated. 7.O.R. joined unit. Strength 8.Off. 199 O.R. 71 animals	R.C.L.
"	20/8/18	—	Morning spent in Coy Training. Op. Order from 52nd Bde received 5.30 p.m.	

Army Form C. 2118.

WAR DIARY
93rd (L) Coy. R.E.
INTELLIGENCE SUMMARY. AUGUST 1918.

SHEET III

(Erase heading not required.)

Instructions regarding War Diaries and Intelligence Summaries are contained in F. S. Regs., Part II. and the Staff Manual respectively. Title pages will be prepared in manuscript.

Place	Date	Hour	Summary of Events and Information	Remarks and references to Appendices
BEAU-QUESNE.	20/8/18	9.30 P.M.	Coy. marched out, arriving at ACHEUX at 1 A.M. and going into Billets. Strength 8 off. 155 O.R. 1 O.R. evacuated. Lt. MacQueen ordered to 77th (3L) Coy RE. as 2nd in Command. 71 animals	Rct.
ACHEUX.	21/8/18	—	Coy. training	Rct.
"	22/8/18	—	Coy. training	Rct.
"	23/8/18	—	Coy. training. 7 Reinforcements joined unit. Strength 8 off., 205 O.R. 71 An's	Rct.
"	24/8/18	—	Coy. training. 1 O.R. joined unit. Strength 8 off. 206 O.R. 71 Animals	Rct.
"	"	9.30 P.M.	Marched out. Arrived Q.17.c.O.S. at 1.15 A.M. & bivouaced	
SHEET. 57.D. Q.17.c.O.S.	25/8/18	—	No. 1.3.& 4. Sections returning road No 2 Section complete marched out at 2 p.m.-8 went to R.33.d. cent. for work on Water Supply in forward area	Off. IX
"	"	7.45 P.M.	Coy (less No 2 Section) marched out & reached R.32.b.2.3. at 11.30 p.m. & bivouaced. O.C. established touch with No 2 Section and reconnoitred for Water.	Rct.
R.32.b.2.3.	26/8/18	—	No. 1 & 4. Sections on Road Repairs No 2.8.3. on Wellsm Forward Area. Repairs	Off. XI Rct.
"	27/8/18	9.30 A.M.	No 3 Section complete marched out to M.25.b.O.G. No 1 & 4. Road Repairs.	
"	"	3.0 P.M.	No 1 & 4 marched out to billets at M.25.b.O.G. arriving 4.30 p.m. Office at M.25.b.	Off. XI Rct.
"	"	—	O.G. Horse lines removed at R 32.b.2.3.	Rct.
M.25.b.O.G.	28/8/18	—	Coy on Water Supply. 2 L.D. horses received. Strength 8 off. 206 O.R. 73 animals	Off. XII Rct. Reports

WAR DIARY

INTELLIGENCE SUMMARY

93rd (Fd.) Coy. R.E.
AUGUST. 1918
SHEET IV

Army Form C. 2118.

Place	Date	Hour	Summary of Events and Information	Remarks and references to Appendices
M.25. b.0.6.	29/8/18	—	Sections on Water Supply. Transport moved up to M.25.d.	App. XIII R.C.L. Report
"	30/8/18	7.30 A.M.	No. 2. Section complete marched out & went into billets at GUADECOURT.	
"	"	8.30 A.M.	No. 1 & 3 Sections complete moved up to billets in FLERS	
"	"	2.0 P.M.	No 4 Section moved into billets in FLERS. Work on Water Supply. Horse lines at M.25.d.	App XIV R.C.L. Report
FLERS	31/8/18	—	Work on Water Supply. No. 2 Section moved from GUADECOURT to FLERS	
			2.O.Rs killed. 2.O.R. wounded. 1 Off (Ghurza ("BABY")) 3 L.D horses	R.C.L.
			2 L.D. mules killed 1 rider wounded & sent to 29th M.V.S. 1 L.D.	
			horse wounded, remained with unit. Strength 8 Off. 202 O.R. 66 animals Reports	App XV

R.C. Pundu Maj. RE.
O.C. 93rd (Fd) Coy R.E.

SECRET

Daily Progress Report of Work being done by 24 Fd Coy 9 Fd (Ind) Aust RE

Sgt i/c	DR	No. per location	Location	Nature of Work	Progress	Present state of work
	48	2	HAYMARKET ST.	Digging	76" long 66" deep	
	1	1		Duckboarding	70' constructed	
10	8	4	Hall Road	Duckboarding	156' duckboards laid 400' prepared	
8				Materials	Picking lines & pits; finishing track work — old & new models	for duck 2 models

Sqd.	Det.	Offrs	O.R.	Location	Nature of Work	Progress	Present state of work
14				9 V.K.c.	Wiring	230 coils due for month	
3					Road System Hal Post	Reviewing wires	
3				Bh		Urgent indents for O.S. (rope)	
3					Working on R.E.A dugouts	Laurencest not made the Second since last Summer	
3					Stenaining Rd for occasions	returned	
2					Working widow Slit Raft 50th Bn		
3					Rest House repairs	unprmed do	
4					Role Khana		
3				1	B.J.Y.	(Sgn) R.H. & Revd Raph R.E.	
1					Ayuda for Shoing	for O.C. 93rd (Fd) Co R.E	

SECRET

12th Division R.E. and Pioneers
Work Progress Report for 24 hours ending
6 am 3-8-18 (93rd (field) Coy R.E.)

Appendix II

No. of Men	O.R.'s Empd	Location	Nature of Work	Progress	Present state of work
Sai. NY Cpl Pios					
24 30	-	W.20.a.59. 6.W.20.a.0.8. W.&.C.	Wiring	490 yds double apron fence completed	
12 40	-			250 yds Wire fence front line	
3	16 10 100 Pios		Support bomb stores Shakespeare at 7.11.5 2x U.S. (m.g's) from line 0.4.1.9		
- 5	-	8. KINGS ST WEST Nothing on standing by	Shakespeare 30" boundaries		
6 3	-		RFA dugouts for ammunitions		

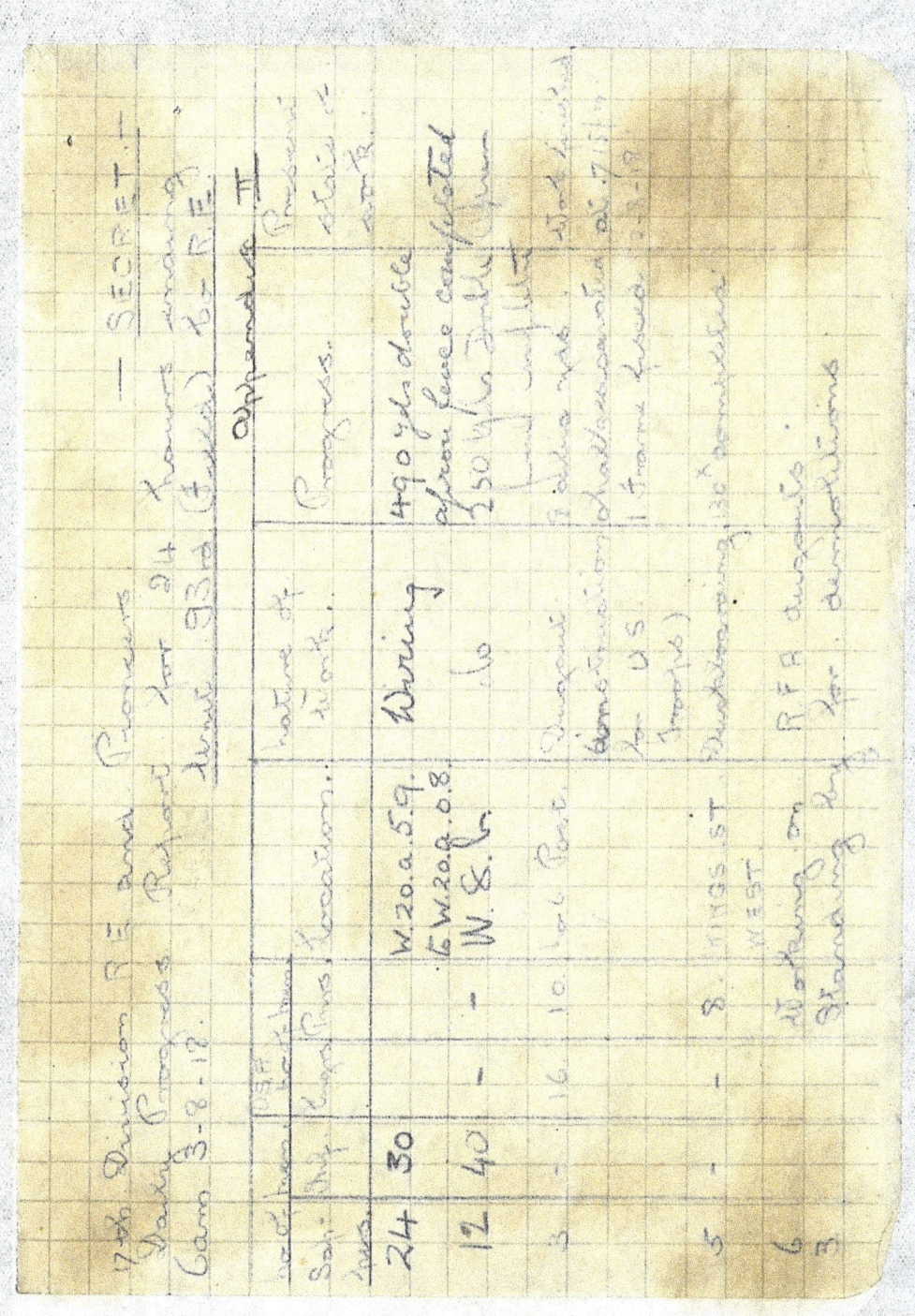

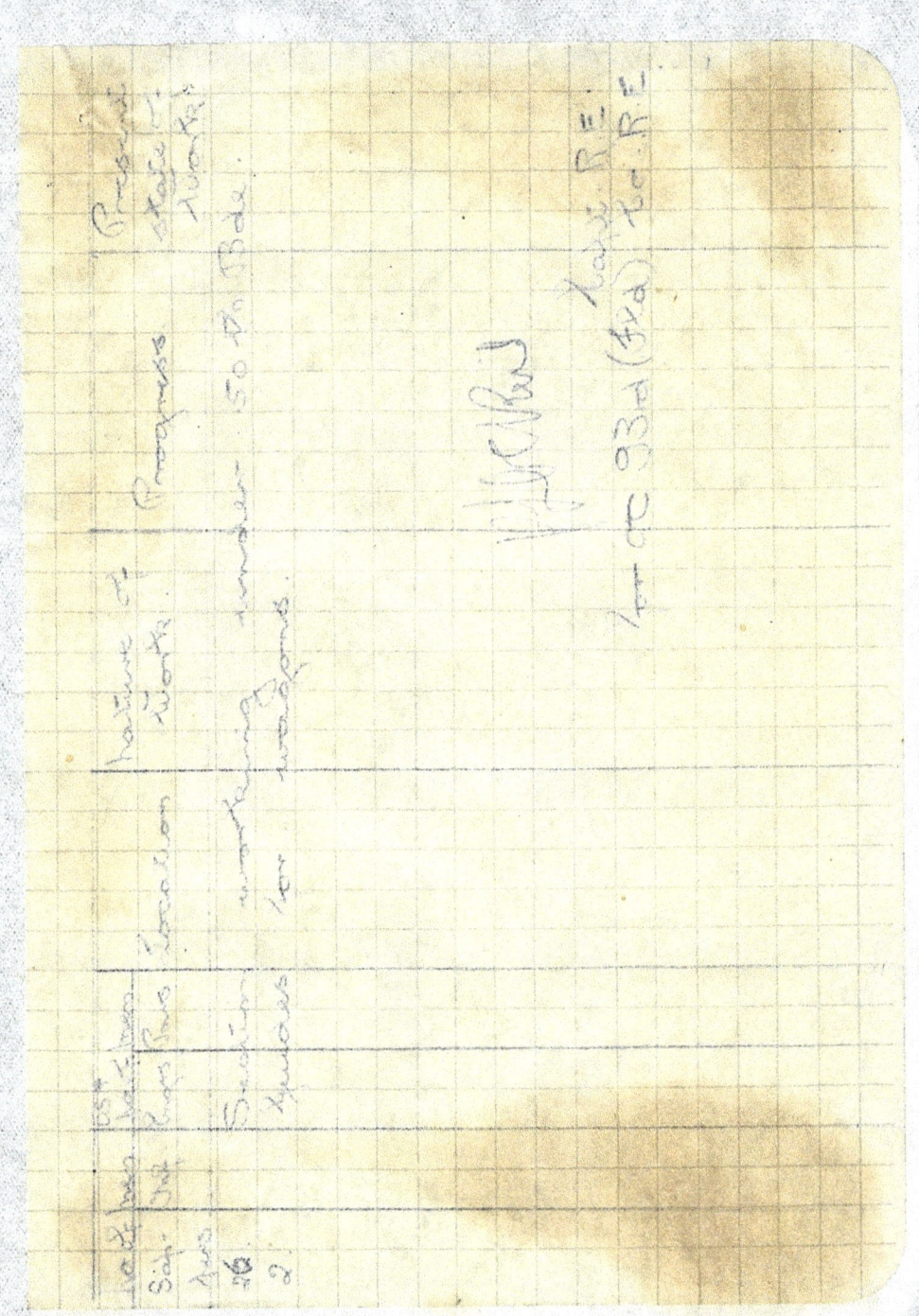

- SECRET -

17th Division R.E. and Pioneers.
Daily Progress Report for 24 hours ending
8 a.m. 4-8-18. that 93rd (Instal) to R.E.
Appendix III

Nor[?]hum Sap. Ty	U.S? te them	Progress	Location	Nature of Work	Progress. Present state of Work
1/4	50	—	MX2IIa.5 W.15.d.8 N of AVELUY ROAD	R.Juns Road Dining	47% Completed
32	150	53	31 AVELUY ROAD		200 yds double apron fence Coy R.E. 250 yds fin- 50% Completed 100 yds double apron fence Coy B.E. 250 yds 55% completed 50 yds Box
26			Sapers working on R.E.A. dugouts		
6			Standing by dumps or change on Long		
3			Houses and BOUZINCOURT		

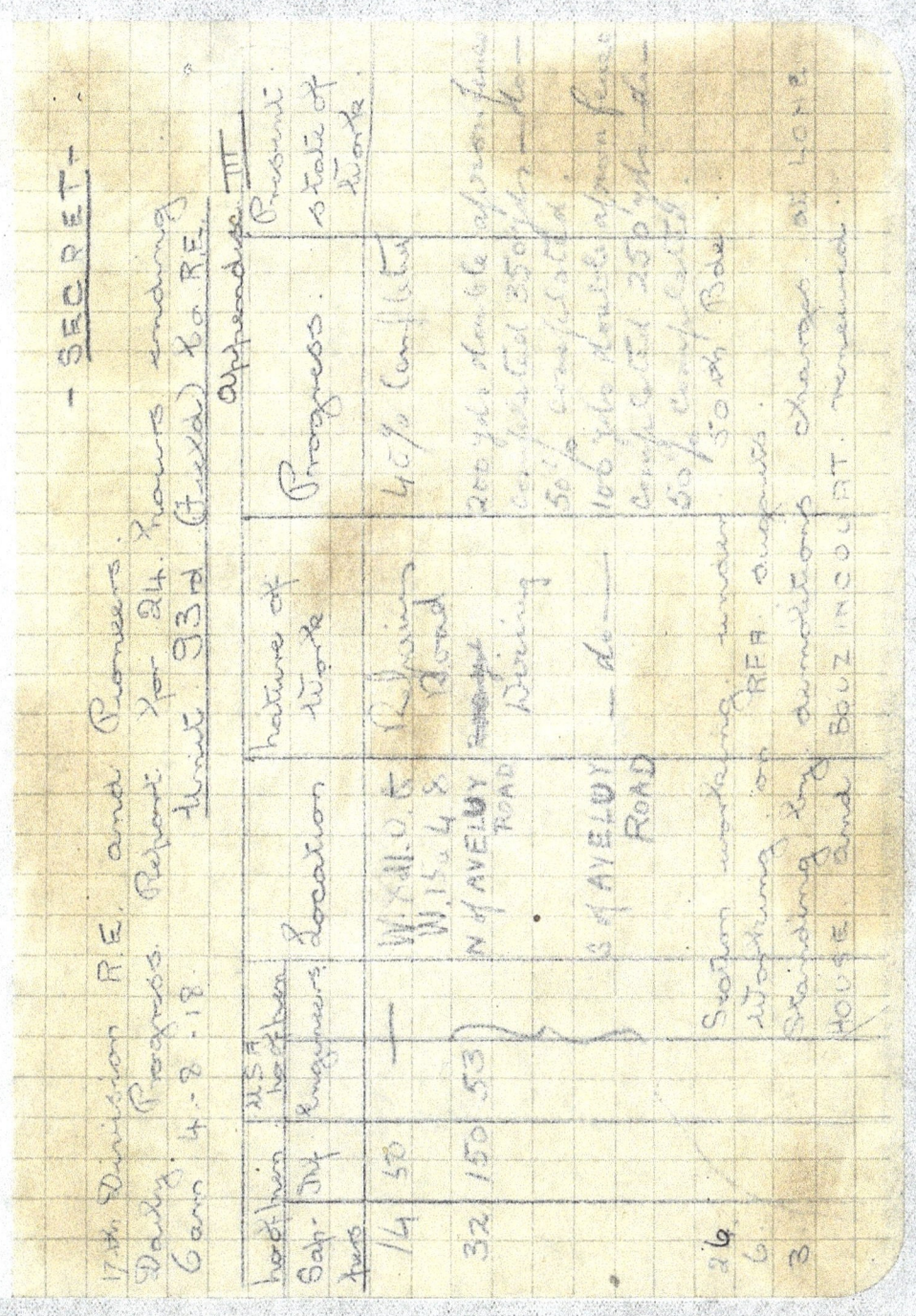

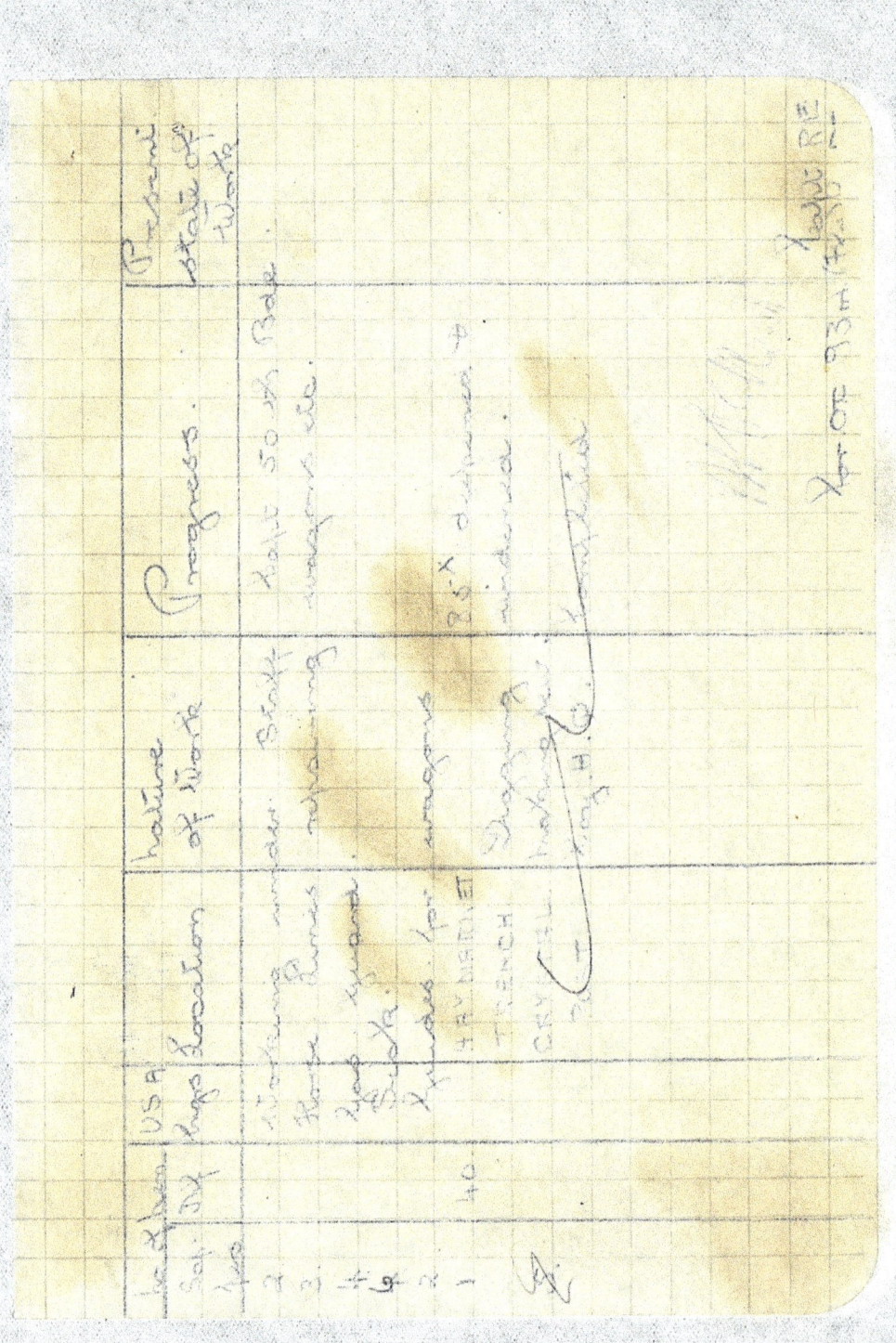

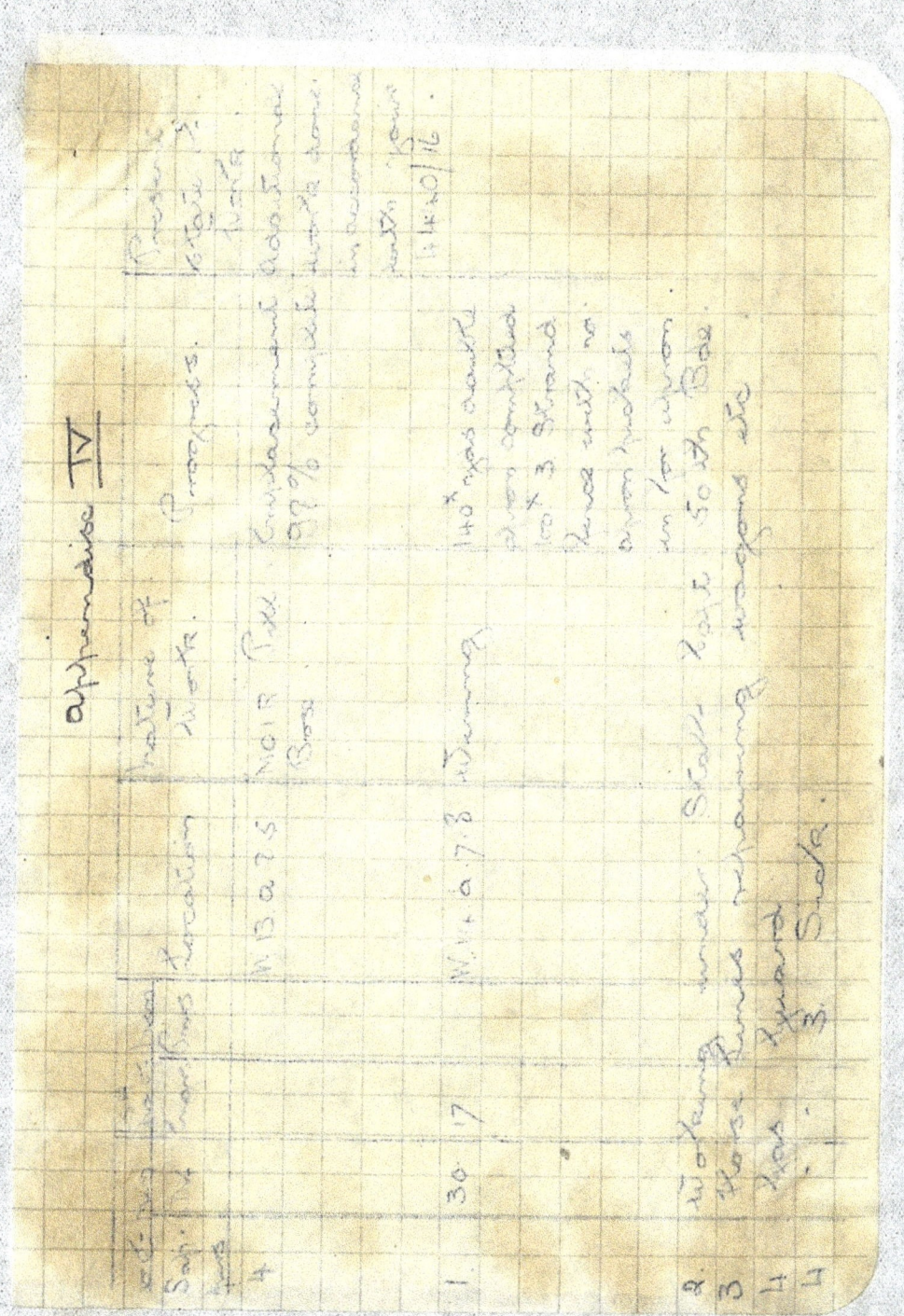

SECRET

17th Division R.E. and Pioneers Progress Report for 24 hours ending 6 am 5-8-18. Sheet 23 m (SW20) 2nd R.E. Appendix ?

No. of hours	Sap-pers	U.S.A	S.W.P	Lewisons	Location	Nature of Work	Progress	Present state of work
2½		50			S of AVELUY Road to W.16.C.4.0	Wiring	250ˣ double apron fence partly done, completed 120ˣ new, completed U.S.A. 365 double apron fence	90% completed
3	25							
9	25	50			N of AVELUY Road to W.10.C.5.3.	Wiring	350ˣ double apron fence partly done, completed 200ˣ new	90% completed

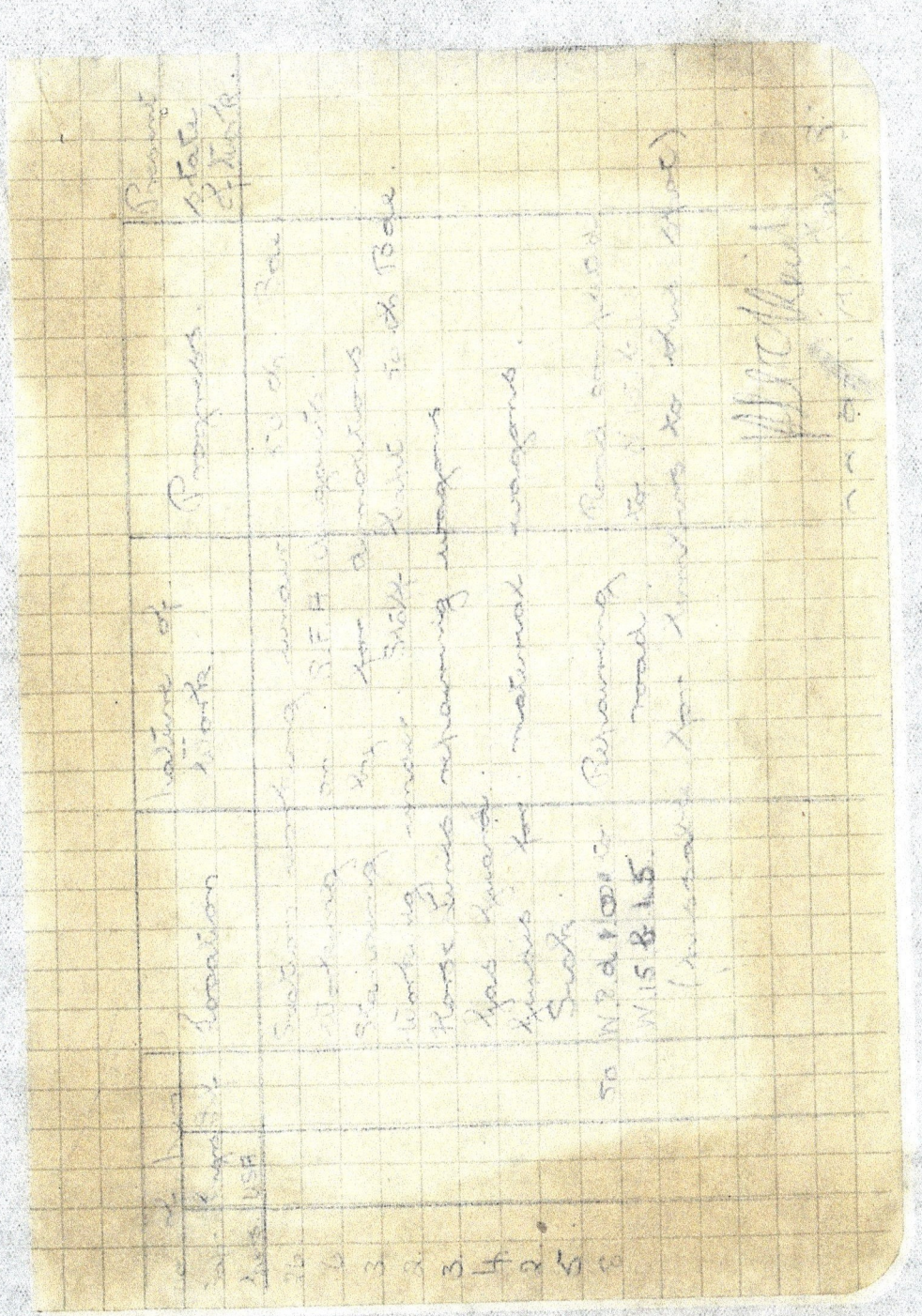

7th Division R.E. and Pioneers Daily Progress Report for 24 hours ending 6 a.m. 14-8-18
Unit 93rd (Suess) 2co R.E.   SECRET

Reference VI   Offensive

No. of men	Location	Nature of Work	Progress	Present state of Work
Sep. 3rd sect. 26	One Section working Gas Guard Sec. (marked duty) Ordered R.27.a	Wiring	under 50th Bde orders	
4, 1, 3, 22	R.20	Wiring	200 yds double fence completed	
41. 1D	central	-do-	400 yds double fence completed. 100 yds of single fence completed. 100 yds progress only	
2	Guides	Infantry carrying		

No. of men	Location	Nature of Work	Progress	Present state of work
Sah. Sep. hers				
2. 1 Rog 80	R.20.a	Digging	Shelled off the trench 30 yds avg 3×2 unfinished	
2.	R.19.c	Supervising		

(Sgn) R. MacGregor hac Quarrie Lt R.E
for O.C. 93rd (Field) Co. R.E.

17th Division R.E. and Pioneers — SECRET
Progress Report for 24 hours ending
Date 16-6-18. Unit 93rd (Field) Co. R.E.
6am 16-6-18.

Appendix VII

No. of Men	Sap	Pnr	Location	Nature of Work	Progress	Present state of Work
	36		No 3 Section Pipe Guard Siask	working	under 50th Bde	Running to hand. Party had to be withdrawn
	4	4	Orderlies			
	3		Leave to U.K.			
	2					
	38	50	R.20.central	Wiring	250 x double fence erected 200 x pickets carted	Twice Rolled off work
	20	47	R.20.d.	Wiring	200 x double fence completed. bot. 75% do	

1. Guide for inf. carrying party turned out
4 guides sent to H.Q. W.R.R. — no party.

(Sgn) R. E. Sundgie, Major R.E.
O.C. 93rd (Fd) Co. R.E.

SECRET

17th Division RE and Pioneers
Daily Progress Report from 2/4 Powers and
6am 15-8-18 — 1 unit 93rd (Cheers) to 1 RE —
OMCWS VIII

Unit	Location	Nature of work	Progress	Below state of Work orders
20		One Section working under 50 m Bde orders		
H		2/4 Pioneers		
—		Sub Quarries (assumed ability)		
13 ¥		—		
22		Quarries — work on boundaries of 2nd tube double line completed		
41 110 R 20		4/00 Ken sundry work Ken 150 yds		
		— No —		
		work 100 yds only		
		B.H.W. — P.b.E.		

Sunday — all Coys at rest.

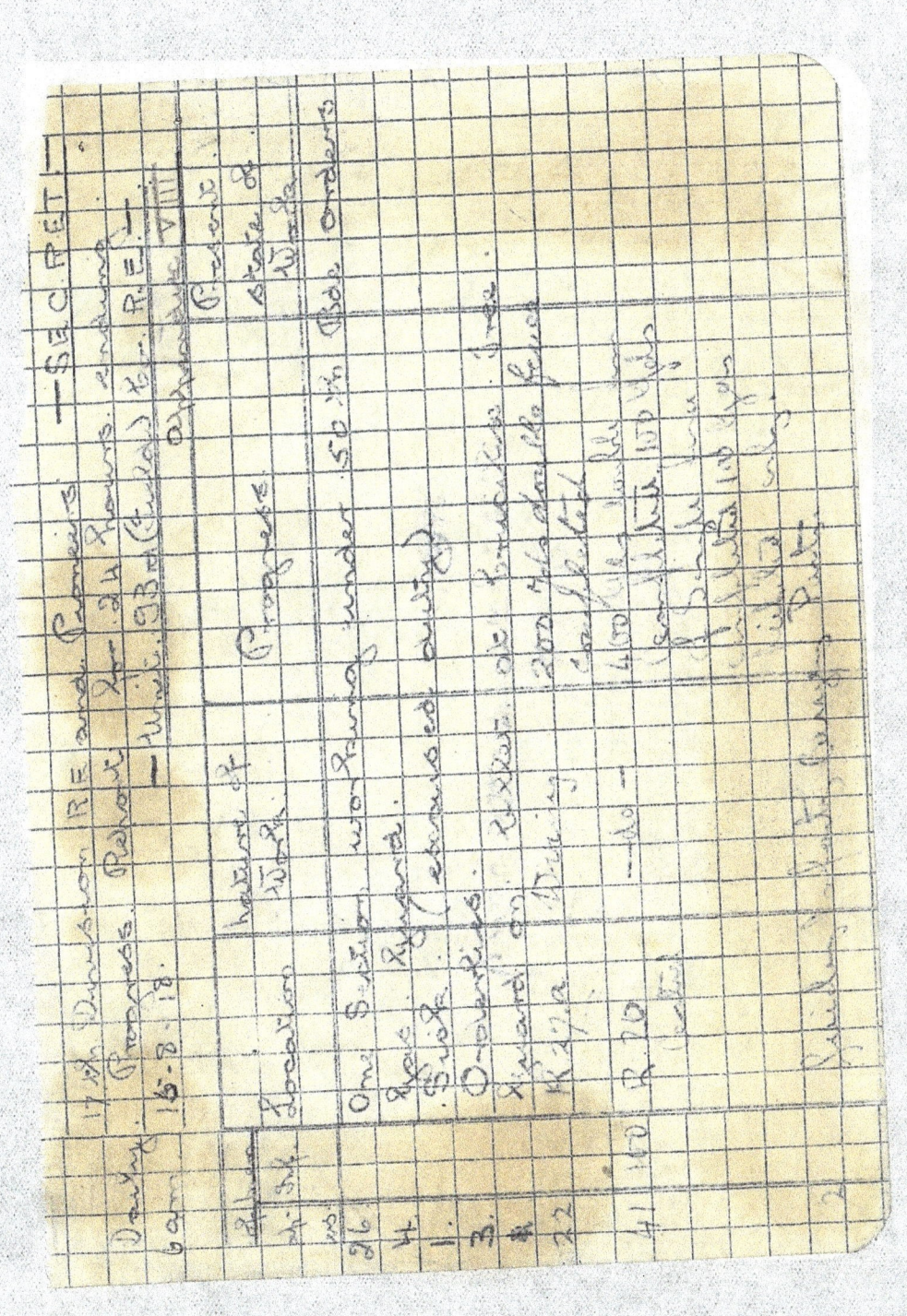

Date	Location	Nature of Work	Progress	Current state of Work
Sat. Aug. 2	(C) R 20 a 80	Digging	Started self two hours 130 yards dug 3×2.	
2	R. 19 a.	Supervision in country for two	Electrician be in work A.K.	L.C. 7, W.T.D in Cy. R.E.

X 25.

Appendix IX

CRE 7th Division   SECRET

Forward Section reports 1 well COURCELETTE 2hii R.20.P.7.3 with windlass & wire rope complete. Put in bucket 108 ft to surface of water. This well appears to have been bombed to about water level, but will be further investigated in the morning. No specimen of water could be obtained.

Well at COURCELETTE SUPERIEURE R.26.a.6.7 was in use (windlass, wire rope & bucket) but supply seemed insufficient to meet the constant demands made on it.

M.O. RE 7th Divn has examined a specimen & finds no trace of metallic poison. A sample for further examination is forwarded herewith.

POZIERES and OVILLERS were reconnoitred without any source of water supply being found. These places will be reconnoitred again tomorrow.

The NCO sent to reconnoitre MARTINPUICH was unable to make a satisfactory reconnaissance owing to enemy activity, if the situation permits further examination will be made tomorrow.

(Sgd) R. E. Lundie, Maj RE
OC 93rd (Field) Co. R.E.

X 25   25-8-18.

Appendix I
SECRET

'X.1.'
C.R.E. 17th Divn.

In continuation of my C.L. 10 of today, I now have to report:-
A well has been found about X.q.a.2.5. This well when discovered was blocked up, it has no elevating gear of any kind, well is 90ft, and had 8ft of water in it. It has evidently been used by the enemy; a specimen of the water has been obtained but has not yet been examined by M.O. R.E.

With regard to COURCELETTE, 3 German wells have now been discovered.

No.I about M.25.b.4.4. is completely destroyed.
No.II R.30.a.5.3 is dry
No.III R.29.b.7.4 is filled with rubbish.

The only 2 wells that appear at all hopeful are at R.30.a.8.8 & R.30.a.5.5. The former has windlass and wire rope complete is 120 ft deep to surface of water & has 18 ft of water in it.

The latter is just beside the road & has evidently been worked by an old French pump which has been broken, but of which the tube is still down the well. Samples of both have been obtained but have not yet been tested.

The well at R.36 a.5.8 has been thoroughly cleaned out right down to chalk bottom, but at present is practically empty, no perceptible rise took place while a sapper was down this well cleaning same out. Well is 140 ft deep.

An N.C.O. made a preliminary reconnaissance of MARTINPUICH without finding any wells, this will be gone into more carefully tomorrow.

Horses were being watered at some large holes beside the road from COURCELETTE to MARTINPUICH on W side near entrance to latter place. A

Great number of horses have also been watered from a Range hole about R.36.a.0.1 but this is now practically dry.

9.15 p.m.

M.O. R.E has now completed his examination of samples mentioned above — all are free from metallic poison but require chlorination. The water from POZIERES is very turbid, while that from R.30.a.5.5 is distinctly good.

(Sgd) P.L. Lundie Maj R.E
O C 93rd (Field) Co. R.E

X.1   26-8-18

SECRET.

C.R.E. 17th. Dumbton

Herewith report on wells in MARTIN PUICH.
Specimens of water from the first two on list
have been sent to M.O. R.E.

Appendix XI

Map Reference	Nature	Method of raising water	Depth to water	Depth of water	Dia	M.O's Report	Remarks
M.30. & 30.95	Particular Brick	Windlass	9'3"	12'	4'	-	? Drum & windlass missing. Water flashing hermonits Glass will be installed tomorrow
M.33 a.1.8.	Particular Brick	nil	80'	-	3'6"	-	Water clear. Wind lass will be installed tomorrow
M.32 & 5.5	Particular Brick	nil	120'	-	4'	-	Water very foul
M.26.d.25.00	Particular Punt	Wind lass	-	-	4'6"	-	Has been used by enemy unsound unsafe to send down.

Map Reference	Nature	Hardness depth of running water	Depth to water	Depth of Dug	M.O's Report	Yield	Remarks
M.32.8.3.3	Perennial Spring	nil	1	1	4'	-	-	not yet examined

Sgn. R.B. Rennie .RE
O.C. 93rd. (Field) 23 .RE

W.1 27-8-18

C.R.E. 17th Division

Report on Water Reconnaissance to 8 h.m. 28-8-18.

Appendix XII

SECRET.

Map Reference	Nature of	Method of raising	Depth to water	Depth of water	Dia.	M.O's Report
P.3b.a.6.6.	Perambr Puits	Pump	143'	69'	6'4"	Clear, tasteless. Odourless. Requires 1 scoop per 110 gals. for chlorination. No metallic poison, no cyanide
Remarks :— M.33.a.1.8	Female Windlass Puits	Female Reports tomorrow	30'	10'	3'6"	Organic XX. almost clear. Small tasteless, odourless. Req. 2 scoops per 110 gals for chlorination, no metallic poison, no cyanide. Well cleaned

Remarks :— Windlass installed & well cleaned.

Map Reference	Nature	Method of raising water	Depth to water	Depth of draw	M.O's Report	Yield
M.26.d.85.00	Rowadar Pant	Wind-lass	100'	4'	4'-6'	Very turbid, tasteless, odourless. Requires screening. 2000 ps per 110galls chlorination. No metallic poison, no cyanide. Unstable.	small
Remarks: M.32.8.33	Well cleaned & windlass					
M.32.8.20.95	Rowadar Kinar	nil Dry	—	—	4'	—	nil
Remarks: M.32.8.20.95 Rowadar Kinar	Windlass	9'3"	12'	4"	Slightly turbid, no sugar of organic life. Tasteless, odourless. Req. 1500ps per 110 galls chlorination. No metallic poison, no cyanide.	?
Remarks: Complete windlass installed						

W.L. 28-8-18.

(Sgd) P.L. Fundie Day R.E/W
O.C. 93rd. (Field) R.E.

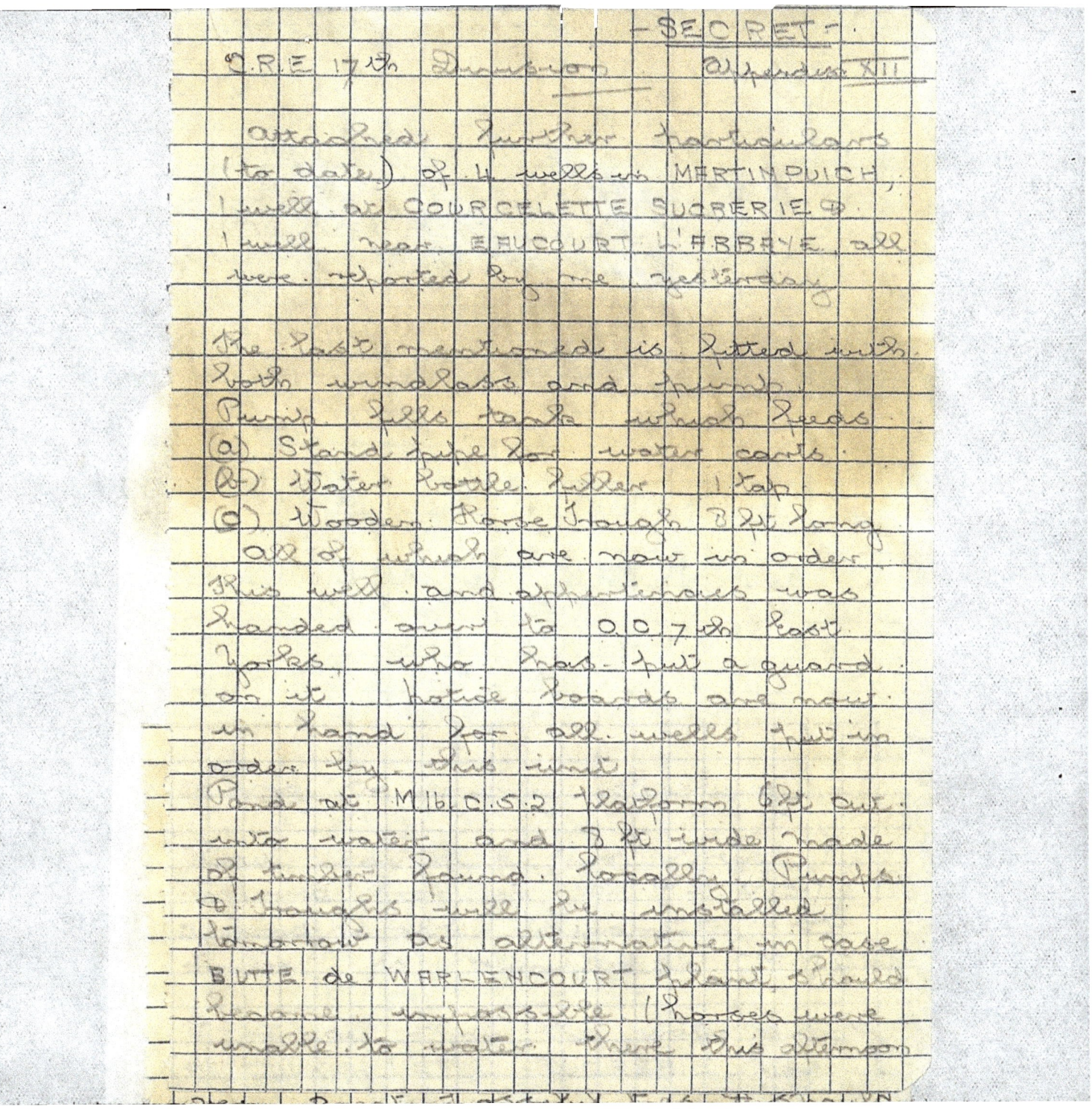

—SECRET—

C.R.E 17th Division   Appendix XII

Attached further particulars (to date) of 4 wells in MARTINPUICH, 1 well at COURCELETTE SUCRERIE & 1 well near EAUCOURT L'ABBAYE all were reported by me yesterday.

The last mentioned is fitted with both windlass and hand pump, fills tank which feeds
(a) Stand pipe for water carts.
(b) Water bottle filler 1 tap
(c) Wooden horse trough 8ft long

all of which are now in order. This well and apparatus was handed over to OO 7th East Yorks who has put a guard on it. Notice boards and now in hand for all wells put in order by this unit.

Pond at M.16.c.5.2. Platform 6ft out into water and 8ft wide made of timber found locally. Pumps & troughs will be installed tomorrow as alternative in case BUTE de WARLENCOURT plant should become impossible. Horses were unable to water there this afternoon owing to enemy shelling.

Road repaired & two trees removed from it at M.21.B.3.7. a considerable quantity of timber is dumped at M.17.C.4.6.

I consider that the water supply at COURCELETTE SUCRERIE has very great possibilities & should be taken in hand by C.E. X Corps as soon as possible

Sgd. R.R. Lundie Maj RE
O.C 93rd (Field) Co R.E.

W.5 27-8-18

Appendix XIII

SECRET

C.R.E. 17th Division
Report on Water Reconnaissance by m 29-8-18
unit 93rd (Field) Co. R.E.

Map Reference	Nature	Method of raising water	Depth to water	Depth of water	Dia.	M.O's Report
T.19.C.7.1.	—	2 man pump	—	—	—	Slightly tinged. Tasteless. Odourless. no metallic poison, no cyanide. Req. 1½ scoops per 110 galls chlorination
Remarks:- M.26.B.57	Working order nil	—	5ft 70'	5ft 10'	—	Clear. Tasteless, odourless no metallic poison, no cyanide. Requires 1 scoop per = 110 galls chlorination
N.26.B.75.	—	Bangalore hand pump	—	—	—	Almost clear. Tasteless. odourless no metallic poison

Map Reference	Nature of raising water	Depth to Depth of water	Dia	M.O's Report	Yield
	Remarks:- Quite good for pumping over well. M32 B25 20 Peruvian Windlass installed	115'	5'	No appearance Req. 1.15.00p per 110 galls. Alumination. concrete cover	
	Remarks:- Unfit for pumping M32 B33 2 Peruvian Windlass brick loss		4'	Very tainted foul smelling, no ransom. Fit for horses. Windlass	
	Remarks:- Soft cleaned, windlass installed				
	W.q 29-8-18			Sgd. R.E. & (Pare) Pant RE. O.C. 93rd (Field) Co. RE.	

— SECRET —

C.R.E. 17th Division
Report on Water Reconnaissance — to 8 p.m. 30-8-18
Appendix XIV   Unit 93rd (Feld) Co. R.E.

Map Reference	Nature of raising	Method	Depth to water	Depth of water	Dia.	M.O's Report	Yield
N.26.b.14.3	Purular Wind-prior Pass		80'	22'	4'	? Sample submitted	?
Remarks:— IN USE. Bucket req. (has been demanded)							
N.26.b.9.b	improvised one in use. Purular Wind-prior Pass.		65'	23'	4'	Clear. Tasteless. odourless. no metallic poison. no organic contamination. Req: 1 scoop for 110 gals chlorination. (has been demanded)	
Remarks:— IN USE (Bucket req.) improvised one in use							
N.26 & 5.7	Purular Wind-prior Pass		70'	10'	4'	O.K. See Report of 29-8-18. Bucket will be fitted	
Remarks:— have numerous made tomorrow							

Map Reference	Nature	Method of raising water	Depth to water	Depth of well	Dia	M.O's Report	Yield
N.26.d.7.5.	Revetted Brick	Large trough. Hand pump	60'	20'	?	O.K. See Report of 29-8-18.	
Remarks:— IN USE. Bucket demanded in use. Improvised one.							
N.31.c.2.5.	Revetted Brick	Wind-lass	90'	18'	6'	Very turbid. no organic life. Tasteless. Slight odour. no metallic poison. Sufft over to cyanide. 2 troops for 110 grass. Chlorination. M.O. Reg. Filtration. M.O. advises use for horses & washing only. Water from used for horses only. Enemy	

Remarks:— IN USE. This well had been demolished by the enemy, but a platform has been built over it & windlass installed. I propose to install a hand pump tomorrow as this camp only source of supply for horses in the immediate vicinity of FLERS.

Map Reference	Nature	Method of raising water	Depth to water	Depth of water	Dia	M.O's Report	Yield
N.26.B.7.3	Purular. Ponds at engines surface pump	Petrol	-	-	3'	That quite clean, tasteless about odourless, no metallic poison no cyanide. 1500g per hour 110 galls chlorination ?	2,500 galls per hour ?
Remarks:- Working order but requires minor alterations & repairs (these are in hand) Second 600 gall tank also required (already demanded). Water strainers is on spots & will be erected shortly tomorrow.							
N.31.C.2.6		-	-	-	-	-	-
Remarks:- Has been thoroughly used by enemy for drinking water, now only used by brasin. I am planting this tomorrow. Pantry for use, thanks of reclaiming which may prove of value. Later on experiments hay R.E.							

(Sgd) O.C. 93rd. (Lord) 20· RE

W.12. 30-8-18

C.R.E. 17th Division.   Appendix XV   SECRET

Report on Water Reconnaissance to 8 h.m. 31-8-18.
Unit 93rd (Field) Coy R.E.

Map Reference	Nature	Method of raising water	Depth to water	Depth of Dia	M.O's Report	Yield
N.31.c.2.b.	Circular Brick lined	Wind Pump Ross.	79'	17'	4'	Water not sufficient clear to test. Sample being taken early tomorrow.

Remarks: hot, not in use. Well has been completely demolished by the enemy. (See Special report K.80. attached.)
See yesterday's report N.26.B.5.7
Remarks :– IN USE. Bucket & cable now fitted.

(Sgd) R. P. Rundle Maj RE
O.C. 93rd (Field) Co RE

W.14. 31-8-18

CRE 17th Division   SECRET.

Appendix XV

Report on Work on Water Panies to 9 p.m. 31-8-18.

M.31.c.2.5. - Two Stages erected in well shaft. Hand Lift & Force Pump on lower stage & second pump (same type as above) erected on stage hanging from baulks across top of well. German Tank (about 300 galls) erected on surface about 4 ft above ground level and holed for 2" pipe. 50 ft. 2" pipe connected to tank, and laid on trestles to horse troughs complete with valves, and off shoot of 1" pipe with tap for supplying washing water. Three enemy troughs repaired and 18 ft new wooden troughs constructed & placed in position. Total length of troughs available for horses 54 ft. (Horses to be watered on one side only) New entrance made to yard in which troughs are situated, to provide distinct routes for horses going to &

...thing from water Bowsers standing alongside trough commenced. (will be continued tomorrow). Notice boards are in course of construction.

N.10.c.7.1. FACTORY CORNER. One sapper spent all day superintending puncturing operations 1" pipe to tap for filling petrol cans, water bottles etc. was cut by shell fire (direct hit) This pipe has been dug up & repairs will be completed early tomorrow.

N.26.B.7.3 Pumping Stn GUEUDECOURT known trough 91ft long repaired & erected standing made beside trough. 1000 gall circular tank salvaged & thoroughly cleaned ready for erection. (This tank has since been seriously holed by shell fire) pumps & engine houses thoroughly cleaned. 600 gall rest tank delivered on site. Work greatly hindered by shell fire intermittent shelling but it is hoped to complete this job (including extensions to horse troughs) tomorrow unless further damage by shell fire has occurred in the interim.

Sgn R.S. Lundie-Loy RE
OC 93rd (Fd) Co. RE

W 15   31-8-17

CONFIDENTIAL

WAR DIARY

OF

93rd Field Co. R.E.

From 1-9-18 to 30-9-18

Army Form C. 2118.

WAR DIARY

~~INTELLIGENCE SUMMARY~~

93rd (2d) Coy. R.E. SEPT. 1918 SHEET (1)

(Erase heading not required.)

Instructions regarding War Diaries and Intelligence Summaries are contained in F. S. Regs., Part II. and the Staff Manual respectively. Title pages will be prepared in manuscript.

Place	Date	Hour	Summary of Events and Information	Remarks and references to Appendices
FLERS	1/9/18	—	Work on Water Supply. Horse Lines at R.25.d. (Sheet 57D.) Strength 8 Off, 202 O.R. 64 animals	Water Report. R.C.L. Oth. I.
"	2	—	As above. Lt. E. MacG. MacQuarrie. M.C. to be 2nd in Command of 77th (2d) Coy R.E. 2 O.R. evacuated. Strength 7 Off, 200 O.R.	Water Report R.C.L. animals Oth II
"	3	—	O.C. made preliminary reconnaissance of LE TRANSLOY for water.	
"		2.30 P.M.	No. 2 & 4 Sections marched out to 0.26.b.42. (Sheet 57c.)	R.C.L.
"		3.0 P.M.	No. 1 & 3 Sections & H.Q. marched out to LE TRANSLOY. H.Q. at 0.25.c.3.6. Sections at SUCRERIE. Work on Water Supply	
LE TRANSLOY	4	—	Horse Lines moved to N.29.d. Water Report. 3 L.D. Horses received. Strength 7 officers 200 O.R.s 67 animals Water Report.	Oth III Oth IV R.C.L
"	5	—	Work continued as above. Nos. 2 & 4 Sections moved from 0.26.b.42. forward to 0.24.a.91. but returned to former location later on account of enemy shelling (H.E. & Gas). Water Report	Oth V R.C.L Oth VI R.C.L
"	6	—	Work as above.	Water Report
"	7	—	Whole Coy. moved to U.G.b.	Report R.C.L
U.G.b.	8	—	Work on Water Supply. 2 O.R. evacuated. 2 L.D. Mules recd. Strength 7 Off, 198 O.R. 69 animals Water Report.	Oth VII

WAR DIARY

INTELLIGENCE SUMMARY.

93rd (Fd) Coy. RE. SEPT. 1918. SHEET 2.

Army Form C. 2118.

(Erase heading not required.)

Place	Date	Hour	Summary of Events and Information	Remarks and references to Appendices
U.G.b. (57.c.)	9/9/18	—	Water Supply. Work continued	R.C.L. A/h VIII
"	10	—	do. do.	R.C.L.
"			O.C. 123rd (Fd) Coy RE arrived to take over work — but not billets.	A/h IX
"	11	A.M. 10.	Water Report. No 1 Section marched to LE TRANSLOY to prepare accommodation.	R.C.L.
"			Remainder of Coy Hqrs at Work.	R.C.L. A/h X
"		2.30 P.M.	H.Q. Nos 2, 3, & 4 Sections marched out to LE TRANSLOY Works Report.	R.C.L.
LE TRANSLOY	12	—	Inspection parades & general fatigues	R.C.L.
"	13	—	Improvements to hutments in Battn Camp of 52nd Bde.	R.C.L.
"	14	—	1 L.D. Mule died (Tetanus) Strength 7 Off. 198 O.R. 68 animals. 2 Sections working, 2 Sections training "Battle Position" Works Report. Work as above X O.C. reconnoitred	R.C.L. A/h XI
"	15	—	2 O.R. joined unit. Strength 7 Off. 200 O.R. 68 animals. Day of Rest. O.C. attended Conference at C.R.E's Office 2 L.D. Mules injured — Strength 70 animals	R.C.L.
"	16	—	Coy training.	R.C.L.
"	17	8.15 P.M.	Coy marched out 15 V.7. & 7.6 and went into billets. Plane lines at U.G.b. 1 O.R. transferred. 1 Rider received.	R.C.L.
			Strength 7 Off. 199 O.R. 71 animals	

WAR DIARY

93rd (3L) Coy R.E.

Army Form C. 2118.

INTELLIGENCE SUMMARY. SEPT. 1918. SHEET 3

Place	Date	Hour	Summary of Events and Information	Remarks and references to Appendices
57.c. V.7.8.7.6	18	—	30 Mobile Bombs to MINE-FIELD made & sent to adv. R.E. dump	R.E.
"	19	12 NOON	O.C. called to CRE's office. Plans lines moved to V.7.b.7.6.	
"	"	4 P.M.	Nos 1,2 & 4 Sections moved to billets at W.3.H. c.7.6.	R.E.
"	"	—	O.C. went round proposed work with CRE. No 3 Section at Store Lines as reserve directly under CRE. Works Report	O.K. XII
W.3.c.7.6	20	—	Consolidation. Works Report	O.K. XIII XIV
"	21	—	As above. 1 O.R. Wounded. Strength 7 Off 157 O.R. 71 annumated. Works Report	R.E.
"	22	—	As above. 1 O.R. No 435556 Sapt DURHAM. T. (B.G. Engineer at 3.) killed. Works Report	R.E. O.K. XV
"	23	9.30 A.M.	CRE went round work with O.C. Work as usual 1 O.R. wounded at W.3.c.7.6. Strength 7 Off 156 O.R. 71 annumated. Works Report	R.E. O.K. XVI
"	24	—	O.C. 126th (3L) Coy R.E. relieved our O.C. on Relief on 25.9.18 No.52472 A.C.S. STATHAM. T. awarded M.M. Works Report	R.E. O.K. XVII
"	25	2 P.M.	Coy moved out- (by Sections) into billets at horse lines V.7.8.7.6.	R.E.
V.7.8.7.6	26	—	Kits etc. unloaded. Continuation of deducted line standings. 30R. joined unit. Strength 7 Off 195 O.R. 71 annumated	R.E.

WAR DIARY 93d (Fd) Coy R.E. Army Form C. 2118.

INTELLIGENCE SUMMARY. SEPT. 1918 SHEET 4.

(Erase heading not required.)

Place	Date	Hour	Summary of Events and Information	Remarks and references to Appendices
57.c. V.7 & 7.6.	27	—	Constructing Band Stand. Horse Lines. O.C. reconnoitred RAILTON Area	R.E.
"	28	—	Coy at W.H Mins Water to horse, feeding, Partiers & Cleaning Wagons. L.D. Mule evacuated. Strength 7 off. 199 O.R. 71 animals	R.E.
"	29	—	As above. 1st Gunner attached to 93d (Fd) Coy RE. for Journal Reconnaissance	R.E.
"	30	—	Coy at W.H Mins Notice "War Savings Certificate" Cambrigan (17th Div.) issued. 753 W.S.C. & 577 Bodd. Ticket Sold.	R.E.

R.E. Sundre Ny R.E.

O.C. 93d Fd Coy R.E.

Army Form C. 2118.
SHEET 1

WAR DIARY
or
INTELLIGENCE SUMMARY. 93RD FIELD COY. R.E.
(Erase heading not required.)

Vol 37

Place	Date	Hour	Summary of Events and Information	Remarks and references to Appendices
ETRICOURT	1-10-18	7 AM	Company marched out arrived at Camp W.6 & 7.8	131
RAILTON DUMP			Sappers employed at RAILTON DUMP fixing up 12 ton axle Cart bridge	
"	2-10-18		" " " "	131
"	3-10-18		1 Rider received. Strength 7 Officers. 90 O.R.s 7 Animals	131
"			Sappers employed at RAILTON DUMP fixing up 12 ton axle Cart bridge	131
"			5 O.R.s join Company Strength 7 Officers 95 O.R.s 7 Animals	131
"	4-10-18		Sappers employed RAILTON DUMP fixing up 12 ton axle Cart Bridge	131
"	5-10-18		Instructions received from O.C. BRITISH RIFLES Coy had orders to Bath Bank of Canal	131
ESCAUT R.		9.20	Mins from C.R.E. to Commence bridging ESCAULT RIVER Nos 1. 2. 7 Sections detail such	131
		10-10	Arrived at HONNECOURT Canerval bridging Canal 575 6-7 No. 8 Section	
		5.30	Arrived HONNECOURT	
	6-10-18		Bridging CARD Branche Boss Bridge Hand to Cavy Suffrs 16-30	117
			Lt GRADY Transferred to 557 AT Coy Strength 6 Officers 201 OR 7 Animals	
HONNECOURT	7-10-18		HONNECOURT Made an bridge approaches. Coy returned to Coumbraements to Afternoon	131
W.16 a.7.8.	8-10-18		No 1 Sect by Cory to HONNECOURT erected stage girder bridge	131
COMPIEGNE-ANNOY		7.00	Operation order. Coy moved out at x 3a 6.r. 20-30 to Compiegne Coy	131
CAMP		8.B. 2. x.3.a.		

Army Form C. 2118.

SHEET (2)

WAR DIARY
or
INTELLIGENCE SUMMARY.
(Erase heading not required.)

93RD FIELD COY R.E

Place	Date	Hour	Summary of Events and Information	Remarks and references to Appendices
X.3a.6.7.	9.10.18	01.01	Operation order issued. Coy situated at OB Hq. Arrived at M33c7.9 at 05.30	
			Ordered at 10.00 to move to HAUT F^m Arrived there at 10.3 Sect on Motor Buses.	154
			Reconnaissance of MAIMCOURT BELIGNY for roles. Horse lelong't captured.	
HAUT F^m	10/10/18	89.70	Nos 1.2 stations and on Motor Buses. MAIMCOURT BELIGNY RUMIGNY Coy marched out at 11.30pm moved at 12 on to Obd 5.8 Sect 3rd Sect'n locating & removing	167
			Area MONTIGNY	
	11/10/18		Move Sect moved at 05.30, worked on Motor Buses TRONCQUOY Nos 1.2.3 Sects noted 6.175.3.5.08"	
J17c.3.5.			Transport followed. Nos 1.3 Sects on footbridges SELLE R. for Infantry attack.	189
			No 4 Sect from OBY. 2 OR's wounded, 1 8 2nd D. Repair 1 R & 2nd D mended	
			Sect 6 29th M.L.5. 2 OFF Chargers L.D. 1 Rider wounded at got.	
			Strength 6 OFF 207 OR's, 64 Animals	
J17c.3.5.	12/10/18		No 1 Sect at Jeancourt Reconstruction of trench road with 1st Manc Gallants. 17th MANC. 30th foot bridge built up	
			And across SELLE R. EVERSWELL. now dismantled Bridge built, across RUMIGNY by C Pion.	193
			2 OR's wounded. Strength 6 OFF 29.2 OR 64 animals	
			5th Con	
J17c.3.5.	13/10/18		Preparation of H.H. bridge by Lt CUMMING R.E, & O.R'S	195
			Strength 7 OFF 296 OR'S 64 Animals	
			Horse Lines withdrawn to AUDENCOURT	

WAR DIARY
INTELLIGENCE SUMMARY

93RD FIELD COY RE SHEET 3

Army Form C. 2118.

Place	Date	Hour	Summary of Events and Information	Remarks and references to Appendices
J.37.c.3.5.	14/9/18		Coy working on foot bridges. MAJ R.C. LUNDIE DSO RE. wounded & died from Sgt LAMB MM RE wounded & later died. (L-30 Km 22.30)	A3.1
	15/9/18		1 OR died of wounds. 2 OR's wounded. Strength 6 OFF, 202 OR's, 60 animals	A3.1
AUDENCOURT	16/9/18		Coy moved back to Iwuy Quin (AUDENCOURT)	A3.1
"	17/9/18		Coy making foot bridges	A3.1
"	18/9/18		"	A3.1
"	19/9/18		4 scouts across SELLE R. Nos 3 & 4 Secs crossed 8 cross SELLE R & reconn. for morning attack. 10 R wounded. 2 LD Aulx Rfft. 2nd Aulx wounded circa 6. 29th MIS Strength 6 OFF 201 OR 60 animals	A3.1
"	20/9/18		2 FLT bridges constructed across SELLE R. 1 OR wounded 30 R found coint. Strength 6 off. 202 O.R. & 60 animals. Maj Lundie's Sig Long bridge recovered.	
	21/10/18		Maintaining bridges. Blowing gundies of K.9.a.1.6. 2nd Lw. 2 LD Hunter recd. Strength 6 offs 202 O.R. 68 animals. Maj Lundie 9 Sigt Long buried at AUDENCOURT.	
	22/10/18		Coy marched from AUDENCOURT to billets in INCHY. Work maintaining bridges	

Army Form C. 2118.

WAR DIARY
or
INTELLIGENCE SUMMARY. 93rd Fld Coy R.E. Sheet 4

(Erase heading not required.)

Instructions regarding War Diaries and Intelligence Summaries are contained in F.S. Regs., Part II. and the Staff Manual respectively. Title pages will be prepared in manuscript.

Place	Date	Hour	Summary of Events and Information	Remarks and references to Appendices
	22.10.18		Strength 6 offs. 201 O.R.s 68 animals	W.4.B
INCHY	23.10.18		Dismantling bridges over SELLE R.	W.4.B
INCHY	24.10.18		Coy resting. I.O.R. trans. to R.E Base Depot. Strength 6 Officers 200 O.R.S 68 animals	W.4.B
"	25.10.18		I.O.R. trans. to R.E Base Depot. Strength 6 Officers 199 O.R.S 68 animals	W.4.B
"	26.10.18		I.O.R. evacuated. Strength 6 Officers 198 O.R.s 68 animals	W.4.B
"	27.10.18	8.00	Marched out, arrived VENDEGIES au BOIS 11.30 hours, and went into billets	W.4.B
VENDEGIES- au-BOIS	28.10.18		No 4 Section making and erecting horse Boards	W.4.B
			No 4 Section making horse Boards. Nos 1,2 & 3 Sections making new roads	W.4.B
			Went at VENDEGIES-au-BOIS	W.4.B
"	29.10.18	15.00	Marched out, arrived NEUVILLY and went into billets at 18.00 hours	W.4.B
			Indents 3 P.D. horses received. Strength/6 Officers 198.O.R.S 72 animals	W.4.B
NEUVILLY	30.10.18		Kit inspection. Training. Capt. W.H Budgett R.E. joined unit and took over command. Strength, 7 Officers 198 O.R.s 72 animals	W.4.B
"	31.10.18		Coy training. I.O.R. joined unit	W.4.B
			Strength/7 Officers. 199 O.R.s 72 animals	W.4.B
			(Wa Budgett) Capt R.E. 31/10/18 O.C. 93rd (3rd) Fd. R.E.	

Secret

Army Form C. 2118.

WAR DIARY
—of—
INTELLIGENCE SUMMARY.
(Erase heading not required.)

Instructions regarding War Diaries and Intelligence Summaries are contained in F. S. Regs., Part II. and the Staff Manual respectively. Title pages will be prepared in manuscript.

93rd Fit Coy RE
WD 3

Place	Date	Hour	Summary of Events and Information	Remarks and references to Appendices
NEUVILLY	1/11/18		Company training	W.H.B.
"	2/11/18		Company moved from NEUVILLY at 17.00 hours & arrived at Orchard west of POIX-DU-NORD at 23.00 hours. Siegfried Section at E.18 d 2.4. 3 ORs killed & 1 OR wounded	W.H.B.
NEAR POIX-DU-NORD	3/11/18		Sections moved from orchard on account of enemy shelling into fields in POIX-DU-NORD	W.H.B.
POIX-DU-NORD	4/11/18		Operation Order No 30 received. 2 ORs killed, 3 ORs wounded. 2/LIEUT W.A. TURNER wounded (gas shell). Company employed in forming corduroy tracks, assisted 3 craters east of KNNE FONTAINE & making water troughs 80 ft run canvas water trough fixed - complete with pump at S 16 c 1.8.	W.H.B.
"	5/11/18		Company working on roads. Orders received at 16.30 hours to move forward from POIX-DU-NORD. Halfmetres & 2 sections at T.20 d 2.9. Two sections & transport lines at S.30 68.9. 4 ORs reinforcements	W.H.B.
LOCQUIGNOL	6/11/18		Company working on roads. Shell holes filled & roads drained off. Stabs. 1 OR transferred to 565 A.T. Coy. O.O. No.31. received.	W.H.B.
"	7/11/18		Sections working on trestle bridge over crates at T.23 c 4.5. Road horses fired & bullet off VACHERY richeses laid on position (not fixed) on 3 days on Eastern side of bridge. Mangancer rast teams in position. Company moved to AYMERIES at hour 20.00.	W.H.B.
AYMERIES	8/11/18		Company moved from AYMERIES at 15.00 hours. Arrived BACHANT 16.30 hours. 1 OR returned sick.	W.H.B.
BACHANT	9/11/18		Rifle inspection & general clean up. No 4 section working on horse troughs. 6 horse troughs erected at U18 63.3.	W.H.B.
"	10/11/18		1 horse troughs erected complete with pumps at U 21 65.2, 2 at U 21 63.3, 3 at U 17 63.5 & 2 at U 18 63.3. Holes bored & hand erected. Lieut OLNEY R.E. admitted to hospital. Lieut LUCAS R.E. awarded M.C. 48409. 2/Cpl Jenkins 189056 2/Cpl Jenkins awarded the D.C.M.	W.H.B.

(A9175) Wt W2358/P360 600,000 12/17 D. D. & L. Sch. 82a. Forms/C2118/15

Army Form C. 2118.

WAR DIARY
~~INTELLIGENCE~~ SUMMARY
(Erase heading not required.)

Instructions regarding War Diaries and Intelligence Summaries are contained in F. S. Regs., Part II. and the Staff Manual respectively. Title pages will be prepared in manuscript.

Place	Date	Hour	Summary of Events and Information	Remarks and references to Appendices
BACHANT	11/11/18		Inspection parade of Company. Washing & cleaning wagons. 1 OR wounded.	W.H.B.
- " -	12/11/18 - 13/11/18		3 sections training. One section working on roads.	W.H.B.
- " -	14/11/18		Company moved from BACHANT at 09.30 hours, arrived ENGLE-FONTAINE at 14.30 hours.	W.H.B.
ENGLE-FONTAINE	15/11/18		Moved from ENGLE-FONTAINE at 09.40 hours & arrived BEAUMONT. 2/LIEUT M. DOOLANS & /LIEUT STEWART joined unit. 2 ORs Reinforcements	W.H.B.
BEAUMONT - INCHY	16/11/18		General clean up of wagons & equipment. 2 ORs Reinforcements.	W.H.B.
	17/11/18		Church parade at 10 H.O. hours. 2 ORs returned from hospital	W.H.B.
	18/11/18		Company had baths & clean change. 1 OR transferred to 45th Light Bty R.E.	W.H.B.
	19/11/18 - 20/11/18		Company training & cleaning of Equipment.	W.H.B.
	21/11/18		Inspection of Company by E.A.E.	W.H.B.
	22-23/11/18		Company Training.	W.H.B.
	24/11/18		Church parade 10.16 hours	W.H.B.
	25/11/18		Company training	W.H.B.
	26/11/18		Inspection by G.O.C. Division at 14.15 hours	W.H.B.
	27/11/18		Company training. 2 ORs Reinforcements. 1 officer & 2 ORs to 3rd Army School of Instruction	W.H.B.
	28/11/18		- " - 1 OR returned from leave.	W.H.B.
	29/11/18		- " - - " -	W.H.B.
	30/11/18		- " - 1 OR to hospital.	W.H.B.

W.H.B.
MAJOR R.E.
O.C. 93RD FIELD COY. R.E.

WAR DIARY or INTELLIGENCE SUMMARY

Army Form C. 2118.

93RD FIELD COY RE

WO 39

Place	Date	Hour	Summary of Events and Information	Remarks and references to Appendices
INCHY	1-12-18	—	3 ORs Leave U.K. 3 ORs to U.K. as miners. 1 OR & U.K. Special Leave. Strength 189 ORs 6 Officers 74 Animals	
"	2-12-18		5 ORs to U.K. as miners. 10 R transferred to 2 L22 Depot. Coy repairing truck floor. Strength 184 ORs 6 Officers 83 ORs 74 Animals. Transport left INCHY with Cycles. Men await to fit. Repairing truck floor	
"	3-12-18		Coy working on floor of church	
"	4-12-18		Church inspected by H.M. THE KING. 2 OR Leave U.K. Strength 6 Officers 183 OR 74 Anim.	
"	5-12-18		Remainder of Coy entrained at CAUDRY. Coy detrained at NURLU and marched to OISEMENT. Transport arrived at PICQUINY. 10 & Cambrai, strength 6 offr 183 OR 74 anim	
"	6-12-18			
"	7-12-18		Transport left PICQUINY. Coy left OISEMENT and marched to LALEU. 2 ORs Leave to U.K. Strength 6 Offrs 183 OR 74 Anim.	
LALEU	8-12-18		Coy working on Camp installments etc	
"	9-12-18		Cleaning ways of	
"	10-12-18		Building Bath Sale at CROQUISON. Coy standing by	
"	11-12-18		2 Sections building drawn hut at LALEU. of remainder moved to CROQUISON	
"	12-12-18		CROQUISON	
"	13-2-18		1 Wiseman hut erected at NETINGY and one at CROQUISON by 2 Offrs, one 1R Joiners. Strength 7 Offrs 184 OR 74 Animals	
CROQUISON	14-12-18		2 OR returned from Leave. 3 OR reinforcements to CROQUISON Strength 7 Offrs 74 & 18 Anim from R.E.B.D.	
"	15-12-18		6 OR " " Strength 7 Officers 197 OR 74 Animal	

Army Form C. 2118.

WAR DIARY
or
INTELLIGENCE SUMMARY.
(Erase heading not required.)

93RD FIELD COY R E

Instructions regarding War Diaries and Intelligence Summaries are contained in F. S. Regs., Part II. and the Staff Manual respectively. Title pages will be prepared in manuscript.

Place	Date	Hour	Summary of Events and Information	Remarks and references to Appendices
CROQUISON	16/10/18		Work. Commenced on railway at Fillièvres (Huitters)	T of
"	17/10/18		"	"
"	18/10/18		IOR reconnaissance Sleep 7 Off un Offs 93 OR 7 Cements. Work on railway bridges continued	
"	19/10/18		" 2 OR'S B U K Huns	
"	20/10/18		Work 93 commenced at FERGUSON	
"	21/10/18		20R. to Dockyard Wk. 175 un. Wk. 95 wagons from Aubigny	
"	22/10/18		30R report from Convic Relay 125 horses to 20 mule Boson Stamp 7 Officers 93 OR 7 Cements Church Parade IOR 6 52 other ranks	
"	23/10/18		Work on railway bridges continued (Huitters Hesdin etc)	
"	24/10/18		"	
"	25/10/18		Coy. Inspected on 9 OR'S found from RFBD Major Budget to R G on leave Stamp 7 Officers 20 OR's 7 Cements Col. Mellor 1 OR returned from leave	
"	26/10/18		Work on Railway Bridges continued LtCol 8s MC 93 returned to Duty for Instructions Str 9t 6 Officers 20 OR 7 Cements	
"	27/10/18		Work Continued	
"	28/10/18		Work Continued in railway Bridges Sunday its orchestra billets	
"	29/10/18		Church Parade 10 6 56 my Morris & Curtis, 1 NCO from leave	

WAR DIARY
or
INTELLIGENCE SUMMARY.

Army Form C. 2118.

Place	Date	Hour	Summary of Events and Information	Remarks and references to Appendices
CROUNON	2/11/18		Work on various fatigues continued. Officers returning to Company on C.R.E. GRB & 1 Captain R.E.	
	3/11/18		Work continued building up D.R. line between K.23.B. & round from D.R. line to village of Presseau 97. 7 hrs.	

Army Form C. 2118.

WAR DIARY
or
INTELLIGENCE SUMMARY.

93 Field Co RE

(Erase heading not required.)

Instructions regarding War Diaries and Intelligence Summaries are contained in F. S. Regs., Part II. and the Staff Manual respectively. Title pages will be prepared in manuscript.

Place	Date	Hour	Summary of Events and Information	Remarks and references to Appendices
CROQUIS N.	1.1.19		Copies Kings Cuday proclamation in work to troops	
	2.1.19		Strength 3 Offs 189 ORs 71 animals	
			2 ORs returned from leave	
			Work on roads	
			2 ORs signed for 15t 52 Co duty	
	3.1.19		Strength 3 Offs 191 ORs 71 animals	
			Work continued	
	4.1.19		4 ORs to hospital	
			Strength 3 Offs 186 ORs 71 animals	
	5.1.19		Work continued	
	6.1.19		Work continued - 1 O.R. to Hospital (1 R returned to England)	
	7.1.19		3 ORs to UK for demob (Pte REBL Sealed)	
	8.1.19		Strength 3 Offs 36/6 1 St ORs 71 animals	
			Work continued 1 O.R. to UK for demob	
			Strength 3 Offs 188 ORs 71 animals	
	9.1.19		Work continued 1 N.C.O. and assistant 3 ORs to UK for demob	
			Strength 3 Offs 185 ORs 170 animals	

Army Form C. 2118.

WAR DIARY
or
INTELLIGENCE SUMMARY.
(Erase heading not required.)

Instructions regarding War Diaries and Intelligence Summaries are contained in F. S. Regs., Part II. and the Staff Manual respectively. Title pages will be prepared in manuscript.

Place	Date	Hour	Summary of Events and Information	Remarks and references to Appendices
CROQUISON.	10.1.19		Work continued.	
	11.1.19		Strength 30 B. 185 ORs. 70 Rumanians.	
	12.1.19		Work continued.	
	13.1.19		Church Parade. Troops R.	
	14.1.19		Work continued 1 Off. 3 ORs. to Cambrai. 1 Observation OP. 1 Off. to Abbeville. 7 ORs to Wimereux. Strength 30 B. 173 ORs. 70 annual.	
	14.1.19.		Work continued.	
	15.1.19.		" 1 OR to E & RO.	
			Strength 3 Off. 172 ORs. 70 annual.	
	16.1.19		Work continued. 1 O.R. to Mirrenst. 1 Off. returned from leave.	
			Strength 4 Off. 171 ORs. 70 annual.	
	17.1.19		Work continued. 3 ORs. to UK on leave.	
			Strength 4 Off. 168 ORs. 70 annual.	
	18.1.19.		Work continued.	
	19.1.19.		Church Parade. No work. 1 Off. joined. 2 OR rejoined from leave.	
			Strength 5 Off. 161 ORs. 70 annual.	
	20.1.19		Work continued.	

Army Form C. 2118.

WAR DIARY
or
INTELLIGENCE SUMMARY.
(Erase heading not required.)

Instructions regarding War Diaries and Intelligence Summaries are contained in F.S. Regs., Part II, and the Staff Manual respectively. Title pages will be prepared in manuscript.

Place	Date	Hour	Summary of Events and Information	Remarks and references to Appendices
CROUCHSON	20.1.19		Work continued. 1 OR Hospital. 18 ORs Demobed.	
			Strength 4 Off. 149 ORs. 70 animals	
	22.1.19		Work continued. Coy. hqrs. 2 ORs U.K. Leave. 7 ORs. Dis	J.
			Rest Camp. 1 OR I Corps School.	
			Strength 4 Off. 155 ORs 70 animals	
	23.1.19		Work continued. 1 OR from H.M. Workshops.	N.
			Strength 4 Off. 156 ORs - 70 animals.	N.
	24.1.19		Work continued. 2 ORs UK Leave.	
			Strength 4 Off. 154 ORs 70 animals.	J.
	25.1.19		Work continued 6 RMRE 2 AT Coy from PIRYNES.	
			Strength 4 Off. 146 ORs 70 animals.	J.
	26.1.19		To Work. 1 OR rejoined from E&M Coy. 1 OR rejoined from	
			PONTREMY sawmill. 1 OR Leave to DIEPPE	J.
			Strength 4 Off. 147 ORs 70 animals.	J.
	27.1.19		Work continued. 1 Off. 16 ORs to Demob. 1 OR to Hosp.	
			Strength 3 Off. 130 ORs. 70 animals	J.

Army Form C. 2118.

WAR DIARY
or
INTELLIGENCE SUMMARY.
(Erase heading not required.)

Instructions regarding War Diaries and Intelligence Summaries are contained in F. S. Regs., Part II. and the Staff Manual respectively. Title pages will be prepared in manuscript.

Place	Date	Hour	Summary of Events and Information	Remarks and references to Appendices
CROCUSON	28.1.19		Work continued. 1 OR to Pont-Remy Convalls. Strength 3 off. 129 ORs. 70 Animals.	
	29.1.19		Work continued. 2 ORs. Hosp. 1 OR. from Base. Strength 3 off. 128 ORs. 70 Animals.	
	30.1.19		Work continued. 1 OR to Hosp. 3 ORs. rejoined from Hosp. Strength 3 off. 130 ORs. 70 Animals	
	31.1.19		Work continued.	

J M Phillips
Capt. R.E.
OC 93 Field Co. R.E.

WAR DIARY or INTELLIGENCE SUMMARY

Army Form C. 2118.

for February 1919

Place	Date	Hour	Summary of Events and Information	Remarks and references to Appendices
	1.		Work in villages continued. 14 O.Rs. to Div Rest Camp for demobilisation (struck off strength). 1 O.R Hospital. Strength 3 officers 115 O.R. 70 animals	NAR
	2.		Church parade a 9.30. 10.R rejoined from Heavy mobile workshops. Strength 3 officers 116 O.R. 70 animals.	NAR
	3.		Work in villages continued	NAR
	4.		Work in villages continued 5.O.R rejoined from PONT REMY sawmills. Strength 3 officers 121 O.R. 70 animals	NAR
	5.		Work in villages continued. 1.O.R returned from leave to DIEPPE. Strength 3 officers 122 O.R. 70 animals	NAR
	6.		Work in villages continued. 7 O.Rs to Div Reption Camp for demobilisation (struck off strength). 1.O.R to Hospital. Strength 3 officers 114 O.R. 70 animals	NAR
	7.		Work in villages continued. H.O.Rs 6 Div Reception Camp for demobilisation. 3 O.Rs to U.K. on leave. Strength 3 officers 107 O.Rs 70 animals	NAR NAR NAR
	8.		Work on villages continued. 11 Bicycles to D.A.D.O.S. 1 L.D horse to 29 Mot Vet Section. 2 O.Rs to Div Reception Camp for demobilisation (struck off strength). Strength 3 officers 105 O.R. 69 animals	NAR
	9.		No parade. 10.R rejoined from leave. 1 O.R rejoined from Hospital. 2 O.Rs to Div Reception Camp for demobilisation (struck off strength). Strength 3 officers 103. O.Rs 69 animals.	
	10.		Work in villages continued. 10.R rejoined from leave. Strength 3 officers 104 O.Rs 69 animals	NAR NAR
	11.		Work in villages continued. 6 O.Rs rejoined from leave. 5 riders 1 L.D horse, 3 L.D mules to 29 Mobile Vet Section. Strength 3 officers 110 O.R. 60 animals.	NAR
	12.		Work in villages continued. 14 O.Rs to Div Reception Camp for demobilisation (struck off strength). Strength 3 officers 96 O.Rs 60 animals	NAR
	13.		Work in villages continued. 3 O.Rs rejoined from leave. 12 O.Rs to Div Reception Camp for demobilisation (struck off strength). Strength 3 officers 87 O.R. 60 animals	NAR
	14.		Work in villages continued. 1 O.R rejoined from leave. No. 1 Section returned to Company H.Q from WARLUS. Strength 3 officers 88 O.Rs. 60 animals.	NAR

WAR DIARY
or
INTELLIGENCE SUMMARY.
(Erase heading not required.)

Army Form C. 2118.

February 1917 (Con.)

Place	Date	Hour	Summary of Events and Information	Remarks and references to Appendices
	15.		Work in villages completed. 3 O.Rs to Hospital. 1 O.R. reporties from leave. Strength 3 officers 86 O.Rs 60 animals	MR
	16.		Inspection parade 09-30. 3 O.Rs returned from Hospital. 1 O.R. reporties from leave in U.K. 1 O.R to Hospital. Strength 3 Officers 89 O.Rs 60 animals.	MR
	17.		Company employed on loading Pontoons and packing wagons.	MR
	18.		Company working on Race Course, painting oiling & greasing wagons. 1 O.R. to U.K. for leave. 6 L.D Horses & 3 H.D mules to 29 Mobile Vet Section. Strength 3 officers 88 O.Rs 51 animals.	MR
	19.		Inspection of Company at 09-30. Work on Race course continued, painting etc wagons continued. 1 O.R. to Hospital. 5 O.Rs to Div Reception Camp for demobilization (struck off strength) Strength 3 officers 82 O.Rs 51 animals	MR
	20.		Work on Race Course, painting etc wagons continued. 2 riders, 2 pack horses 3 draught horse to Corps Horse Camp for demobilization. 1 O.R transferred to G. Depot Company War Hospital Knightley struck off strength. Strength 63 officers. 82 O.Rs 44 animals.	MR
	21.		Work on Race course, painting etc wagons continued. Serg. Rendars to ALLERY to investigate damage to Baths. 1 O.R to Div Reception Camp for demobilization (struck off strength) Strength 3 officers. 81 O.Rs 44 animals.	MR
	22.		Work on Race Course, painting wagons continued.	MR
	23.		Church parade @ 9-45	MR
	24.		Company employed working in Camp, cleaning harness etc	MR
	25.		Company working in Camp cleaning up returning stores from Div Race Course. 2 O.Rs returned from Leave. 1 O.R to Hospital. Strength 3 officers. 82 O.Rs 44 animals.	MR
	26.		Company working on Brigade Race Course. Fatigues in Camp.	MR
	27.		Work on Bgd Race Course and in Camp Continued. 1 O.R to Hospital. 1 L.D mule to 29 Mobile Vet Section. 1 O.R reporting from leave Strength 3 officers. 82 O.Rs. 43 animals.	MR
	28.		Work on Bg Race Course in Camp continued. Strength Unchanged	MR

C.R.E. 17th Division　　　　　　　　　　　　　　　　　　　　　— SECRET —
Report on Water Reconnaissance to 8 pm 1-9-18
W.16　　　　　　　　　Unit 93rd (Field) Co R.E.　Appendix 1

Map Reference	Nature	Method of raising water	Depth to water	Depth of water	Dia	M.O.'S Report	Yield
N.31.a.35.20	Circular rough chalk & brick	Windlass	73'	13'	4'	Sample submitted M.O's report not yet received	

Remarks:— In use for horses. Reclaimed after demolition

N.31.a.5.3.
　Remarks:— Demolished by enemy. Digging out operations commenced
N.31.c.2.6. See yesterday's report　　　　　　　　Milky in colour due to lime salts.
　　　　　　　　　　　　　　　　　　　　　　　Tasteless, odourless, no metallic poison
Remarks:— In Use　　　　　　　　　　　　　No cyanide. Requires 1 scoop per 100 galls
W.16　　　R.C. Sundie Maj R.E.　　　　for chlorination. Water is excellent for
1-9-18　　O.C. 93rd (Field) Co R.E.　　　drinking purposes

C.R.E. 17th Division   SECRET.
                                                  Appendix a

Water Supply report to 10p.m. 1-9-17.

GUEUDECOURT Pumping Stn. N.26.b.7.3.

Engine has been running, and tank has been kept full all day, except when party was shelled off the job about 1.30 p.m. 36ft. rubber horse trough fitted in wooden frames on trestles. Standings improved. Box drain put in. Supporting structures of tank under-pinned. Second 600 gall. tank placed in position. One 1,000 gall. tank (holed by shell fire yesterday) repaired and placed in position.
Work on Piping for new tanks commenced.

FLERS.
Great difficulties have been encountered at horse water point at N.31.c.2.5. as reported earlier in my X 34, but tank has been successfully filled to night and I do not anticipate much further trouble. Present arrangement of hand pumps is however most unsatisfactory, both as regards waste of labour and flow of water; so far there has been no sign

of any intention on part of the Corps
R.E. to install a canvas built
"water lifter".

A number of horses have been watered
during the day by bucket from well
at N.31.c.2.6; and also horses have
been watered to-night at newly
opened well at N.31.a.35.20.

FACTORY CORNER. N.19.c.7.1.

Pipe to tap for filling petrol cans etc,
cut by shell fire yesterday was
repaired this morning.

N.17.   R.C. Lundie Maj RE
1-9-18   O.C. 93rd (Field) Co. RE

Appendix II

C.R.E. 17th Division — SECRET —
Report on Water Reconnaissance to 8 p.m. 2-9-18.
Unit 93rd (Field) Co. RE

Map Reference	Nature	Method of raising water	Depth to water	Depth of water	M.O's Report	Yield
N.31.a.35.20	See Report of 1-9-18				Slightly turgid. Traces of organic matter. Tasteless. Slightly foul odour, no metallic poison, no cyanide. Requires 1½ scoops per 110 galls for chlorination. Should be filtered, then boiled or chlorinated before being used for drinking.	
W.19 2-9-18					R C Lindie, Major RE O.C. 93rd (Field) Co. RE	

Appendix II
SECRET

C.R.E. 17th Division
Report on Water Supply to 11 p.m. 2-9-18.

Horse Water Point at FLERS N.31.c.7.5.

200 horses watered today. Troughs full for morning. Middle of the 3 pumps Hoovered 8' fly and 2 pumps thoroughly over-hauled.

Wells in FLERS
N.31.c.26. — Staging erected to level of road over well, and sides revetted with C.G.I. windlass fixed IN USE for drinking and cooking.
N.31.a.35.20. — Emergency horse trough fixed with wooden gutter from well IN USE — horses only. See M.O's report attached.
Crater N.31.a.43. — Well could not be found, work stopped after 7 hours.

GUEUDECOURT
Permanent party on Pumping Stn. Notice boards erected. Brick standings constructed round trough and well. Piping work continued on new tanks and water jacket of engine. Many horses watered 12 m.n. Pumping plant has just arrived for FLERS
W.20.
2-9-18.

R S Lundie Major RE
O.C. 93rd (Field) Co RE

C.R.E. 17th Division.   Appendix VI
                                         SECRET.

Water Report to midnight 3-9-18.
ROCQUIGNY.
Q.27.b.42. — M.O.RE reports:—
Turbid tasteless odourless, no signs of
organic life, no metallic poison, no
cyanide. Requires 2 scoops per 110 galls
chlorination. Must be boiled or
chlorinated before use, but recommended
for horses.
Q.27.b.13. — M.O.RE reports.
Clear tasteless odourless, no metallic
poison, no cyanide. Req 1 scoop per
110 galls chlorination. Must be boiled
or chlorinated before use. Excellent
for human consumption.
Officer i/c Advanced Sections reports
work on 2 wells proceeding windlass
for well at Q.27.b.4.2. has been sent
up to him by wagon.

LE TRANSLOY.
N.30.a.26.   M.O.RE reports:—
Cloudy, organic debris, no organic
life. Tasteless, odourless. No metallic
poison, no cyanide. Req 1½ scoops
per 110 galls for chlorination. Must be
boiled or chlorinated before used for

human consumption.
N.30.d.08. - M.O. R.E. reports :-
Slightly cloudy. Tasteless. Odourless, no metallic poison, no cyanide. Req 1 scruple H110 falls chlorination. Must be boiled or chlorinated before drinking.
N.30.d.08. Depth of well to water 30', depth of water 13', dia 3'6". Work in LE TRANSLOY had been discontinued owing to lack of Lignite, but will be re started at full strength at 5 a.m.
4 Troughs were erected about O.25.c.80 and have since been successfully filled by motor lorry. no troughs were brought by motor lorry, please say what is to be done with these troughs in the event of a forward move tomorrow.

3-9-18.

R.C. Lundie Major RE
O.C 93rd Field Co RE

C.R.E. 17th Division   Appendix III
                                  SECRET

I have this morning reconnoitred BUS from the Water Supply point of view, but cannot find anything of importance in the portion which falls within the 17th Divisional area, except a good block of horse troughs about O.24.c.8.2. which I have ordered to be repaired for filling by lorries.

I twice attempted to get into LECHELLE but was turned back by gas in both cases. A large overhead tank at O.23.d.2.0. appeared to be in good order and there are 2 good metal tanks in the same area.

X 53   R C Lundie Major RE
4-9-18   O C 93rd Field Co. RE.

Appendix IV

C.R.E. 17th Division — SECRET

Report on Water Supply Situation

An engine and belt pump has been installed by 559th A.T. Co R.E. at O.27.b.1.3 to fill 2 canvas tanks and 3 canvas horse troughs. Installation was running at 8.45. p.m. to-night.

The belt pump originally issued to this unit for use in FLERS is not now required at ROCQUIGNY but will be erected temporarily as an experiment at O.25.c.4.7 in the meanwhile a gantry will be erected over the well at O.25.c.2.6. in case it is required to install belt pump there. Wells have been opened and are now in operation at N.30.a.2.6 and N.30.d.0.8.

This evening I successfully reconnoitred Water Point at LECHELLE P.25.c.9.0; it consists of:

(a) 1 Standard for filling water carts
(b) 1 Small tap "   "   "   biscuit tins
and about 200 ft of horse trough (semi circular iron section) most of which up to now is undamaged. Storage tank of flimsy construction about P.25.d.5.1. also seems undamaged. Owing to heavy shelling I was unable

to approach the Pumping Stn on P.32.d.
Lieut Thomas reports that reinforced
concrete troughs at O.17.d.9.6. have
now been made fit for use. Total
length of trough level 72 ft including
1 corrugated iron tank laid down by A.T. Coy
R.E. Troughs at BUS. O.-4.c.8.2.
will be taken in hand tomorrow.
More windlasses are urgently required.
Capt Reid reports Pumping Stn at
GUEUDECOURT running well but in
my opinion this plant has undoubtedly
been overworked. Will you please
hasten relief of my 2 engine drivers
there.
M.O.R.E. reports as follows on specimen
of water from CANAL DU NORD forwarded
by 50th Bde (map ref not stated)
Quite clear no organic life. Tasteless
odourless, no metallic poison, no
cyanide. Requires 1 scoop per 110 galls
for chlorination – must be boiled or
chlorinated before use.

        R.C. Lundie Major R.E.
4-9-18   O C 93rd (Field) Co R.E.

Appendix VI
SECRET

C.R.E. 17th Division

Map Reference	Dia	Depth to Water	Depth of Water
O.27.b.4.2.	3'	111'	18'

Remarks:- New windlass installed - completed

| O.27.b.1.3. | 3' | 129' | 24' |

Remarks:- New rope and bucket fitted. Windlass repaired.

M.O.R.E reports on both these wells were submitted last night.

X 46.
5-9-18

R.C. Lundie Maj R.E.
O.C. 93rd Field Co R.E.

C.R.E. 17th Division	SECRET
Report on Water Reconnaissance to 11 p.m. 6-9-18
	Unit 93rd (Field) Co. R.E. Appendix VI.

Map Reference	Nature	Method of raising water	Depth to water	Depth of water	Dia	M O's Report
ROCQUIGNY						
O.27.b.1.3	Already reported					

Remarks:— Taken over by 559 A.T. Co. R.E. this morning. Engine and belt pump installed 2 canvas tanks & 3 canvas Horse Troughs erected. Was working O.K. 8.45 p.m. to-night.

| O.27.b.4.2. | Already reported | | | | | |

Remarks:— IN USE. Horses only

| O.27.c.3.6. | Circular brick | Wind-lass | — | 26 | | Slightly clouded (chalk) Tasteless, odourless. No Metallic poison No cyanide Req 1 scoop per 110 galls for chlorination. Must be boiled & chlorinated before use. Excellent for horses |

Remarks IN USE

Map Reference	Nature	Method of raising	Depth to water	Depth of water	Dia	M.O's Remarks	Yield
O.27.c.9.1.	Circular brick	nil	116'	15'	4'	Unfit for use of any kind	

Remarks:- Notice board FOUL will be fixed tomorrow

O.27.c.5.6.	brick	Windlass	108'	8'	4'	Excellent water - must be boiled or chlorinated before use. Req 1 scoop per 110 galls chlorination	

Remarks:- No windlass available to-day, same will be installed tomorrow

O.27.C.2.7	brick	Windlass	90'	12'	4'	Fit for horses only	

Remarks:- No windlass available today, same will be installed tomorrow

LE TRANSLOY

N.24.b.2.1.	brick	Hand pump (demolished)	80'	2'	3'	Requires 4 scoops per 110 galls chlorination. Fit for horses only	

Remarks:- Work discontinued on account of shortage of supply of water. A slightly larger charge than usual seems to have been employed and a large quantity of bricks and other debris have gone down the shaft stuffing it up

Map Reference	Nature	Method of raising	Depth to water	Depth of water	Dia	M.O's Report	Yield
O.25.c.3.6	Circular brick	Engine & pump engine required and Windlass now installed	30'	20'	3'-6"	Cloudy, organic life. Tasteless, odourless, no metallic poison, no cyanide. Req 1 scoop per 110 galls for chlorination. Must be boiled or chlorinated before use	

Remarks:- Not yet in USE. Gantry for belt pump if required will be installed to-morrow.

M.30.d.0.8 Already reported

Remarks:- IN USE Windlass installed today

| N.30.a.2.6 | Circ brick | Windlass | 60' | 16' | 4' | Already reported |

Remarks:- IN USE - Windlass installed today

| O.25.c.4.7 | Circular brick | Windlass | 66' | 6' | 3'-6" | Requires filtration & 1½ scoopsful per 110 galls chlorination, without any treatment is fit for horses & washing |

Remarks:- IN USE - Belt pump (water lifter) is to be installed experimentally tomorrow

6-9-18

R.C. Lundie Major RE
O.C 93rd Field Co. RE

C.R.E. 17th Division   SECRET
                           App. VI.

Water Report to 11 p.m. 8-9-18.

1 N.C.O. & 5 men assisting with belt pump in ROCQUIGNY.

Two sections less above number now located at O.30.b.1.9.

Well at O.25.c.3.6 - engine and canvas belt pulley erected, latter connected to 2" pipe to supply existing water troughs. Belt round pulley "laced" and ready for lowering. Engine has been run.

Well at O.25.c.4.7 - complete water lifting plant installed and has been successfully run. 1 large canvas tank & 2 canvas water troughs erected. Final Report follows.

M.O. R.E. reports as follows:—

2nd Specimen of WATER, CANAL DU NORD.
    (Supplied by 77th Field Co R.E.
Quite clear, no organic life, tasteless, odourless, no metallic poison, no cyanide. Requires 1 scoop per 110 galls for chlorination - must be boiled or chlorinated before use.

WELL No.2. N.30.a.2.6. by Capt MacQuarrie M.C. Submitted. Requires 1½ scoops for chlorination. Must be boiled or chlorinated before use. Excellent for horses without treatment.

                          R.C. Lundie Major R.E.

8-9-18   O.C. 93rd Field Co R.E.

C.R.E. 17th Division   SECRET
app. VIII

Well at O.25.c.4.7.

Belt pump going well, large number of horses watered there this morning.
Well at O.25.c.3.6. - installation completed.
Belt pump has been run and water delivered at trough, minor alterations now in hand.
Urgently required 8 ⅝" bolts complete with nuts and washers 7" long or over.
½ lb resin for preventing belt slipping.
Canvas tank at O.25.c.4.7 now being filled.

X 64.   R.C. Lundie Major RE
9-9-18   O.C. 93rd Field Co RE

C.R.E. 17th Division   app. IX   SECRET-

Report on water situation to 11 p.m. 10-9-18.

LE TRANSLOY.
O.25.c.3.6. – Belt pump installed complete, and has been running intermittently since midday, and many horses have been watered. One bad fall took place about 5 p.m., and the belt was broken and fell down the well, but another was installed and pumping resumed. Tank and troughs now full.
O.25.c.4.7. Belt pump has been running practically all day and many horses have been watered. Slight falls of clay have taken place. Tank and troughs now full.

ROCQUIGNY.
559th A.T. Coy R.E. have moved belt pump to O.27.b.4.2. where it was working well at 2 p.m.

GUEUDECOURT.
Engine broken down magneto trouble, repairs being executed locally at adjacent A.S.C. workshops.
1. 20 ft horse trough with L & F. pump fixed at pond at P.25.c.3.
Sample has been examined and passed for horses by M.O.

2 canvas horse troughs and 1. 3,000
gall canvas tanks erected at P.33.C.0.1-
fed by 2 L&F pumps with intermediate
tank, horses watered here.

Repairs to LECHELLE Water Point
in hand.

                        R C Lindie Major RE
10-9-18   O C 93rd Field Co R E

CRE 17th Division   SECRET.

Works Report to Noon to-day.
Water Point P.32.d.9.6.
  35 yds brick standing laid at troughs.
  60 yds scraped clear of mud.
Water Point P.32.d.9.1.
Circular track from main roads across Ry tracks all staked out.
Drainage continued.

11-9-18.   R C Lundie Major RE
           O.C. 93rd (Field) Co RE

W 10.

App XI

C.R.E. 17th Division
H.Q. 52nd Bde (for information)

Following huts have been repaired by this unit to date:

12th Manchester Regt — 3 Nissen huts
BEAULENCOURT — 2 large wooden huts

10th Lancs Fus — 6 Nissen huts
N.24.b.

9th Duke of — 3 Nissen huts
Wellingtons   2 large
O.25.d.   wooden huts

      R.C. Lundie Major R.E.
W.16. O.C. 93rd Field Co R.E.
14-9-18.

SECRET

17th Division R.E. and Pioneers
Daily Progress Report for 24 hours ending 6am
20-9-18.   Unit. 93rd. (Fd) Co RE.

app. XII

No of Sappers employed	Location	Nature of Work	Progress
Half No I Section	W.5.a.1.9	Digging & Firestepping	13 Firesteps 5 yds of trench dug to 5ft
Half No I Section	W.5.b.1.3	Digging & Firestepping	15 yds of firing stepping & 30 yds of tr. dug down to 5'6"
No 2 Section	W.5.c.8.6	Digging & Firestepping	5 Firesteps Completed 65 yds trench deeper @ 5'-0"
No 4 Section	W.5.d.1.2	Digging & Firestepping	9 Firesteps Complete 56 yds trench deep @ 5'-0"

W.20.
20-9-18.

R. ?????? RE
O.C. 93rd. (Fd) Co RE

-SECRET-

17th Division R.E and Pioneers
Daily Progress Report for 24 hours ending 6am
21-9-18. —— Unit. 93rd (Field) Co. R.E.—

app XIII

No. of men employed.	Location	Nature of Work	Progress	Present state of Work
No 1 Section	W.6.c.0.8	Digging	48" dug 3'6" x 4'0" up & Camouflaged	
No 2 Section	W.5.b.7.2	Digging S.P	60 yds dug 3'0-3'0 & Camouflaged	
No V Section	W.5.b.4.5	" "	55 " " "	

Note:- Trench was taped from W.16.d. central South West to about W.12.a.3.4. (about 250 yds from LOWLAND Trench), and "B" and "C" Coys. Pioneers commenced work.

No of men employed	Location	Nature of Work	Progress	Present state of work
	Trench in which were commenced for the most part removed; same W.6.c.5.8. to W.6.c.9.1.	Supporting Points	is extremely sketchy, only a trace with turf may be said of Trench from	as above

W.21.
21-9-18.

R. B. Smith
Maj. R.E.
O.C 93rd (Fd) Co R.E

SECRET

17th Division R.E. and Pioneers.
Daily Progress Report for 24 hours ending 6.a.m.
22-9-18 — Unit. 93rd (Field) Co. R.E. —

Appendix XIV

No of men employed	Location	Nature of Work	Progress	Present state of Work
No 1 Section	W.6.c.0.8.	Wiring	270ˣ Double apron fence Completed.	
No 2 Section	W.5.b.4.5.	Wiring	300ˣ double apron fence Completed	
No 4 Section	W.5.b.7.2.	Wiring	300ˣ double apron fence Completed.	

Note:- As no other labour was available, all materials had to be carried by Sappers from dump at W.S.d.8.8 to site of wire.

W.52. 22-9-18.

OC 93rd (Fd) Co. R.E.

17th Division R.E. and Pioneers.   SECRET
Daily Progress Report for 24 hours ending 6 a.m
23-9-18. —— Unit. 93rd (Field) Co. R.E. ——

App XV

No. of men employed	Location	Nature of Work	Progress	Present state of Work
No.1 Section	W.6.c.0.8.	Wiring	230ᵒ double Apron fence Completed	
No.2 Section	W.5.b.4.5.	"	280 " "	
No.4 Section	W.5.b.7.2.	"	280 " "	
Note	Work hindered by enemy shell fire.			

R.C. Lundie
O.C. 93rd (Field) Co. R.E.

Maj: R.E.

17th Division R.E and Pioneers.   —SECRET—
Daily Progress Report for 24 hours ending
6am. 24·9·18 — Unit 93rd (Field) Co R.E

App XVI

No of men employed.	Location	Nature of Work	Progress	Present State of Work.
8 R.E. (NCOs) 30 N.I.H.	W.4.b.	Filling in Crater	Crater 50% filled in.	50% comp.
10 R.E. (NCOs) 30 N.I.H.	W.5.a.	" "	Work commenced.	

No. of men employed	Location	Nature of Work	Progress	Present state of Work
No 1 Sect.	S.P. W.5.a.1.8.	Wiring	200' double apron fence Completed	
		Repairing Old Wire	80' "	
No 2	S.P. W.5.a.2.0.	Wiring	290' double apron fence completed	
"		Strengthening Old Wire	50' "	
No 4	S.P. W.5.c.7.2.	Wiring	280' double apron fence Completed	
		Strengthening Old Wire	120' "	

W.25.
24-9-18

R C Lumdon
Maj
O.C 93rd (a) Co. R.E.

17th Division R.E. and Pioneers   SECRET
Daily Progress Report for 24 hours ending 6 a.m.
25-9-18   Unit 93rd (Field) Co R.E.

App XVII

No of men employed	Location	Nature of Work	Progress	Present State of Work
18 R.E. 50 N.I.L.	W.4.b	Filling in Craters	Crater 75% filled in	
	W.5.a	" "	10% completed	
No 1 Sect	S.P. H5a1-8	Wiring	50" double apron complete 100" thickened & strengthened 400" old fence thickened making apron & belts in front of the front	
No 2 "	S.P. H5a.2.0	"	100" new fence erected 900" old fence repaired & thickened	
No 4 "	S.P. H5d.1-2			

Shortage of pickets with wiring

R.C. Lundie
OC 93 (F) Co
Maj R.E.

WAR DIARY or INTELLIGENCE SUMMARY

Army Form C. 2118.

Place	Date	Hour	Summary of Events and Information	Remarks and references to Appendices
CROQUOISON	1.3.19		Fatigues and work on Brigade Racecourse. 2 O.R. To Divn. Rest Camp RAFTON. Strength 3 Offs. 77 O.R. 43 animals	R2
	2.3.19		No parades. 2 O.R. Cadre park LONGPRE.	R2
	3.3.19		Fatigues. 1 O.R. Cadre Camp 21 Avy.	R2
	4.3.19		Fatigues. 1 O.R. Returned from hospital. 2 O.R. Xferred to 29 Mtd Yorks Bde. Strength 3 Offs 77 O.R. 3 animals	R2
	5.3.19		Fatigues. 1 O.R. admitted to hospital. 6 L.D. Mules to FRIXCOURT	R2
	6.3.19		Fatigues. 1 O.R. Returned from hospital. 2 L.D. horses to 29 M.V. Sect. Strength 3 - 78 - 29	R2
	7.3.19		Fatigues. 1 O.R. Identified in England (Struck off strength) 8 L.D. Mules to 33 M.V. Sect. " 3 - 78 - 21	R2
			25/1/19	
	8.3.19		Union River Meeting. Work on Divn'l Race Course.	R2
	9.3.19		Fatigues & work at HENCOURT. 1 O.R. proceed from leave. " 3 - 78 - 21	R2
			1 O.R. to Divn'l Resp'n Camp (recreate)	
	10.3.19		Fatigues. Billeting party to HANGEST. 1 Rider Y. } To HANGEST " 3 - 77 - 19	R2
			1 A.D. knee Xtransferto SH.	
	11.3.19		Fatigues. Work at WARCUS. 1 O.R. Returned from hospital.	R2
	12.3.19		Ditto. 1 O.R. To Divn'l Resp Camp. " 3 - 78 - 19	R2
CROQUOISON	13.3.19		Marched 13.00 hours arrived HANGEST 16.30 hours. 5 O.R. Reinstated at CROQUOISON	R2
HANGEST			A.L.D. Patrols to BOURDON in Sect.	
	14.3.19		Fatigues. 3 O.R. To Cadre parks LONGPRE	R2
			1 O.R. To Cadre park LINNEPRE. " 3 - 73 - 15	
	15.3.19		Fatigues. 1 Off. posted from 77th Field Cy R.E. 1 Off. attached to 7th Div'n aa Cy " 3 - 70 - 15	R2
			1 Off posted from 77 " " R.E. 1 O.R. Xferred from Brigade.	
	16.3.19		No parades. " 1 - 71 - 15	R2

WAR DIARY
or
INTELLIGENCE SUMMARY

(Erase heading not required.)

Army Form C. 2118.

Instructions regarding War Diaries and Intelligence Summaries are contained in F. S. Regs., Part II. and the Staff Manual respectively. Title pages will be prepared in manuscript.

Place	Date	Hour	Summary of Events and Information	Offrs	Rations Men	Strength	Remarks and references to Appendices
HANGEST	17.3.19	09.15	Baths. 2 offrs joined unit from Base				
			1 O.R. ditto	4	72	15	
	18.3.19		Fatigues. Work at LE MESGE				
	19.3.19		Fatigues. 1 O.R. rejoined unit from hospital	4	73	15	
	20.3.19	9.30	Clean arms Inspection. 5.L.D Marks to 29 M.V. Section	4	73	8	
	21.3.19		Fatigue. 5 O.R. to Devn'k H.D. 2 L.D Marks to 5" V.E.S. for sale	4	68	8	
	22.3.19		Fatigue. 1 O.R. to Hospital. 1 O.R. Transferred R.U.A. 25.1.19 (struck off)				
			9.3.19 " " " " at CROUY-WILSON alloy	4	65	8	
	23.3.19		No parade. 2 O.R. to detachment at CROUY-WILSON. 1 X Rider to HANGEST for dinner.	4	65	7	
	24.3.19		Fatigue. 24 O.R. To unit from 78th Fld Coy R.E. 23 O.R. from 77 Fld Coy R.E.	4	93	7	
	25.3.19		Fatigue. 2 O.R. Leave to U.K. 1 O.R. to hospital	4	90	7	
	26.3.19		Clean arms Inspection. 4 O.R. rejoined from leave. 1 Off (att 78th Fld (Gy)) Sent to dent.				
			1 O.R. to Main repl. Camp.	4	93	7	
	27.3.19		Bath. 1 O.R. from detachment at CROUY-WILSON. Leave to U.K.	4	91	7	
	28.3.19		Fatigue. 1 O.R. to 77 F Field Coy R.E.	4	91	7	
HANGEST	29.3.19		March off 11:30 hours arrive BOURDON 12.00 hours. 1 O.R. rejoined from leave. 1 off rejoined from				
BOURDON			leave. 1 O.R. Leave to U.K. Leave to Codyport	4	91	7	
	30.3.19		Fatigues. 1 off (Capt. Cocksfonk) Leave to U.K. 1 + 2 Rates reported missing from Codyfk. 4	90	6		
			1 O.R. Leave to U.K.				
	31.3.19		Fatigues. 4 O.R. rejoined from detachment CROUY-WILSON. 3 Z Riders to Renewal party to	4	95	3	
			1 O.R. " " Leave ABBEVILLE				